Dispatches *from* Bermuda

The Civil War Letters
of Charles Maxwell Allen,
United States Consul at Bermuda,
1861–1888

Edited by Glen N. Wiche

Kent State University Press
Kent, Ohio

© 2008 by The Kent State University Press, Kent, Ohio 44242

All rights reserved

Library of Congress Catalog Card Number 2008014200

ISBN 978-0-87338-938-9

Manufactured in the United States of America

Library of Congress Cataloging-in-Publication Data

Allen, Charles Maxwell.

Dispatches from Bermuda : the Civil War letters of Charles Maxwell Allen, United States consul at Bermuda, 1861–1888 / edited by Glen N. Wiche.

    p. cm. — (Civil War in the North)

Includes bibliographical references and index.

ISBN 978-0-87338-938-9 (hardcover : alk. paper)∞

1. United States—History—Civil War, 1861–1865—Blockades.

2. Blockade—Bermuda Islands—History—19th century.

3. Allen, Charles Maxwell—Correspondence.

4. Consuls—United States—Correspondence.

5. United States—History—Civil War, 1861–1865—Personal narratives.

6. United States—History—Civil War, 1861–1865—Naval operations.

7. Confederate States of America. Navy—History.

8. Bermuda Islands—History, Naval—19th century.

9. Atlantic Ocean Region—History, Naval—19th century.

10. United States—Foreign relations—1861–1865.

I. Wiche, Glen Norman. II. Title.

E600.A44 2008

973.7′5—dc22

                2008014200

British Library Cataloging-in-Publication data are available.

12 11 10 09 08   5 4 3 2 1

In loving memory of Susan Z. Wiche, who found Charles Maxwell Allen's last resting place on a warm Bermuda afternoon and encouraged me to tell his story.

Engraved portrait of Charles Maxwell Allen
(Courtesy of Bermuda National Trust Collection, Bermuda Archives,
Hamilton, Bermuda)

Let us have faith that right makes might, and in that faith let us,
to the end, dare to do our duty as we understand it.

ABRAHAM LINCOLN

Simple duty hath no place for fear.

JOHN GREENLEAF WHITTIER

Contents

Preface

My quest for Charles Maxwell Allen began on a warm Bermuda afternoon in 1992. My wife and I had gone to the island for a short holiday and were charmed by its beauty, the hospitality of the people, and its curious history, so strongly connected to that of the United States. That Sunday we worshipped at St. Mark's Anglican Church in Smith's Parish. After the service, we strolled across the narrow road and through the picturesque old cemetery. Our attention was drawn to a tall handsome obelisk. Closer inspection revealed it to be the last resting place of Charles Maxwell Allen, who, according to the inscription, had been the U.S. consul to the Island of Bermuda from 1861 until his death in 1888.

We were touched to discover the grave of this American who had served his country for so many years on foreign soil. I had long been interested in the international aspects of the American Civil War, and particularly the maritime history of the period. I was well aware of the important part that Bermuda had played in the conflict as a haven for Confederate blockade-runners in their attempts to bring vital war materiel from Europe through the Union blockade of Southern ports and into the Confederate states. But, in all my reading on the subject, I could not recall any references to Allen's own wartime activities in Bermuda.

I decided to review the printed sources on the subject when I returned home. In doing so, I discovered that there had been no books or scholarly monographs devoted to Allen's Civil War career. I wondered whether his story, if it could be pieced together, might make a valuable contribution to the literature of the war, and my wife urged me to tell his story.

Not long after, I was delighted to discover that Allen's diplomatic dispatches survived and had, in fact, been microfilmed by the National Archives in Washington, D.C. I quickly purchased the microfilm reels and began to make transcripts of the original documents. It soon became apparent what a rich source of information Allen's dispatches were. Here was a new, largely unused, eyewitness account that shed important light on the diplomatic and naval aspects of the conflict.

This book gathers together all of Consul Allen's Civil War diplomatic dispatches. Many of the dispatches are published here for the first time since Allen penned them in wartime Bermuda. They tell a fascinating story of diplomatic and military intrigue. They also illuminate the character of a proud, patriotic New Englander who represented his country skillfully and ably for more than a quarter of a century. It is a testament to Allen that, although he was greeted with scorn upon his arrival in pro-Confederate Bermuda in 1861, he became a beloved figure in the postwar years and was genuinely mourned by Bermudians when he died on Christmas Eve 1888.

Acknowledgments

My chief debt of gratitude is to Kathleen Moore of Chicago—indefatigable researcher, candid counselor, prudent critic. When the editor became legally blind, she became the project's chief transcriber and researcher. Without her efforts and encouragement, the story of Charles Maxwell Allen would yet remain unwritten.

The Allen Family Papers at the Vermont Historical Society were made available through the courtesy of Alice Ross de Kok. A descendant of one of Charles Maxwell Allen's brothers, Ms. de Kok generously shared Allen family letters, photographs, and memories. A special thank you is due to Bettye Hitchcock Allen, who preserved all of the Allen family history.

Paul Carnahan of the Vermont Historical Society provided valuable research assistance on the Allen family in Vermont. Marlene Wightman of Belmont, New York, provided much material on the history of the Republican Party in Allegany County, New York. My thanks to Charles B. Smith of the Orono, Maine, Historical Society for providing information on Anson Allen and the Allen Match Manufactory. I also wish to acknowledge the assistance of the staff of the Bermuda Archives for making the Allen papers in their possession available to me. My thanks are also due to the Bermuda Library in Hamilton, which provided microfilm copies of the *Bermuda Royal Gazette*.

I wish to thank John Aubrey, Ayer librarian of the Newberry Library, for his many assistances and the expediting of important interlibrary loans.

To my friends and colleagues, Tom Drewes, Edward Gordon, Robert Guinan, Bruce Kirstein, Professor Deirdre McCloskey, Kathleen Occhipinti, Charles Priestley, Sandra Sadler, Frank C. Schell III, Edgar Self, and Robert

Sharp, who read portions of the manuscript, I am grateful to each for their valuable comments, suggestions, and encouragement.

I am indebted to the following individuals and institutions for the illustrations they provided for this book: Horst Augustinovic, Dr. Charles Peery, Alice Ross de Kok, St. George's Historical Society, the Bermuda National Trust, and the Chicago History Museum.

Editor's Note

The diplomatic dispatches of Charles Maxwell Allen, from the time of his appointment until the assassination of President Lincoln, have been transcribed in their entirety. The enclosures with Allen's quarterly reports have been omitted, being numerous and lengthy ledger sheets. Also omitted are letters from various persons that Allen forwarded to the Department of State along with his official dispatches. These omissions can be found in the microfilmed dispatches.

Consul Allen was required by the Department of State to number each dispatch consecutively. Omissions in the consecutive numbering indicate dispatches that were not microfilmed.

Allen generally wrote in a very clear hand, unlike many of his contemporaries. He made few errors in spelling, and where these occurred, corrections have been made. In a small number of instances, where a word or phrase is illegible, a question mark within brackets is used.

From time to time, Allen made minor mistakes in spelling the names of the vessels about which he wrote. These errors in spelling have been corrected for uniformity.

Every effort has been made to be as accurate as possible.

Maps and Illustrations

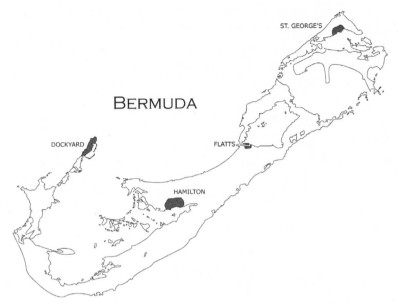

Line drawing of Bermuda showing the location of St. George's, Flatts, Hamilton, and the Dockyard (Courtesy of Horst Augustinovic, Hamilton, Bermuda)

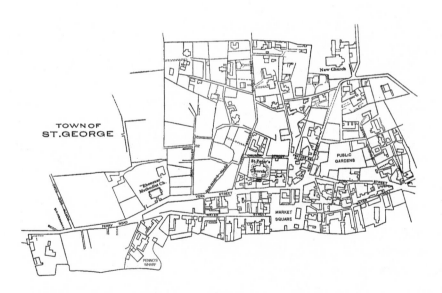

Line drawing of St. George's, Bermuda, ca. 1890 showing the principal streets of the town and Penno's Wharf (Courtesy of Horst Augustinovic, Hamilton, Bermuda)

CHAPTER I

"The most self-effacing of men"

Charles Maxwell Allen, who served his country as U.S. consul at Bermuda from 1861 until his death in 1888, was the most self-effacing of men. It is ironic that the very qualities that helped make him the skillful and articulate diplomat that he was—his even temperament, his steady habits, and his personal modesty—were the very qualities that help explain his reticence in telling his own fascinating story.

Allen's post at Bermuda was of vital importance to his government during the years of the American Civil War, and he was often thrust into sensitive, difficult, and sometimes dangerous personal circumstances in the performance of his consular responsibilities. Nevertheless, he did not leave a memoir of his wartime experiences as did so many of his contemporaries. It is fortunate that his diplomatic dispatches to the U.S. Department of State survive. These dispatches, and the few surviving letters to his wife, provide a unique perspective on the important part that Bermuda played in the American Civil War. And in them we can discern, if sometimes only faintly, what life was like for Consul Allen as he lived it, day by day, far from family and country, during its greatest national crisis.

Throughout his long, colorful, and sometimes controversial career, both at home and abroad, Allen was never far from his New England roots. The Allen family came to America early in the seventeenth century, and many of their names appear in the historical records of the Massachusetts Bay Colony. The family emigrated from England and arrived in Boston Harbor in 1635. They lived first in Weymouth, and then in Braintree and Sandwich on Cape Cod Bay. They were permanently established in Bridgewater, Massachusetts, about thirty-five miles southeast of Boston, by the year 1660. The Allens prospered in Bridgewater, and the community was indebted to them "for the burying ground, meeting house lot, and common or training field, which were given by them" to the town.[1]

The Allens had lived in Massachusetts for over a century when Charles's grandfather, Silas Allen, was born in Bridgewater in 1754.[2] Silas was the son of James Allen and Mary Packard, the ninth of their ten children. The Boston Tea Party and other events that led to the American Revolution took place during Silas's impressionable youth. Following his older brother's example, the twenty-three-year-old Silas also joined the Patriot cause. During the conflict, Silas saw military service on three separate occasions during 1777–78.[3]

In 1778, Silas purchased land in the far northwestern frontier of Massachusetts in what is now Franklin County.[4] After returning to civilian life, he settled on his land. Here, in the town of Charlemont, in about 1780, he met and married Esther Hastings. Silas and Esther lived in Charlemont where five of their children were born.[5] The family moved a few miles north of Charlemont to the village of Heath in about 1788–89,[6] where the last six of their eleven children were born.[7]

Heath, situated near the New Hampshire-Massachusetts border, is about 120 miles northwest of Boston. In this small community, incorporated in 1785, Silas made his mark as a housewright.[8] He must have been prosperous, for he paid taxes on one hundred acres in 1791 and transacted a good deal of business in real estate. Many of the early Heath homes were built by Silas. He built a substantial two-story home for his large family, the stone foundations of which survive.[9] Silas lived in this home until his death at the age of eighty-seven in 1841.[10]

Charles's father, James Allen, the sixth child of Silas and Esther, was born in 1792 in Heath.[11] Choosing not to follow the occupation of his father, James became the owner and operator of a grist mill[12] in Dell, employing two young men and a young woman.[13] Dell was a small community about a mile from the center of Heath, comprised entirely of the grist mill owned by James, a fulling mill, and a few scattered houses.

James was twenty-eight years of age when he married Sarah Howe in the Congregational Church of Heath on October 26, 1820.[14] Sarah Howe was also descended from an early New England family; one of her ancestors was Edward Rawson, secretary of the Massachusetts Bay Colony, who came to New England in 1636.[15] A son, James, was born to James and Sarah, followed a year later by the birth of Charles Maxwell on July 28, 1822.[16]

With a wife and two small children to support, James sold some, if not all, of his land to his brother David and his friend Hugh Maxwell Jr. "The wording of the deed shows a warmth and expansiveness seldom encountered in such documents, and not encouraged by lawyers. The new owners were 'To Have and to Hold the said demised premises . . . for and during the time that trees shall grow and brooks shall run to be fully and ended,' and were to promise to pay $5."[17]

James and Sally moved north to Vermont with their two sons. They settled no more than sixty miles from Heath in Winhall, a small town in the eastern part of Bennington County situated on the Winhall River, where five more children were born to them over the next ten years.[18] By 1836, James and Sally had five sons, James, Charles Maxwell, William Dennis, Jonas, and Anson, and two daughters, Sarah Elizabeth and Amanda Malvina. With seven young children to care for, Sally became pregnant with her eighth child. Her eldest son, James, was seventeen, and Charles was fifteen. Amanda, the youngest, was just one year old. The Allen family suffered a great bereavement when both mother and daughter died in childbirth on April 9, 1837.[19]

Fifteen months after Sally's death, James remarried. He married Mary (Polly) Vaile, the daughter of Col. Jonathan Vaile and Mary Rawson of Winhall.

In 1840, the town of Winhall had a population of 576. It had grown since James and Sally had arrived in the early 1820s. The population had been only 428 in 1820. At the time of James's second marriage, there were four school houses in Winhall. There was a grist mill and seven saw mills, a general store, three taverns, and a tannery. Two small union meeting houses, one belonging to the Congregationalists and one to the Baptists, offered spiritual comfort to the citizens. Methodists were tended by circuit preachers.[20] Most of the inhabitants of Winhall, including James Allen, earned their livelihood from farming.

Polly Vaile Allen, twenty-nine years of age, took on the duties of caring for James's seven children and, within the next ten years, became mother to five of her own. James's second family of three sons, Jonathan Vaile, John Harvey, and Henry Seldon, and two daughters, Mary (Polly) Ogilvia and Elsie Jane, were as close to their older half-brothers and half-sisters as if they were all born of the same mother. The fourteen children stayed in touch with each other to the end of their lives.

Charles was part of a typically large early nineteenth-century American family. During his adolescent years, he helped out with family chores and learned the values of family responsibility, helping his father and brothers on the Allens' hardscrabble farm. The rugged terrain of Vermont was not well suited to agriculture and yielded a living only reluctantly. A photograph of the house where Charles and his siblings were reared shows a weathered, two-story clapboard farmhouse on a bleak treeless landscape.[21] Charles suffered from asthma all his life, which must have made work on the farm more onerous for him than it might otherwise have been.

The few surviving family letters make it clear that the Allen children were well educated. Not only was the grammar, punctuation, and spelling in their letters above the average for that time, but they used Latin occasionally and periodically quoted Shakespeare. At least three of Charles's siblings became teachers in villages near Winhall, and perhaps Charles also taught.[22] The education that the children received allowed them to improve their prospects and seek wider horizons than the small and often unprofitable family farm.

The older Allen children left Winhall one by one. By 1848, Charles's brother, William Dennis, had left for California to try his luck in the Gold Rush. Charles and his older brother James were established in Orono, Maine, almost 250 miles from Winhall, where they became partners in a match manufacturing business. Their sister Sarah Elizabeth lived in Orono with them. Brother Jonas was still at school, and the younger children were at home in Winhall.

The large frame Allen Match Manufactory, situated on Spring Street near the canal in Orono, provided an essential commodity for every home and farm. The Allen brothers made a success of their undertaking, and the business flourished for more than a quarter of a century. The Orono Match had a large sale outside the state. The matches were at least six inches long and about the thickness of a lead pencil. The wood was pine, and they were tipped with sulfur. The making of these matches was both a dangerous and an unhealthy occupation, given the constant exposure to phosphorus and sulfur, and must have had an ill effect on the asthmatic Charles.[23]

It was while in Maine that Charles met and married Susan Elizabeth Richards. Susan was born in Norridgewock, Maine, in 1827. Her father, Amos Richards, was a Methodist circuit preacher, and her mother, Betsey Witherell, was the granddaughter of a prominent Congregational minister.[24] The Richards family settled in Milo, Maine. Susan's early years paralleled those of her future husband's in many respects. When Susan was seventeen, her mother died. Susan and her older sister stayed in the home to care for their six younger brothers and sisters until Amos Richards remarried a few years later. As a preacher's daughter, Susan probably received more of an education than most women of her time and place. She naturally would have had access to a number of books, although they were, perhaps, mainly theological in nature.

By the time Susan had reached her teens, Milo, Maine, was a growing community. There were three churches in the town, several mills, a two-room schoolhouse, several stores, and a burying ground. In many respects, it developed in the same way that Winhall had, with the same industries of milling and lumbering.

It is not known how or when Charles met Susan, but they were married in Maine by 1849 when their first child, Charles Fletcher, was born. In that same year came the sad news that Charles's brother, William Dennis, had died of lung fever at the young age of twenty-five, far away from family and home, in the gold fields of California.[25]

Despite Charles's strong New England roots, he was not destined to remain in the rugged and unforgiving land of his forefathers. By mid-1850, Charles and his young family were settled in western New York State. Enumerated in the 1850 census of Amity, Allegany County, New York, Charles's occupation was listed as "merchant." At the time of this census, Charles and Susan did not yet have a home of their own, having just arrived from Orono.[26] Brother James and his wife also had left Orono, following William Dennis in the wake of the Gold Rush of 1849. Young Anson Allen, then twenty-one years of age, took over the match manufactory and operated it until his death in 1884.

It is not known with any certainty why Charles settled in western New York State, more than five hundred miles from Orono. Though both Charles and Susan had family ties in New England, family was not enough to stop them from seizing the opportunities of a widening world.

By the 1840s, journeys westward were made less arduous by the establishment of both the Erie Canal and the Erie Railroad. The Erie Canal, crossing New York State from Albany to Buffalo, made it possible for the first time to travel across the state by water, and the Erie Railroad had reached Allegany County in 1850. News of the rapid development of the Genesee Valley accelerated the migration of economically hard-pressed New Englanders into the western part of the state, in what has been called the "Yankee Invasion of New York."[27]

The Genesee River, with its heavily timbered valley, was ideally suited for the development of the lumbering industry. Because of the area's natural resources and its geographic location, Amity grew rapidly during the 1850s. The sawmills on the Genesee River were capable of producing from fifty to seventy-five thousand feet of lumber per day.[28] One of these sawmills was owned by Daniel Crabtree, who was soon to become a close political ally of Charles Maxwell Allen. The arrival of the Erie Railroad in Amity brought many Eastern merchants to supply the needs of the town's growing population.

The Allen family settled in the part of Amity that lay east of the Genesee River, in an area known as Miltonville. The heart of the community was on the west side of the river, and here was located the courthouse, the town clerk, the post office, and the train station. A single bridge, spanning the Genesee River, was the only link between the eastern and western sections of Amity.[29] When the Allen family arrived in Amity, its population was nearly eighteen hundred souls. Charles's success as a merchant enabled him to purchase property in the quiet residential section of Miltonville at the corner of Triana and Charles streets.[30] To the north, Charles's neighbor was Augustus Miller, who became the husband of Charles's sister, Sarah Elizabeth. His neighbor to the west was Silas Richardson, a good friend for many years.

By 1854, the Allen family had grown with the birth of two daughters, Henrietta Elizabeth (Hettie), born in 1851, and Mary Eva (Myra), born in 1853. But as the Allens were enjoying these peaceful and prosperous years in Amity, a political crisis was threatening the peace and prosperity of the entire nation. The national debate over the extension of slavery was reaching a critical point.

People opposed to slavery had hoped that the institution would die a natural death if restricted to the Southern states where it already existed. Their hopes were dashed when the Kansas Nebraska Act of 1854 was passed. This legislation allowed each new territory to decide for itself whether or not slavery would be allowed. The compromise failed miserably, resulting in civil strife in the territories between proslavery and antislavery factions. Recriminations over the escalating violence in the territories further polarized the national political parties, both North and South. Opposing the extension of slavery into the territories, antislavery forces recognized the necessity for a new national political party to advance their cause.

The political affiliation that was to take Charles Maxwell Allen to Bermuda had its origins in these attempts to settle the issue of slavery. Throughout this period, some of the more active opponents of slavery became involved in the Underground Railroad to circumvent the Fugitive Slave Act of 1850.[31] This loose network of men and women sheltered runaway slaves. The slaves were passed along from one safe house to another until they could cross into Canada, where they were beyond the reach of American law and could live in freedom, for Great Britain had abolished slavery in the empire in 1832. The Underground Railroad was particularly well established in New York State. Here the cities of Niagara and Buffalo made access to Canada relatively easy. In western New York, the Underground Railroad ran through Allegany County, and William Sortore of Amity,[32] a friend and neighbor of Charles and Susan, participated in this secret and illegal activity.[33]

Asahel N. Cole, editor of the *Genesee Valley Free Press*, was the leading antislavery figure in western New York. The number of his adherents was small, said to be no more than three hundred. William Sortore, Daniel Crabtree, and Charles Allen were well known in Amity as supporters of Cole.[34]

The principal objective of this small group was to field a slate of candidates statewide in New York running on an antislavery platform. Though an unsuccessful attempt was made to organize politically in 1852, Cole and his supporters persevered and succeeded two years later. On May 16, 1854, a meeting was held, since known as the Friendship Convention. A contemporary account, published just six years after the convention, recalled the meeting and Charles Maxwell Allen's involvement in it: "A little after there appeared in the columns of the *Free Press,* a call, humbly signed by five men.[35] Here are their names: A. N. Cole, Robert Snow, Elias P. Benjamin, Charles M. Allen and Joseph Shuart. This was the first call for a Republican convention in the State of New York. The convention was held on the 17th day of October, 1854, birthday of the great party of freedom in this State.[36] It was held on the soil of our glorious old Allegany, at the old court-house in Angelica; was not numerously attended, only a half score or so of Whigs in the entire county having pluck enough to participate in its proceedings, together with fifty or sixty Free Democrats."[37]

The year 1854 was a watershed not only in American political life but also in the lives of millions of Americans, including a thirty-two-year-old merchant of Amity. Charles's service on the committee demonstrates that he had quickly made his mark in the town and county to which he had arrived fewer than four years before. He was, in fact, the only member of the committee from Amity and the only one who was not born in the state of New York.

Similar political activities were held in several other Northern states at this time, and by 1856, the new Republican Party held its first national convention at Pittsburgh.

The Allen family welcomed the birth of a daughter, Mary Genevieve (Jenna) in 1857. Also in this year Susan's sister Mary Ann died at the age of twenty-five in Milo, Maine.[38] By 1860 the Allen family was well established in Amity. Charles, whose occupation was now that of a lumberman, was thirty-eight years of age. His real estate was valued at two thousand dollars, with personal property valued at one thousand dollars. Susan was thirty-three, Charles Fletcher was eleven, Hettie was nine, Myra seven, and Jenna three years old. Residing with them at the time was Susan's younger sister, Alice Richards, a schoolteacher.[39]

While Charles was hard at work with his family, his business, and his politics, events were beginning to take place that would change his life and the lives of his family forever.

The year 1860 saw the first election of a Republican president. The success of the Republican Party gave real political power to the antislavery movement. The Democratic Party had broken into several factions over the issue of slavery, which resulted in the election of Abraham Lincoln. Lincoln's victory left many Southerners feeling that the only way they could protect what they saw as their property rights was to secede from the Union. Five days before Christmas 1860, South Carolina became the first Southern state to secede and was quickly followed by other Southern states. When President Lincoln took the oath of office on March 4, 1861, all compromise seeming to have failed, the nation was poised on the brink of civil war.

It is often easily forgotten just how young the American nation was on the eve of the Civil War. The Republic to which Charles Maxwell Allen had pledged his allegiance and service was not yet seventy-five years old, and the Republican Party he had helped to found in the state of New York had been in existence for a mere seven years.

After ten years of Democratic rule, the first Republican president was confronted not only with secession and the prospect of armed conflict but also with the need to fill virtually all government offices with loyal party members.

There were more than sixteen hundred government positions to fill, and within a few days the new administration had managed to fill more than fourteen hundred of them, in this way paying off political debts, both large and small. Even the first battles of the Civil War did not seem to slow the steady stream of office seekers. The huge number of applicants for the relatively small number of offices led the humorist, Artemus C. Ward, to wryly note that "the retreat of the Union Army at Bull Run was based on a rumor that several vacancies existed in the New York Customs House."[40]

Many of these office seekers were nominated to be United States consuls abroad, representing the commercial interests of their country. Diplomatic positions abroad were especially popular because "a consulship could be a commercial advantage, a social distinction, and a possible source of revenue from consular fees."[41] Throughout most of the nineteenth century, the role of U.S. consuls in facilitating trade with the United States remained constant. It is rather surprising that these men did as well as they did considering that most of them did not have any prior diplomatic experience and that they had received little if any instruction from the Department of State as to how they were to perform their consular duties.

Both Lincoln and his secretary of state, William H. Seward, were aware that should war come, there would be a greater need for international diplomacy.[42] At the outset of the war, the president and his secretary of state had fundamentally different views of the role of U.S. consuls. Lincoln used his power of patronage by appointing consuls in recognition of their political service without great regard for their professional credentials.[43] In contrast, Seward, in pursuing an assertive foreign policy, envisioned the consuls as intelligence gatherers. Seward hoped that those consuls serving in countries that were in some measure sympathetic to the Confederate cause would report on Confederate procurement efforts, in effect, becoming the eyes and ears of the Federal government abroad. It was fortunate for the Lincoln administration that the consuls who were appointed to what became posts of first importance during the war rose so well to the challenge.

On July 23, 1861, just two days after the North's defeat at the Battle of Bull Run, the U.S. Congress showed foresight as to the international implications of the conflict when a resolution was adopted to increase the consular representation of the United States during the present insurrection. In the past, consular appointments had often been given without regard to the candidate's diplomatic skills. Now, in wartime, consular appointments needed to be filled by astute men of patriotic character who could effectively represent the interests of their country abroad in the most trying of circumstances.[44]

Seward was from New York State, which had played a crucial role in the Republican victory. Charles Maxwell Allen, being a founding member of the Republican Party in that state, had an advantage in securing a political appointment. The events that would take Allen to one of the most isolated islands in the world began when an earlier candidate declined the office.[45] Fewer than two months later, on August 7, 1861, during the first congressional recess, Charles Maxwell Allen was nominated as U.S. consul at Bermuda.[46]

The confirmation process was a lengthy one.[47] The U.S. Senate confirmed Allen's appointment on April 14, 1862, more than eight months after his nomination and five months after his arrival in Bermuda.[48] But Allen had not waited for confirmation from the Senate. Within two months of his nomination, he had settled his business affairs in Amity, now known as Belmont, and had submitted the surety bond required by the U.S. government. In preparing himself for his new duties, Allen relied principally on the book of consular regulations, which set forth the responsibilities of a U.S. consul.[49] The duties and responsibilities of the U.S. consul had not materially changed since the Consular Act of 1792.[50] In fact, the first book-length manual of consular regulations did not appear until 1856.

The principal duties of a consul were, as they always had been, to protect the interests of U.S. commerce and her citizens abroad. These duties, which were regularly reported by Allen in his dispatches, included aiding U.S. ships in distress, providing for destitute or ill American seamen, notarizing documents for U.S. citizens abroad, and reporting to the department on the arrival and departure of American vessels. But Allen could hardly have envisioned what his role would be as a wartime consul in Bermuda, and little could have prepared him for the long separation from his wife and young family.

Having provided for his family's welfare while he was away, he said his farewells to his wife and five children, for a son, William Henry, had been born a few months earlier. Charles Maxwell left for St. George's, Bermuda, passport in hand.

The journey to Bermuda was not a pleasant one. Winter storms in New York delayed his departure, and the schooner *St. George,* which had brought him to Bermuda from New York harbor, encountered two severe gales, one of which lasted eighteen hours and resulted in the loss of the schooner's anchor.[51] Ironically, the schooner and her captain were later to become involved in blockade-running.

From the very beginning of the war, it quickly became apparent that in order to wage war against the industrial North, the agrarian South would be dependent upon obtaining war materiel from Europe, especially from industrialized Great Britain. To prevent this, the Lincoln administration established a blockade of Southern ports. Great Britain was officially neutral during the American Civil War and never recognized the Confederate states. There were, however, British political and commercial interests sympathetic to the Southern cause, and the British island of Bermuda was destined to play an important part in the conflict.

Neither the granite hills of Vermont nor the expansive forested lands of western New York could have prepared Charles Maxwell Allen for Bermuda. The small fishhook-shaped island, located nearly seven hundred miles east of the Southern port of Wilmington, North Carolina, is only twenty-two miles in length and at no point more than two miles wide. The entire parish of St. George's is only 2.3 square miles.

Before the American Civil War, Bermuda's commerce was about equally divided between the ports of Hamilton, the capital of Bermuda, and St. George's, a tired laid-back village on the eastern tip of the island chain. Shortly after Allen's arrival, the easily accessible St. George's harbor was to become a center for blockade-running and consequently became the commercial hub of Bermuda.

St. George's was founded in 1612 and is the oldest, continuously inhabited English settlement in the New World. Consul Allen must have been surprised and perhaps a little disappointed by his first sight of the diminutive and un-

View of St. George's, Bermuda. Painting by Edward James (Courtesy of St. George's Historical Society, St. George's, Bermuda)

prepossessing little village perched along the harbor. The consulate was almost in sight of the town square. The Bermuda State House, built in 1620; St. Peter's, the oldest Anglican Church in the Western hemisphere; and the many small stone cottages and buildings, little changed from the eighteenth century, were to become familiar sights to him as he walked the crooked little lanes and narrow alleys of the old town.

When Allen arrived, the town obviously had seen more prosperous times. From its beginnings, Bermuda was engaged chiefly in maritime trade. Strategically located between England, the American Colonies, and the Caribbean, the islanders were soon known for their expertise in building and repairing sailing vessels. St. George's became a boomtown during the Civil War, as it had, on a much smaller scale, during the War of 1812, when privateers had made the port a lively and prosperous community, if only for a few years.

Surrounded by vast expanses of ocean on all sides, Charles's first and most important adjustment was to learn to live as an islander. After having traveled from the Vermont mountains to northern Maine and then westward to New York, it must have seemed strange to him to live in such a confined and isolated place. The former lumberman would have been pleased with Bermuda's prolific growths of cedar trees, but little else would have reminded him of the Genesee Valley. Having experienced the harsh winters of New England, the temperate climate of Bermuda would have appealed to him, but the oppressive summers always carried the possibility of the dreaded yellow fever.

In letters to Susan, Charles expressed his surprise and delight at the abundance of flowers and fresh fruits available throughout the year. Seafood was always available, but the climate was not conducive for keeping fresh butter and other perishable staples. The high humidity and prevalence of insects were frustrations to which he would have to learn to adapt.

In the annals of American diplomatic history, perhaps few consuls assumed their post in such trying circumstances as did Charles Maxwell Allen. When, in November 1861, he arrived in the British Crown Colony of Bermuda, the government he represented was engaged in a war that threatened its very existence. The Bermudians, with commercial and family ties to the American South, were for the most part sympathetic to the struggle for independence by the Confederate states. The war years were to see Allen nearly bereft of friends, the object of open hostility from the people of Bermuda, and unable to obtain more than token cooperation from British and Bermudian officials.

Allen found himself enmeshed in the American Civil War he thought to have left behind. Bermuda was the closest British territory to two important Confederate ports, Wilmington, North Carolina, and Charleston, South Carolina. The large, slow-moving, transatlantic steamers that brought Confederate supplies from Europe were not able to pierce the Union blockade of these Confederate ports. In overcoming this obstacle, Bermuda became an important center for the transshipment of goods to the Southern states. Cargoes from Europe were transferred in Bermuda to smaller, faster vessels designed and built to run the blockade and deliver vital war materiel.

The importance of this traffic through Bermuda quickly became apparent to the neophyte diplomat. He was to spend the next four years attempting to thwart the blockade-runners and reporting on their activities in detail to his government.

The establishment of the Union blockade of Southern ports, the efforts to build Confederate ships in English and Scottish shipyards, and the growth of the lucrative blockade-running trade, centered in the Bahamas and Bermuda, can justly be called the "Atlantic campaign" of the Civil War. U.S. consuls on both sides of the Atlantic played crucial roles in this campaign. Thomas Haines Dudley, a lawyer from New Jersey, was appointed consul at Liverpool, England. Freeman H. Morse, a carver by trade and former congressman from Maine, served as consul at London. Mortimer M. Jackson, a Wisconsin jurist, was consul at Halifax, Nova Scotia.

Dudley, with a large network of paid informants, worked to prevent the delivery of ships secretly destined for Confederate service. Morse had the advantage of working in the same city as the U.S. minister to Great Britain, Charles Francis Adams. Jackson, in Nova Scotia, who saw a surprising number of Confederate ships that had arrived for repairs, had the advantage of reporting these activities to the Department of State by telegraph.

By contrast, the consuls at the centers of blockade-running, Capt. Samuel Whiting, who served at Nassau, and Charles Maxwell Allen, who served at Bermuda, had no such advantages. The hostility of the people in the Bahamas overwhelmed Consul Whiting, who took solace in drink. Similar treatment received by Allen in Bermuda seems to have strengthened the resolve of the Yankee consul. Without a large secret service budget, without the advantage of telegraphic reporting, and little knowledge of the actions of his consular colleagues, Allen labored virtually alone.

Allen's dispatches to the secretary of state were often forwarded to the Department of the Navy and quickly sent on to the blockading squadrons.[52] Occasionally, Allen wrote directly to the blockading squadron commanders and to other U.S. consuls alerting them to the movements of the blockade-runners. These diplomatic dispatches have been preserved on microfilm at the United States National Archives.[53]

Allen also wrote letters to his wife. Much to our regret, we do not have the originals of his letters to her, but his daughter, Edith Wistowe Allen, read excerpts from the letters at a Bermuda festival in 1930. Thirty years later, Allen's granddaughter-in-law, Patricia Allen Chaplin, provided a second reading of the letters. The original letters have, since that time, disappeared.[54]

Much has been written about Confederate blockade-running through Bermuda, but little has been written about the diplomatic war waged against these activities by the United States in Bermuda. It is hoped that the Civil War letters of Charles Maxwell Allen will contribute to a more complete picture of Civil War Bermuda. The letters that follow chronicle these events in great detail from the point of view of an American diplomat who rendered great service to his country, though on foreign soil, in what has been called the "Offshore Confederacy."

CHAPTER 2

"Such a God-forsaken place"

▩ Dated twelve days after he received notice of his appointment, Allen's first dispatch to the Department of State was written from his home in Belmont, New York. By the time he wrote this dispatch, every Southern state from Virginia to Texas had withdrawn from the Union. President Lincoln had issued a call for seventy-five thousand volunteers to put down the rebellion, and the Union armies had suffered reverses in both the Eastern and Western theaters of war.

Belmont, N.Y.
Aug. 19th 1861

F. W. Seward Esqr[1]
Assistant Secretary of State, Washington, D.C.

Dear Sir

The blank bond with enclosure came duly to hand.[2] I have had it executed and sent it to the U.S. Attorney at Potsdam for his approval.

The Consular Regulations of which you speak have not arrived. Have they not been yet sent?

I was born in Mass., County of Franklin, and was appointed from New York.

I have always resided in the U.S.

Yours &c,
Chas. M. Allen

▨ Allen's early dispatches to the secretary of state indicate that he prepared himself well for his appointment and, in fact, appears eager to begin his new assignment. Even before Allen left for Bermuda he began to investigate the many facets of the position to which he had been appointed.

Belmont. N.Y.
Sept. 6th 1861

To the Assistant Secretary of State
Washington, D.C.

Sir

   Your enclosure with passport and other papers came to hand today. You request me to furnish the department with the information called for in its letter of Aug. 27th. I have rec'd no such letter. The only papers rec'd being those enclosed with passport, and blank bond with notice of appointment under date of Aug. 7th. The information therein called for was at once forwarded to the Department. I will repeat it. I was born in Franklin Co., State of Mass., and appointed from the State of New York. I have never resided in Great Britain or any of its dependencies.

   Will it be necessary for me to have a consular agt? If so would it be advisable to appoint one before going to Bermuda?

   I would prefer to remain here till the 1st of October if consistent.

Very respectfully &c,
C. M. Allen

▨ Allen's appointment did not come at a particularly propitious time in his personal life. As he was preparing to leave for Bermuda, news arrived of the death of his father-in-law, Amos Richards. Fortunately he was still at home to offer sympathy and comfort to Susan. Also in this year, Charles and Susan's fifth child, a son, William Henry, was born.

   A few days before his departure, Charles sold some of his land to a neighbor.[3] He most likely sold the property to provide for Susan and the children while he was in Bermuda. The property he sold did not include the Allen home for his family remained in Belmont until the end of the war.

   After settling his affairs in Belmont and having been delayed by a severe storm, Allen began the first leg of his journey to Bermuda, arriving in New York City eleven days after this dispatch was written.

Belmont, N.Y.
Sept. 29, 1861

To The Assistant Secretary of State
Washington, D.C.

Sir

Enclosed I send consular bond approved.

I shall leave here as soon as there is any trans. over the road.

The storm of yesterday has destroyed most all the bridges in this vicinity and it may be some days before I can get away.

Any communications will reach me at No. 51 Mangin St., New York till I leave then which will be the first opportunity.

Your obedient servant,
C. M. Allen

▨ The newly appointed consul must have been reassured by the receipt of this document requesting his safe conduct and welcome to Bermuda. The document ensured his safe conduct but could hardly ensure a friendly welcome in pro-Confederate Bermuda.

United States of America, Department of State

To all whom these presents shall come, Greetings:

Know Ye, that the bearer hereof, Charles Maxwell Allen, Esquire, Consul of the United States, at Bermuda, is now proceeding thither.

These are therefore to request all whom it may concern to permit him to pass freely without let or molestation; and to extend to him all such friendly aid and protection as would be extended to Consuls of Foreign Governments, resorting to the United States.

In testimony whereof, I, William H. Seward, Secretary of State of the United States of America, have hereunto signed my name, and caused the Seal of this Department to be affixed, at Washington, this seventh day of October, A.D. 1861, and of the Independence of the United States, the 80th.

William H. Seward

▨ Charles wrote to Susan as soon as he arrived in New York City. His journey of more than three hundred miles must have been arduous due to the damage caused by the severe storm. This may very well have been his first visit to the city of New York.

It is unfortunate that the letters Charles wrote to Susan exist only in two heavily edited transcripts. Each of the transcripts was prepared by a family member who omitted much of the original text, which was probably of a personal nature.[4]

October 9, 1861

I arrived here this morning after a very hard passage. I am well and like the appearance of things.[5]

▨ The cause of the Union had suffered its first major military defeat at the Battle of Bull Run just three months before Allen's arrival in New York City. As volunteers hurried into the ranks, the newly appointed consul to Bermuda waited impatiently for a ship to take him to that isolated Atlantic island. After three weeks in New York, Allen was finally able to book passage on a Bermuda-bound schooner.

No. 51 Mangin Street, New York
Oct. 9, 1861

To The Assistant Secretary of State
Washington, D.C.

Sir

Yours of the 5th inst. with circular &c is at hand. The book of consular regulations of which you speak came to hand some time since. There is no vessel to leave this port for Bermuda before the 23rd inst.

I will ascertain if there is any from Boston before then and, if deemed important I will go there should I find an opportunity to go sooner.

Your obedient servant,
C. M. Allen

⬚ Allen was at last ready to leave for Bermuda. It is ironic that, within a year, the schooner that took him there became a blockade-runner.

New York
Oct. 31st 1861

To The Assistant Secretary of State
Washington, D.C.

Sir,

I expect to leave this port today in the British Schr. *St. George* for Bermuda.

I have been here most of this month and this is the first opportunity I have had to go thence.

Enclosed I send oath of allegiance.

Your obedient servant,
C. M. Allen

⬚ Allen arrived safely in Bermuda and quickly acquainted himself with the town of St. George's, established a residence and made himself known to the public officials. He then began to work with Frederick B. Wells, his predecessor, on the transition of consular duties.[6]

St. George's had been the original capital of the islands, but the seat of government had moved to the more centrally located city of Hamilton in 1815. The U.S. Consulate, however, remained at St. George's until 1872, inasmuch as this place was the principal port of the islands.

It is not known exactly where the consulate was located in St. George's, but Allen submitted quarterly rent receipts to the secretary of state for an office in the town. A watercolor circa 1864 provides a clue to the office location, for there was a U.S. flag waving from a tall flagpole outside a large building near Penno's Wharf.[7] There would have been no U.S. flag in St. George's in 1864 except at the U.S. Consulate. The wharf was on St. George's harbor at the western edge of the town.

A view of U.S. Consulate on Penno's Wharf, St. George's, Bermuda. Painting by Lt. H. S. Clive ca. 1864 (Courtesy of Bermuda National Trust Collection, Bermuda Archives, Hamilton, Bermuda)

Consulate of the United States at Bermuda
Nov. 15th 1861

To The Secretary of State
Washington, D.C.

Sir

In conformity to Article 79 of Consular Regulations I herewith enclose Inventory of the property of the United States at this Consulate. I have this day entered upon my duties.

In a communication from the Assistant Secretary under date of Sept. 9th he expressed as the opinion of the Department that I will not require the services of a Consular Agent.

The ports of Hamilton and St. George are twelve miles apart and nearly an equal amount of official business at each.

Will you please direct what course I shall follow.

Mr. Josiah T. Darrell held the appointment under Mr. Wells as Consular Agent at Hamilton and received his authority to so act from the British Government last June. He is an American citizen and I think him a good and loyal man well calculated to fill the place should it be thought necessary to employ any one. I have requested him to act as heretofore until such time as I can hear from the Department.[8] He has had for his services such fees as he could by law collect which I am informed amount to about two hundred dollars per year.

There is no stationary at this Consulate and but very few blanks of any kind.

I am sir, Your obedient servant,
C. M. Allen

Inventory of Property belonging to the U.S. at the Bermuda Consulate
November 14th 1861

1 Book Case
12 Vol. Statutes at Large
13 Record Books viz
Arrivals & Departures
Seamens Register

Statement of Fees
American Seamen Relieved
Record of Relief
U. S. Treasury Fees
Passports
Invoices
Ships Daily Journal
Marine Note of Protest
Marine Extended Protest
Register of official Letters Recd
Register of official Letters Sent from
5 Vol Commercial Relations
Digest of Revenue Laws
12 Pamphlets Laws
2 Packages unbound official correspondence
5 Vol Bound official correspondence
21 Books Marine Protest extended
5 Vol. Surveys
4 Packages surveys unbound
1 Package old Letters
1 Package old Pamphlets
3 Pamphlets Consular Returns
3 Vol Consular Records
2 U.S. Arms
2 U. S. Flags
1 Flag Staff & fixture
Consulate Seal & Press
2 old books of Returns
1 Vol unbound consular regulations
Blank Forms, certificates, returns, etc.

C. M. Allen
F. B. Wells

No copy of "Wheaton's Digest" was found in this office when I came here, & none has been received since that time.[9]

.

F. B. Wells

✶ Just a week after he began his official duties, Consul Allen was confronted by the first of many blockade-running activities that he would contend with for the next four years. His predecessor, Frederick B. Wells, had felt that little could be done to stop this traffic. In a dispatch to the Department of State dated November 1, 1861, Wells wrote: "All that it has been in my power to do to prevent the *Nashville* from obtaining a supply of coal here has been done. The person who has engaged to supply her has been deaf to my arguments and remonstrances, and I can only now fold my hands, and hope and pray that one of our vessels of war may come here before her departure."

By contrast, Allen took a much more vigorous course of action in these matters. With few resources at his command, Allen became skillful at gathering intelligence from a wide variety of sources. He would prove to be a perceptive observer, an articulate correspondent, and an effective advocate for the interests of his country.

Consulate of the United States at Bermuda,
November 23rd 1861

To The Assistant Secretary of State
Washington, D.C.

Sir,

Capt. B. F. Perkins Master of Brig *A. B. Cook* of New York who arrived here yesterday informs me that on the 19th inst. in Lat. 30° 40' Long. 73° 50' he fell in with the British bark *Neptune* of Falmouth, England. The Master told him he was bound from Glasgow to Quebec with 500 tons of coal but said it was so late he thought he would try to go to Charleston. He wanted to know if the blockade had been raised and made many other inquiries as to the chance of getting into a Southern port, said he was willing to stay about there two months if he thought he could get a load of cotton home.[10] Capt. Perkins says one of the men on board said bark told him their cargo consisted of 300 tons of coal, 200 tons hardware in cases and 40 rifled cannon, that they had been in that vicinity about a week and were expecting a vessel from Charleston to take their Hardware and cannon then they were going to some northern port to sell their coal. Capt. Perkins says judging from the appearance of things the master did not tell him the truth but thinks the man did. He was also informed that when they left the English channel they stood to the southward and passed south of Madeira, says the bark draws about fifteen feet of water.

Captain Perkins appears to be a candid and well informed person. I send the statement as I receive it thinking it possibly may be of service.

I am Sir, Your obedient servant,
C. M. Allen

⊞ Allen spent his first Christmas in Bermuda without family or friends. Shortly after his arrival in Bermuda, he began to experience the open hostility of the local people and officials. He wrote to Susan of the problems he faced, including the possibility that the United States might go to war with Great Britain.

The "difficulties" that Allen referred to in his letter was the *Trent* affair. The Confederate states' commissioners to Great Britain and France, James M. Mason and John Slidell, were in transit to England on the British mail steamer *Trent*. On November 8, 1861, the ship was stopped by the USS *San Jacinto* under the command of Capt. Charles Wilkes. Wilkes seized Mason and Slidell and took them to Boston, where they were imprisoned. This breach of British sovereignty brought the United States and Great Britain close to war. Mason and Slidell were held until January 1, 1862, when they were released by order of Secretary of State Seward. When President Lincoln was questioned about the perceived capitulation to British demands, he was reported to have said, "One war at a time."[11]

December 30, 1861

I have for some days being in a very unsettled state as regards to my remaining here. Everybody here thinks there is no escape of war between England and the United States and if it should prove so of course I should be compelled to leave but I am more hopeful than most others and think the difficulties will in some way be settled without War. The present state of things makes it very unpleasant for me here just now as there is a very bitter feeling against everything and everybody belonging to the United States and many here seem to go upon the supposition that I am responsible for the whole difficulty. I am denied privileges that heretofore have been allowed me and everybody takes the ground that War actually exists.

The Military men of which there are a great many are very busy and I am informed they have been at work all day today making cartridges and mounting guns. They seem to be of the opinion that our people will be after this Island first thing. I told them today at the dinner table "they need have no fear, as our people would not have such a God-forsaken place as this if they could get it for nothing." I hope the next arrival will bring us something definite as to the result of the complicated state of things.

I cannot imagine what has become of the letters I send to you. I sent 3 and I think 4 before the one by the *Princess Royal*. I have written every time a vessel has left here. I am sending this by the Captain of the Ship *Devonshire* who will leave his vessel here and go home by steamer to Halifax.[12]

P. S. The *Excelsior* has just arrived from New York. News, no war.[13]

CHAPTER 3

"They are a big lot of scamps"

As the year 1862 began, British-American relations were probably at their lowest point at any time during the Civil War. The *Trent* affair had not yet been resolved, and the new U.S. consul must have been acutely aware of his delicate position in the British Crown colony of Bermuda.

The quarterly reports that Allen had to submit to the Department of State required meticulous record keeping on a daily basis. Each consular dispatch is numbered. All dispatches were required to be numbered consecutively for each calendar year.

No. 1
Consulate of the United States at Bermuda
January 6th 1862

To the Secretary of State
Washington, D.C.

Sir
Enclosed herewith, I beg to hand you the following returns, for the fraction of the Quarter, ending December 31, 1861 viz[1]

Navigation and Commerce No. 1
Cases of Relief afforded to destitute American Seamen No. 2
Detailed list of Seamen Shipped and Discharged No. 3
Arrivals and departures of American Vessels No. 4

The cases of relief were all to the seamen of the Ship *Jas. W. Fanning,* wrecked on the reefs off these Islands in November last.

No. 12, John Smith, was found on board at the time of the wreck, sick with Small Pox and was immediately sent to quarantine, together with eight others of her crew, who were released after remaining one week.[2]

The whole quarantine experience is included in No. 12 amt. as they were all supplied in common while there, and the amount expended for each could not be definitely ascertained.

The Quarantine Authorities provided nothing except the building. Every thing beside was supplied by the consulate.

The Account Current of No. 2, has been transmitted to the Fifth Auditor of the Treasury, and the return of Fees to the Secretary of the Treasury, also one half of the Register of the late Ship *Jas. W. Fanning.*

I am Sir, Your Obedient Servant,
C. M. Allen

▨ The "very bitter feeling against everything and everybody belonging to the United States" about which Charles wrote to Susan extended to frequent criticism printed in the weekly editions of the *Bermuda Royal Gazette.* It must have given the consul some small measure of satisfaction that the pro-Confederate *Bermuda Royal Gazette* did at least publish his letter, written to correct misrepresentations that appeared in their column.[3]

Consulate of the United States of America
St. George's, Bermuda
Jany. 7th, 1862

Mr. D. McPhee Lee,
Editor of the Royal Gazette, Hamilton:

Sir:

In your issue of Dec. 24th, in an article headed, "United States Ships of War" you say "The Pilot complains they gave him nothing to eat or drink during the 9 hours he was on board the *Quaker City,* and that he was paid but 4s, 2d per foot instead of the regular allowed of 5s per foot for his services."

The Pilot T. Cann who makes the above complaint did not go on board the *Quaker City* as I am reliably informed till after 10 o'clock A.M. and left about 1 o'clock P.M., consequently could not have been on board over three hours instead of 9. The amount paid him was but 4s, 2d per foot, but the fault was his own that he did not get more as he showed no list of charges and [did] not seem positive as to what he ought to have. The Commander of the *Keystone State* was appealed to and said he had just paid Mr. Richardson 4s, 2d for taking him out, and they, supposing that to be right, paid him that amount, which he took without making any objection. In regard to the *Quaker City* taking soundings along your southern shore you seem not to be aware of the fact that it is customary for all our Government vessels to take soundings whenever they can off any shore.

I am, Sir, Yours respectfully,
C. M. Allen, U.S. Consul

◙ Within ten days of their release from prison, the Confederate commissioners, Mason and Slidell, arrived in Bermuda on the HMS *Rinaldo* to great acclaim, and the possibility of war between the United States and Great Britain abated.

No. 2
Consulate of the United States of America at Bermuda
January 10, 1862

To the Secretary of State
Washington, D.C.

Sir,
    I beg to inform you that the Steamer *Rinaldo,* with Mason & Slidell and their Secretaries on board, arrived here yesterday, the severe weather having prevented their getting to Halifax.
    I understand they are to dine today with Admiral Milne, and tomorrow proceed on their voyage to Europe by way of St. Thomas.[4]
    The sympathy of the people of these Islands is almost entirely with them and their cause; and they are very bitter against the government of the United States.

I am Sir, Your Obedient Servant,
C. M. Allen, U.S. Consul

◈ Charles's next letter to Susan conveys his indignation when a secession flag was raised on the grounds of the U.S. consulate. This would not be the only time that the U.S. consulate at St. George's would be violated.[5]

January 13, 1862

Slidell and Mason arrived here in the *Rinaldo* last Thursday; dined with the Admiral and next day went on to St. Thomas. They were Lions here.

I found a Secession Flag on my Flag-staff yesterday morning; it was a new one and as I was up early I captured it before anyone saw it; there was a most miserable, dirty apology for the Stars and Stripes underneath it—Union Down! There is a Secession vessel in Port under British Colors and one Steamer which is going to run the Blockade if they can.[6]

◈ Allen's actions in alerting the authorities to the distressed American vessel, the *Wheatland,* saved the ship but in so doing created a host of problems that would consume an inordinate amount of his time over the next six months.[7]

No. 3
Consulate of the United States of America at Bermuda
February 4th 1862
To the Secretary of State
Washington, D.C.

Sir

I beg to inform you that the Bark *Wheatland* of Baltimore from Palermo bound to New York anchored off these Islands on the evening of the 2nd inst. in distress, having lost sail, and otherwise disabled, and entirely out of provisions. There being at the time a strong wind, she parted both chains, and in attempting to make sail to regain the land lost all the sail she then had and was driven to sea.

I immediately made known this situation to Sir Admiral Milne, in Her Majesties Service, who only on the following morning ordered two steamers under his command to proceed at once in search of the said Bark. They returned this morning having found her some distance to the south, and took her in tow, and brought her safely into the port of St. George.

I am Sir, Very respectfully, &c,
C. M. Allen, U.S. Consul

◩ Throughout this period there was also ongoing routine consular business that claimed Allen's attention. He spent a surprising amount of time dealing with American ships that arrived in Bermuda in distressed circumstances. When the American ship *Devonshire* arrived in Bermuda and was unable to be repaired, it fell to the U.S. consul to provide for the destitute American seamen. With so few people in St. George's sympathetic to the government Allen represented, the arrival of these American vessels would have provided welcome company from "home" for the consul from New York. They also often raised complex issues of maritime law. Allen invariably demonstrated his clarity of thought and expression in these cases.

Consulate of the United States of America at St. George Bermuda
Feb 7, 1862

To the Fifth Auditor of the Treasury
Washington, D.C.

Sir,
    Your communication of Jan 10th with copies of correspondence with Capt. J. W. Shaw in relation to the claim made by him for taking home destitute American Seamen from the Ship *Devonshire* was received at this consulate on the 4th inst.
    I immediately addressed a letter inquiring into this matter to Thomas Anderson late Master of same ship, and received from him a reply, of which I herewith enclose a copy.
    From all I can learn, I think his statement is in accordance with the facts in the case, and trust the information he furnishes will enable you to see the claim of Capt. Shaw in its true light. Should you require Capt. Anderson's Affidavit, or wish to communicate with him, he can be found care of E. E. Morgan Esqr South Street, New York, he leaves here for there in a few days.

The ship *Devonshire* has had a survey upon her, and the surveyor's report what should be done to put her in order for the continuance of her voyage. The Master does not propose to make her sea worthy but simply to repair her enough that with the aid of steam pumps he may get her to New York. I have taken for my guidance in regard to the crew of said ship the 12th 13th & 14th sections of the act of July 1840 and required the payment of one month's extra wages each for the seamen discharged, and one month's pay each for the government. If I am wrong will you please instruct me, and shall not I claim the same amt. for each of the six men sent home in the Brig *J. C. Shaw?*

I am, Sir, Your obedient servant,
C. M. Allen, U.S. Consul

▨ Allen was to face many difficult issues as consul, but the incident reported in this dispatch clearly shows that there were some matters to which the statute books could give no answer.

No. 4
Consulate of the United States of America at St. George Bermuda
February 10, 1862

To the Secretary of State
Washington, D.C.

Sir
The Bark *Wheatland* of Baltimore, J. R. Peacock, Master, forty two days from Palermo laden mostly with Brimstone, and same to be bound to New York, recently put into this port in distress, has on board a rebel flag. The Master says he had it made expecting to find the port of New York blockaded, and in that case he would use it to get into a southern port.

Complaint has been made to me, by some of his crew that the same Master is guilty of Sodomy, or Buggery, committed upon the person of a boy fifteen years of age, a native of Denmark, and shipped on board his vessel at Copenhagen. The said act is alleged to have been committed at sundry times, both on the high seas, and in port on the Mediterranean. I think the evidence is conclusive of his guilt, but as I am unable to find any Federal Statute making the charges a crime, and as in all probability the said vessel will not leave here for some weeks, will you please instruct me what action if any I shall take in the premises.

The Schr. *Emma de Russie,* Capt. Neil hailing from Sydney, New South Wales, and as I am informed, has an English register, flies both the British and rebel flag in port here. The vessel and master formerly belonged to Pensacola and if my information is correct, the Master is still the owner. She is loaded with molasses and will sail in about two weeks, said to bound to New York. On her arrival here she reported herself sixty two days from Havana.

With much respect, Your Obedient Servant,
C. M. Allen, U.S. Consul

More confident and comfortable after three months in hostile Bermuda, Charles's next letter to Susan must have pleased her. The roommate to which he refers in this letter was Edward James, an English artist who had arrived in Bermuda about the same time as Allen.[8] James would become one of Allen's only friends in St. George's during the war. The paintings and sketches that James made of blockade-running vessels were to be of great assistance to Consul Allen.

February 10, 1862

The climate has agreed with me; I have gained 18 lbs. My roommate is an artist. Business at the Consulate has been very slack—for instance, the law says I shall appoint surveyors for the ships here but the first after I came was surveyed before I knew anything of it and I found that the Agent of the vessel appointed the Surveyor so that he may get just the report to suit himself, etc.; consequently greatly displeased with the new Consul. An American vessel anchored just outside the harbor last week about nightfall. A Storm came up and she was driven off without provisions. I had to get to the Admiral's at the other end of the Island and was all night getting there;[9] he sent two steamers after the vessel; they found her and brought her in the next day.[10]

As blockade-runners arrived in Bermuda in increasing numbers, Allen began to send detailed reports of their activities to his government. After little more than three months in Bermuda, Allen was becoming adept at gathering intelligence. Without being privy to a blockade-runner's papers, he was able to report on the ship's captain, cargo, origin, and destination, gleaned from the weekly *Bermuda Royal Gazette* and Custom House cargo manifests as well as from conversations with captains and crews conducting business with the consul.

No. 5
Consulate of the United States of America at Bermuda
17th February 1862

To the Secretary of State
Washington, D.C.

Sir

I beg to inform you that the Schooner *Pearl* of Newborn [New Bern], N.C., Beneridge, Master, arrived at these Islands on the 15th inst. having on board 540 bbls Spirits Turpentine, 2 tons of Beeswax, and a quantity of Tobacco. The master reports having ran the blockade off Beaufort [North Carolina] on the night of the 7th inst. She came here under United States colors, and the Master reported himself at the custom house from the United States, but has not deposited his papers in this Consulate.

She was on the rocks off these Islands and is badly injured, will require some three weeks to get ready for sea.

I am very respectfully, Your obedient servant,
C. M. Allen, Consul

▨ Vessels often called at Bermuda in order to resupply with coal, quantities of which were kept there for this purpose. The proclamation of neutrality issued by the British government prohibited the establishment of coal depots by either the United States or the Confederacy in any of the British colonies. However, inasmuch as blockade-runners were receiving coal from private Confederate agents in Bermuda, the United States Navy Department shipped quantities of coal to Allen for their own use. Governor Ord's letter to Allen, dated February 19, 1862, confirmed that coal depots were not to be established in any British colony "for the use of their vessels of war, either by the Government of the United States or of the so-styled Confederate States."[11]

Brief handwritten notes appear at the top of almost all of Allen's dispatches to the Department of State recording the date each dispatch was received. Ord's letter occasioned an additional remark to be affixed to this dispatch, noting, "Please copy for Congress."

No. 6
Consulate of the United States of America at Bermuda
20th February 1862

To the Secretary of State
Washington, D.C.

Sir

I beg to inform you that the Rebel Steamer *Nashville* arrived at these Islands this P.M. reported seventeen days from Southampton, short of coal. I shall do all I can to prevent her getting coal.

I am informed her armament is the same as when here last fall, but the vessel has changed some in appearance, having had her masts shortened, and some alterations about her head. She has but little cargo if any. I herewith enclose paper No. 1, copy of a communication recd this day from Gov'r. Ord in relation to the formation of a Coal Depot here.

I have received four cargoes of coal amounting to about 1150 tons shipped by the U.S. Navy Department from Philadelphia, but have received no instructions as to its disposition. I have a very good place to store it at an annual rent of $100 per year.

With much respect, I am sir, Your obedient servant,
C. M. Allen, Consul

▨ Because of the prohibition against U.S. and Confederate warships receiving coal from established coal depots on the island, the CSS *Nashville* obtained its coal from a British ship lying in St. George's harbor.[12]

No. 7
Consulate of the United States of America at Bermuda
Feby 22nd 1862

To the Secretary of State
Washington, D.C.

Sir

I have the honor to inform you the Steamer *Nashville* is still here and is obtaining a supply of coal from the British Ship *Mohawk*.

They report having seen no vessels on the passage hither from England. I understand it is their intention to go from here immediately home.

I am Sir, With much respect, Your obedient servant,
C. M. Allen, Consul

🀫 Charles's correspondence was via U.S. military and commercial vessels. These letters were often written under the pressure of a ship's imminent departure, as with this letter to Susan.

February 22, 1862

This is Washington's birthday and the news from home is the most cheering of anything since the war commenced. I mean the result of the Burnside expedition.[13] I cannot write more now. The Capt. is waiting for this impatiently and I have had so much to do I could not find time to write more.[14]

🀫 Allen reports on the success of the *Nashville* in obtaining fuel as the ship departs Bermuda under British escort with 150 tons of coal. Although technically not a blockade-runner, the CSS *Nashville* successfully ran the blockade and arrived at Beaufort, North Carolina, just four days after leaving Bermuda.

No. 8
Consulate of the United States of America at Bermuda
February 25th 1862

To the Secretary of State
Washington, D.C.

Sir
I beg to inform you that the Steamer *Nashville* left here yesterday, after taking on board 150 tons of coal and all of the crew, and master, of the Schooner *Pearl,* recently arrived here from Newbern, N.C.
She left these Islands under escort of their Majesties Steamer *Spiteful* and from all the information I can gather, I think she will go directly to Charleston or vicinity.

I am reliably informed that a large portion of her crew were confined below deck while in port here.

I am sir, Your obedient servant,
C. M. Allen, Consul

🔲 Recognizing the importance of U.S. consuls as sources of intelligence, by the spring of 1862 Secretary of State Seward had requested that consuls provide more detailed descriptions of blockade-running vessels. In addition to physical descriptions of the vessels, the content of Allen's dispatches now include such details as their colors and insignia, which would assist the United States Navy in identifying these vessels.

No. 9
Consulate of the United States of America at Bermuda
5th March 1862

To the Secretary of State
Washington, D.C.

Sir

I have the honor to inform you that the British screw-steamer *Economist,* having on board a full cargo, and the 1st Lieut. of the Southern Steamer *Nashville* and two pilots belonging to the Southern States, arrived at these Islands on the 28th ult. having cleared at London on the 29th of January last for Melbourne. She is owned as per register, by Richard G. Brisberg of Liverpool, is 472 tons burden, is bark rigged and draws 10 feet of water. She is a long narrow Steamer with no topmasts or spars, and reported very fast.

She came here to replenish her coal, and as I am informed, intended to leave at once after doing so, but the late news from the Southern States seems to have disarranged their plans and at present they seem undecided what to do.[15]

I am unable to learn anything reliable in regard to her cargo.

I am sir, With much respect, Your obedient servant,
C. M. Allen, Consul

⊞ Within six months of his arrival in Bermuda, Charles was busily engaged in forming a small circle of friends and associates sympathetic to the cause of the Union. After an initial period of loneliness and frustration, he was able to write to Susan about his improved domestic and social circumstances.

March 10, 1862

Rec'd 3 letters written by you in January & none since. I expect some to-night as a steamer has just gone into Hamilton from New York. The vessels that I sent my last 3 letters by have all come back; they had a terrible storm. The *Princess Royal* went about the same time & I hope that she got there safe; four came in here in one day with masts gone. I have gone to housekeeping & am getting on very nicely; the barrel you sent after a long time came safe to hand, not a thing broken & the things were just what I wanted. One Captain gave me 2 good pillows & 2 nice good hair mattresses & one white spread & a looking-glass. The Captain of a steamer bound to China went from here yesterday & he gave me a keg of prime good butter which is a great treat here as we seldom get any fit to eat. I have a boy of 14 years who stays with me for his board & he does everything. We have our dinner at 6 P.M. & it is the only cooked meal. Since I have been writing a Captain has come in & told me to send on board his ship & get a kit of mackerel. Do not think that I shall starve.

I have a good deal of trouble with some of the Captains here; they are a big lot of scamps, many of them. I expect to send one home in "irons" soon; another shot two men last night, killing one instantly. He will stand a good chance to get his neck stretched before he gets away from here.[16]

It has been more than 5 months since I left home & I cannot realize that you have been having a cold winter. The weather is beautiful here most of the time; yesterday was the coldest I have known yet; everything is green and beautiful, plenty of flowers; I wish I could send you a bouquet.

At the Captain's request, I invited all my friends on board his steamer last week & he gave us an elegant dinner & we had quite a gay time. The steamer is a new one called the *Kiang-Tsi,* built in New York for China & on her pas-sage she broke her wheel & came in here to repair.[17]

◉ Despite political tensions between the two countries, Allen writes to Washington about a U.S. vessel rescued by a British vessel.

No. 11
Consulate of the United States of America at Bermuda
March 18th 1862

To the Secretary of State
Washington, D.C.

Sir

I have the honor of informing you that the British Ship *Mohawk*, F. W. Fuller Master, on a voyage from these Islands to New York on the 9th inst. in Lat. 43–38, Long 64–30 fell in with the Bark *Hyperion* of New York with everything above decks gone excepting the lower main mast and a part of the mizzen mast. The master had his arm broken and having lost all his nautical instruments begged to be taken off.

Capt. J. B. Richardson of this place who was their acting mate on board the *Mohawk* volunteered to go on board the bark and try to take her into some port. Capt. Fuller allowed him to do so and sent four men from his vessel to assist him. He succeeded in bringing her safe into port here on the 12th inst.

I am Sir, With much respect,
Your Obedient Servant,
C. M. Allen, Consul

◉ The British steamer *Bermuda* arrives at St. George's laden with arms and ammunition. In the autumn of 1861, the *Bermuda* became the first vessel to successfully run the blockade at Savannah, Georgia. Her success in bringing large quantities of cotton through the blockade to England led many British ship owners to engage in blockade-running.

No. 12
Consulate of the United States of America at Bermuda
March 20, 1862

To the Secretary of State
Washington, D.C.

Sir

I beg to inform you that the British Screw Steamer *Bermuda,* nineteen days from Liverpool, arrived here this morning. I learn that she has some mdse. for these Islands, but her principal cargo is arms and ammunition, and I think there is but little doubt that their intention is to run the blockade of some Southern port. She has on board some very heavy rifled guns. She draws fifteen feet of water if full. Brig rigged, with the exception of bowsprit, of which she has none. She is the same vessel that took a cargo of cotton from Charleston some time since.

I am Sir, Your Obedient Servant,
C. M. Allen, Consul

▣ Blockade-runners brought more war materiel into St. George's than the small community was able to accommodate. Vessels laden with powder were often prevented from unloading their dangerous cargoes until secure storage on shore could be found. Storage of any kind was very limited in St. George's.[18]

No. 13
Consulate of the United States of America at Bermuda
22nd March 1862
To the Secretary of State
Washington, D.C.

Sir

The British Iron Screw Steamer *Sedgewick* arrived here last night, reports twenty five days from London bound to Nassau with a general cargo.[19] She is about 500 tons burden, and draws fifteen feet of water. Her Hull is dark red. She has one smokestack with a large white diamond on two sides. From appearances I think she has a cargo for the Southern States.

The *Bermuda* I am informed wants to discharge her cargo here, but having a large quantity of powder, she cannot as yet get storage.

I am Sir, Your Obedient Servant,
C. M. Allen, Consul

P. S. I have just learned that the *Bermuda* is to remain here till some vessel or vessels come for her cargo. I am informed at the Custom House that the *Sedgewick* has a full cargo of Shot & Shell. C. M. A.

John Tory Bourne, a Bermudian, was the Confederate commercial agent in Bermuda to whom many of the blockade-running ships were consigned, including the British steamer *Herald*. At this early stage of blockade-running, one unforeseen risk to the owners was that of a master who refused to take the ship through the blockade. The master of the *Herald*, who had signed ship's articles specifying a different destination, had not been told that the ultimate destination was a Confederate port. In seeking Consul Allen's assistance in making an official protest, he set off a series of legal maneuverings between the shipowner and Bermudian government officials that would occupy them and Allen for the next three months.

No. 14
Consulate of the United States of America at Bermuda
24th March 1862

To the Secretary of State
Washington, D.C.

Sir

I beg to inform you that the British Side wheel Steamer *Herald* of Dublin reported fourteen days from Madeira arrived here this morning. She is consigned to J. T. Bourne agent for the so called "Southern Confederacy." She is a long narrow iron vessel of about 600 tons burden and draws but 9 feet of water, is white below water line, and black above, has one smoke stack and two masts, with yards on the foremast. It is reported she is to take the cargo of the *Bermuda*, but from her appearance I should think she has on board a full cargo. The Steamers *Bermuda* and *Sedgewick* are still here. I think the

Sedgewick will leave soon, and presume the cargo of the *Bermuda* will be re-shipped. They have tried to get storage for it, but as there is a large quantity of powder the authorities will not allow it to be landed. Fourteen men came as passengers in the *Bermuda,* they are supposed to be Southerners.

I am Sir, Your Obedient Servant
C. M. Allen, Consul

⊕ Learning of the shipowners' intent to run the blockade, Captain Tate, master of the *Herald,* requests the intercession of the U.S. consul.

No. 15
Consulate of the United States of America at Bermuda
28th March 1862

To the Secretary of State
Washington, D.C.

Sir

I beg to inform you that the British Steamer *Southwick* left these Islands on the 25th inst. with the rebel flag flying at her main peak. In my dispatch No. 13 I incorrectly reported her as the *Sedgewick.* Since the Steamer *Herald* arrived here on the 24th I have had several confidential interviews with her Master. She was chartered to come here and to go to ports in the West Indies not to be absent more than twelve month.

She has on board munitions of war but not a full cargo. Her supercargo this morning ordered her to go along side of the *Bermuda* and take in shot and shell and go to Charleston.[20] He did not refuse but came to me and I went with him to the Mayor and he entered a protest which was signed by the Chief Engineer also.[21] He has now gone on board the *Bermuda* to [ask?] the Master for an [order?] as the risk is greater to go to Charleston than the W.I. [West Indies.] If he gets it and I think he will I shall have him where the authorities here will have to take hold. If they order him to Havana he declares he will smash his engines before he will leave as there is four of the *Nashville*'s men on board and the pilot who took the *Bermuda* into Charleston before. The vessel is now underway that takes this. I will write by the first opportunity the results.

I am Sir, Very respectfully,
C. M. Allen, Consul

◼ Allen was not deterred in his efforts to prevent the *Herald* from running the blockade. Having appealed to the governor he was told nothing could be done unless the ship's cargo was unloaded. A determined Allen continues his efforts. John Tory Bourne's colorful firsthand account of this affair can be found in his letter to the shipowners dated April 8, 1862.[22]

No. 16
Consulate of the United States of America at Bermuda
1st April 1862

Hon. Wm. H. Seward,
Secretary of State, Washington, D.C.

Sir

The Steamers *Bermuda* and *Herald* are still in port here and are yet in trouble. A person calling himself Lewis Mitchell from one of the Southern States and super cargo of the Steamer *Herald* appears to be the managing man. I learn it was his intention to run the *Herald* between this place and Charleston. The Master has in his possession a power of attorney to two men in Charleston authorizing them to sell the vessel. The master is willing to go where the vessel was chartered to go, but he will not go to the Southern States unless he goes as a prisoner, neither will he leave this port for the W.I. with the fourteen Southern men who want to go as passengers. They have used every exertion in their power to induce the Master to leave the vessel but he says he will not give her up. Her cargo is entered at the Custom House as stationery which is false. I have laid all the facts before the authorities here but they say they can do nothing unless the cargo is landed. The ship *Ella* forty days from London or Liverpool arrived here on the 3rd ult. She has a general cargo to be reshipped to the Southern States.

I am sir, Your Obedient Servant
C. M. Allen, Consul

◼ Though hard pressed with the affairs of the *Herald,* Allen submits his meticulous quarterly report in a timely manner.

No. 17
Consulate of the United States of America at Bermuda
4th April 1862

To the Secretary of State
Washington, D.C.

Sir

I have the honor to enclose herewith the following accounts and vouchers for the quarter ending March 31st 1862 numbered from 1 to 12. No 1, Arrivals and Departures, and Statement of fees, No. 2, Seamen Shipped and discharged, No. 3, Navigation and Commerce, No. 4, Account for Postage, No. 5, Account for Letters Sent, No. 6, Letters Received, No. 7, Account of Office Rent, No. 8, 9, 10, 11, Accounts rendered by J. T. Darrell Consular Agent, at the Port of Hamilton and copied on to the books of the Consulate, No. 12, Vouchers for Office rent.

I am Sir, Your Obedient Servant,
C. M. Allen, Consul

▨ As blockade-runners continue to arrive at St. George's, the *Herald* takes on a new crew, but the dispute remains unresolved.

No. 18
Consulate of the United States of America at Bermuda
19th April 1862

To the Secretary of State
Washington, D.C.

Sir

I beg to inform you that the British Steamer *Economist* arrived here yesterday with 700 Bales of Cotton and 800 Bbls Naval Stores. She reports having left Charleston on the 2nd inst. and came by way of Nassau. The Steamers *Herald* and *Bermuda* are still here. The *Herald*'s entire crew have been discharged and a new one shipped. It is reported they will both leave for Charleston immediately. The Ship *Ella* has not discharged her cargo. A Barque has just arrived from Europe with coal consigned to J. T. Bourne, the agent here for the

Southern States. I am informed the *Economist* will not discharge here but go directly to England. The master reports no difficulty in running the blockade at Charleston.

I am Sir, Your Obedient Servant,
C. M. Allen, Consul

⬚ The British steamer *Stettin* joins the *Bermuda* and the *Herald* as they prepare to run the blockade. Allen's mention of Tampico refers to blockade-running through Mexican ports such as Tampico, from which goods were then transported across the Rio Grande and into Confederate Texas.

No. 19
Consulate of the United States of America at Bermuda
19th April 1862

To the Secretary of State
Washington, D.C.

Sir
    The British Iron Screw Steamer *Stettin* has just arrived here with a cargo for the Southern States. I am informed she will proceed from here to Tampico and the *Bermuda* and perhaps the *Herald* will accompany her.[23] I think their destination as above is correct.

I am Sir, With much respect,
C. M. Allen, Consul

⬚ With the departure of the *Stettin* and the *Bermuda,* Charles takes the opportunity to write home. This affectionate letter provides a glimpse into the personal interests and activities of Charles and Susan.[24]

April 24, 1862
    My office furniture I bought of the former Consul for $50. Did you see the piece in the *Herald* of the 14th April about Bermuda? I have not seen it but heard it spoken of.

Three steamers left here yesterday, 2 for Southern States, one for Europe from Charleston with cotton and turpentine.

I saw the whales playing but a short distance from the land a few days ago; they came out of the water at least 50 feet & threw their fins up so that they looked like boat sails. It was worth going a great way to see. I have not yet been fishing but I hope to go soon. I have had so much to do I have not painted any lately but when I get through with distressed vessels and wrecked seamen, which I hope will be soon, I shall go at it again.

We had news here from Charleston that the "South had whipped the Northern Army & killed and taken them all prisoners." There was great rejoicing here & everyone seemed to believe it. The next day a steamer came from New York with some days' later news & it appeared that the victory was on the other side but no one would believe it. It is wonderful to see how ready they are to believe anything that favors the South and ready to disbelieve anything that favors the North. The fact is they are afraid of the growth of our country & want to see it divided. I don't know of a person here that expresses an idea that the States will ever be united again. I have no patience to talk with them so I have learned to keep quiet and enter into no arguments. Every hole & corner is filled up with Southerners, some have left today but there are plenty left. If they will only catch the steamers *Bermuda* and *Stettin* that have gone today I shall be thankful.

Please send some newspapers; there is no postage on them from New York here. There are plenty of fleas and cockroaches here; ants everywhere and all victuals have to be hung up by a rod with a cup around it filled with oil. I have 4-lbs of ice a day for which I pay $3 a month. I am boarding with colored folks[25] for 60 cents a day & sleep myself.[26] I have been full of business with distressed vessels, rebel steamers and shipwrecked sailors. I have now on hand 22 who were part of the crew of the *Ocean Monarch* of New York; they were picked up in an open boat at sea and brought in here. There are in port 2 steamers and one ship with cargoes for the Southern States.

I have a bad job on hand, I am afraid; some of the men off the *Ocean Monarch* have things belonging to the Captain; one of them says there was money taken and that the Captain was left on board helpless having been struck by some of the men. I shall have an examination & try to get at the facts. The master of the vessel that picked them up thinks that the Captain was murdered.

There are a great many Southern people here; 14 came in the steamer *Bermuda.* They & their friends are down on me & have threatened to whip me. I have made them a great deal of trouble and got them into a fix they cannot get out of very easily & I intend to follow them up close.

I learn the [USS] *Vermont* was seen two days ago about 60 miles north of here in tow of a steamer. We had a terrific gale here yesterday.[27]

I should love to see you and the children but if this Southern business continues I am not sure that I can get leave of absence. Ladies wear silks some here but musters never; all their dresses are flounced; there are not many bonnets worn; they wear flats more.[28]

▣ As blockade-runners depart St. George's, the fate of the master of the *Herald* remains unresolved. The day after this dispatch was written, the *Bermuda* was captured between Bermuda and the Bahamas. It was converted into a U.S. ship and saw service with the Gulf Blockading Squadron.

No. 20
Consulate of the United States of America at Bermuda
April 26th 1862

Hon. Wm. H. Seward
Secretary of State, Washington, D.C.

Sir

The Steamers *Bermuda* and *Stettin* left here on the 23 inst., they cleared for Tampico. The *Economist* left on the same day for England. The *Herald* is still here and cannot go until they get authority from England to remove her master.

I am sir, Your Obedient Servant
C. M. Allen, Consul

Allen's authority to act in consular matters was questioned in Bermuda, because up until this time, he had been acting without the benefit of his official consular papers. This placed the consul in a diplomatically ambiguous position. The receipt of his commission confirmed his appointment by the U.S. government. According to Benjamin Moran, assistant secretary at the U.S. embassy in London, Consul Allen's exequatur, although requested in September 1861, was received more than a year later in October 1862. Moran's diary comments on the long delay, noting, "This gov't seems to have no rule in these cases, caprice usually governing."[29]

No. 21
Consulate of the United States of America at Bermuda
6th May 1862

To the Secretary of State
Washington, D.C.

Sir

Your communication of the 17th of April, with commission enclosed, has been this day received.

I am, with great respect,
Your Obedient Servant,
C. M. Allen, Consul

This dispatch, regarding the Barque *Wheatland,* is the beginning of a lengthy correspondence between Allen, the secretary of state, Governor Ord, the U.S. representative from New York, and the New York Board of Underwriters. Allen's attempts to replace the Rebel captain resulted in threats of bodily harm to Allen and demonstrates not only his legal persistence but also his willingness to place himself in harm's way in the performance of his consular responsibilities. Allen's actions forced Governor Ord to support him, although unwillingly, in light of the continued absence of his exequatur.

Allen's actions resulted in the removal of the captain and the rescue of the *Wheatland* and also brought to the attention of the Board of Underwriters a scheme to defraud the board. Allen's involvement brought recognition of his efforts from both the secretary of state and the New York Board of Underwriters.

No. 22
Consulate of the United States of America, Bermuda
24th May 1862

To the Secretary of State
Washington, D.C.

Sir

I have the honor to submit for your consideration and advice, the following circumstances connected with the Barque *Wheatland* of Baltimore. On the 29th of April, the said vessel then lying in the port of St. George, Bermuda, I was waited upon by Mr. W. C. Poe and Mr. A. V. Fraser, who presented to me letters, and a power of attorney, by which it appeared that the former was duly empowered by the owner of the said Barque, to supersede in the command thereof, J. R. Peacock, the then master and that the latter was authorized by the underwriters to cooperate with the former.[30] On the 30th I consequently proceeded in the presence of the three above named gentlemen, to attach to the ship's register the usual certificate removing Mr. Peacock from command, and appointing Mr. Poe in his place. On the 2nd of May, Mr. Poe obtained peaceable possession of the vessel, and on the same day was ejected from it by Captn. Peacock, assisted by others. I therefore applied to the local authorities for assistance in reinstating Mr. Poe, but was met by a distinct refusal. On the 3rd I addressed to the Governor here a letter (Enclosure No. 1) asking his protection in the matter. It will be proper here to mention that in consequence of the non arrival of my commission, or exequatur, I had been in some difficulty as to the recognition of my position here, and had mentioned the matter to the Governor at a previous interview, and he informed me that he considered me as Consul of the United States. On the 8th I received a reply from the Governor (Enclosure No. 2) informing me he had directed the magistrates to afford such aid as might appear to them necessary to keep order and to maintain the peace. On the 10th I made a second application to the magistrates and a constable, and his assistant having been dispatched to the vessel, I proceeded in company with Mr. Poe, and Mr. Fraser, for the purpose of reinstating the former in command, but was met by the former Master and forcibly prevented from going on board, the Constable standing passive. On the 12th I called on the Governor with Mr. Poe and Mr. Fraser. The Governor requested a private interview, at which he informed me he had no jurisdiction to interfere further, and the remedy was in the courts of law. I inquired if he had come to that conclusion from the fact that I was not recognized by the British Government; he replied that he had not taken that ground, but might be compelled to do so. I then handed him my commission for perusal, and addressed him another letter (Enclosure No. 3). On the 13th I received a reply (Enclosure No. 4) and in consequence on the 14th I made a further application to Mr. Fisher, Police Magistrate, which resulted in my being accompanied on board the vessel by him and being enabled peacefully to reinstate Mr. Poe in command, and to remove Captn. Peacock. I would mention that I was the more urgent in my proceedings from the fact that the cargo of the vessel had been illegally sacrificed to meet the repairs. A cargo of brimstone insured for $12,000 was sold for less than $2,000 above the expense incurred on the same here, and was then being shipped on board a vessel formerly owned and belonging to Pensacola, and now owned by the same person under the British flag, and flying the Rebel flag at the fore, from all the information I could get it appeared to be the intentions of the parties interested to get the cargo into a Southern port of the United States, and I had been informed the agent had publicly announced his intention of selling the vessel as well. My object in submitting these facts to you is to ascertain whether in what has occurred I have exceeded or kept within the limits of my consular authority; in the absence of any consular treaty between the government and our own. I understand the broad principle to be, that I am empowered to do any act on board an American vessel in this port, not conflicting with the laws of the United States, or with any local law. I have been careful not to do any act which can in any way be interpreted as thus conflicting, but as considerable doubt does appear to exist, as to the exact intent of consular jurisdiction in such a case, and as an exactly similar state of things may arise tomorrow, I have thought it best to lay the facts before you for instruction and advice. The points involved appear to me to be of great importance as bearing on our Mercantile and Maritime interest in general.

I am Sir, Your most obedient servt,
C. M. Allen, U.S. Consul

Beginning to develop a network of informants, Allen discovers the true identity of the new master of the *Herald*. Lewis Mitchell Coxetter, the man who replaced Captain Tate on the *Herald* and one of the most successful of all blockade-runners. As commander of the *Jefferson Davis* and later of the *Herald*, he made twenty-four successful voyages through the blockade.[31]

No. 23
Consulate of the United States of America at Bermuda
June 4th 1862

Hon. Wm. H. Seward
Secretary of State, Washington, D.C.

Sir

The owner of the Steamer *Herald* which vessel has been in port here since about the 20th of March arrived here yesterday. I learn the master Capt. Tate will be displaced today and a man calling himself Mitchell who I am satisfied is no other than Capt. Coxsetter formerly of the *Jeff Davis* will take command.[32] He has been here for some weeks and has been several times identified. A person this morning informs me he has known him for seven years and knows him to be the same.

There is no doubt in my mind but that the vessel when he leaves here will go direct to Charleston. How soon she will get away is uncertain but I should think within ten days. She is a very fast side wheel steamer, long and low and draws but nine feet of water. Five of her crew will not go unless compelled by the authorities here to do so. From present appearances I think they cannot escape. Their names are George Murry, Robert Burchell, John Fegan, Patrick Clark & Patrick Fegan. The Schr. *Jane Campbell* has been in port here for some days awaiting orders.

I am sir, Your most obedt. sevt.
C. M. Allen, Consul

Encountering further difficulties, the *Herald* is still unable to run the blockade for want of a crew.

No. 24
Consulate of the United States of America at Bermuda
June 10, 1862

To the Secretary of State
Washington, D.C.

Sir

The schr *Anna E. Berry* arrived here on the 7th inst. from Wilmington, N.C. with cotton & tobacco.[33]

The Steamer *Herald* is still here, a large portion of her crew having left her. They cannot get a crew, and will I think be detained some days.

I am, with much respect,
Your obedient Servant,
C. M. Allen, Consul

◼ Having secured a crew, the *Herald* at last leaves for Charleston. Allen's intervention, while not ultimately successful, did delay for more than three months a large cargo of arms and ammunition destined for the Confederate states. As more and more blockade-runners arrive at St. George's, Allen reports that they are having difficulty securing coal.

No. 25
Consulate of the United States of America at Bermuda
June 11th 1862

Hon. Wm. H. Seward
Secretary of State, Washington, D.C.

Sir

The Steamer *Herald* left here yesterday under command of Capt. Coxsetter who shipped by his real name. She cleared for Nassau.

The iron screw steamer *Stanley* of Aberdeen arrived here on the 11th inst. reported twenty four days from Liverpool bound to Nassau with a full cargo. She is about 500 tons burden, has three masts, with yards on the foremast.

The iron side wheel steamer *Leopard* of Glasgow, arrived here on the 12th inst., reports fifteen days from Cork. She is about 350 tons burden of light draft, Schr. rigged, and apparently a very fast vessel. The *Leopard* has taken all the coal in the hands of individuals which is only about fifty tons and I am informed will leave early next week. The *Stanley* is in want of coal but cannot get it as the Government refuses to supply them.

The three above named vessels belong to what is called here "Wilson's Southern line" and are consigned to J. T. Bourne the Southern agent here.[34]

The crew of the Schr. *Anna E. Berry* all left here in the Steamer *Herald* after having shipped their cargo to London.

I am Sir, Your obedient Servant,
C. M. Allen, Consul

◼ Charles observed many Allen family anniversaries without the love and companionship of his wife and children. He writes to Susan a few days after his fortieth birthday. Here he comments on the capture of the *Bermuda* and the *Stettin*.[35] This news must have given him some measure of satisfaction.

June 26, 1862:

Will they keep the Steamer *Bermuda* or let her go?[36] I see the *Stettin* has been caught.[37]

🌐 By the summer of 1862, the vast number of blockade-runners through Bermuda had exhausted coal supplies on the island. A relieved consul reports that Governor Ord has taken a strong stand "against these islands being made a depot for those in the interest of the rebellion."

No. 26
Consulate of the United States at Bermuda
June 26th 1862

Hon Wm. H. Seward
Secretary of State, Washington D.C.

Sir

The British iron side wheel steamer *Adela* of Belfast arrived here on the 19th inst. She is a very long narrow vessel with two masts and two large white smoke stacks one forward of the other, draws seven feet 6 inches of water.

There is no coal here except in the hands of the government and while they have invariably supplied merchant steamers when they could not get it from other sources the Governor has refused it to this steamer, also the *Stanley* now in port here.

They are buying wood at a heavy expense.

It gives me pleasure to state that Governor Ord has taken a very decisive stand against these islands being made a depot for those in the interest of the rebellion.

He has recommended a bill to the Assembly now in session here to enable him to prohibit if necessary the exportation of arms and military store from the Colony.

I am Sir, Your obedient Servant,
C. M. Allen, Consul

◈ When ship captains presented incomplete or suspicious papers for Allen's authorization, as in the case of the *Lodona,* the consul was especially vigilant and did not give his approval easily.

No. 27
Consulate of the United States of America at Bermuda
July 2, 1862

Hon. Wm. H. Seward
Secretary of State, Washington, D.C.

Sir

I have the honor to inform you that the British Barque rigged iron screw steamer *Lodona* of Hull, of the burden of 573 tons, arrived here on the 29th ult. purporting to be bound to Beaufort, N.C., under a consular license from James W. Marshall, U.S. Consul at Leeds, dated May 30th.

It seems from the statement of the master that no bond was given and no oath was made to the Manifest. Neither is the consular certificate endorsed on the manifest or crew list. The license does not state the master has made oath to the manifest, but gives permission upon the affidavit of one Pierson[38] (who purports to be the owner of the vessel that she is intended for a lawful voyage) to proceed to Beaufort, N.C., Port Royal, S.C., or New Orleans, La.[39] She has a cargo principally of Ardent Spirits, some drugs, amongst which is a large quantity of quinine, clothing and other mdse.

The master has requested me to endorse his license which I have refused to do, on the ground his cargo is principally contraband and further their associations are such here as to leave little doubt in my mind that their license was not obtained in good faith. It would appear from their [dockets?] when their cargo was taken on board they were bound to Tampico.

They have received here a letter of instructions from one J. M. Tompson of New York, advising them to let their intentions be made known to the fleet here before leaving and stating whatever the result of the voyage he will be satisfied.[40] The British iron brig rigged screw steamer *Columbia* has just arrived from some port of England. I should judge her to be about 400 tons burden. The master had when he came on shore a small Rebel flag in his hat.

The steamer *Stanley* left on the 28th ult. after having obtained a supply of wood. The *Adela* is still here. They were expecting coal by the mail steamer from Halifax which arrived last night, but none came. They cannot get coal here.

I am Sir, Your obedient servant,
C. M. Allen, Consul

Allen's suspicions that the *Lodona* was a blockade-runner are confirmed when he learns that the master had orders to sink the ship rather than let it fall into Union hands. The captain's attempts to persuade the consul that the *Lodona* was not a blockade-runner continues, but Allen is not convinced.[41]

No. 28
Consulate of the United States of America at Bermuda
July 3rd 1862

Hon. Wm. H. Seward
Secretary of State, Washington, D.C.

Sir

Since writing you yesterday I have learned that the steamer *Lodona* purporting to be bound to Beaufort under a U.S. Consular license, has six screw plugs in her bottom, which when taken out will sink her in twenty minutes. The master I am also informed has orders to sink her rather than let her fall into the hands of the United States.

The letter of instructions which I spoke of in my communication yesterday I did not see, but it was read to me. The name may be J. N. Tompson instead of J. M. Thomson, or Tompson.

From the nature of that letter I infer he (Tomson) is the owner of the cargo, or is largely interested in it.

The master has made himself particularly familiar with me in hopes I could be induced to let him have some coal. It is uncertain when they will leave here as they cannot go till they get coal.

The vessel draws eleven feet of water and is full Barque rigged.

I am Sir, Your humble servant,
C. M. Allen, Consul

◈ With his usual efficiency, Allen's reports for the second quarter of 1862 are submitted. His quarterly reports were never late. It is clear from his correspondence that he did not have the assistance of a clerk during the war years. Nevertheless, his reports were all written in a clear and practiced hand.

Consulate of the United States of America at Bermuda
July 5th 1862

Hon. Wm. H. Seward,
Secretary of State, Washington, D.C.

Sir
    Herewith enclosed I transmit the following returns for the year ending June 30th

Arrivals & Departures of American vessels No. 1
Navigation & Commerce No. 2
Also Account for office rent No. 3
With voucher No. 4
Return by J. T. Darrell Consular Agt at the port of Hamilton of Arrivals and
    Departures No. 5

    Is it required I should make a return as per form 44? I do not fully understand.

I am Sir, Your obedient servant
C. M. Allen, Consul

◈ The potential profits of a blockade-runner could be so enormous that every effort, legal and otherwise, was made to ensure success. The Consul's adversaries, having inflicted social and physical abuse upon him, next attempt to bribe him as the case of the *Lodona* illustrates. Though the bribe could have been taken unnoticed, as Allen wrote to his wife a few days after this dispatch, he repeatedly refused the temptation. Allen's subsequent actions in the *Lodona* case were described by his son, Charles Fletcher Allen:[42] "The Consul, in the meantime, feeling sure that the vessel intended to enter the Confederacy, communicated with the Naval Department through Consul Jackson at Halifax.

The fleet was instructed to watch for the *Lodona,* as she carried a cargo worth nearly $800,000 currency. After long delay, after being painted white, and unloading some of the cargo, took a lot of ship wood on board for fuel, sailed and was captured and condemned. For his efforts in the matter, the Consul received the personal thanks of the President."[43]

No. 33
Consulate of the United States of America at Bermuda
July 7th 1862

Hon. Wm. H. Seward
Secretary of State, Washington, D.C.

Sir

The Steamer *Lodona* now in port here, has on board twenty five tons of salt-petre, and I have good reason to believe she had other contraband goods besides spirits, among which are some Enfield rifles.

The master after most emphatically declaring he had no cargo contraband of war on board, when I asked him about it (the saltpeter) said it was taken by mistake supposing it was salt. There are two strangers here said to be officers of the late Rebel steamer *Sumter* and one left on the *Adela* said to be Capt. Semmes.[44] Whether they came in the *Lodona,* or the *Columbia* I cannot ascertain. They are stopping most of the time on board the *Lodona.* The master of the *Lodona* flew the Stars & Stripes and was extremely northern in his expressions till he found he could not induce me to let him have coal when he pulled them down.

Every scheme human ingenuity could invent has been resorted to induce me to let him have coal. He went as far as to offer me $1000 if I would go to the other end of the islands and remain two days and leave my business in the hand of a merchant here. The name of the person claiming to own the vessel and who obtained the consular license is Z. C. Pierson of Kingston on Hull.

Both the *Lodona* and *Columbia* are getting wood, but it is ascertained that with their furnace they cannot keep half a head of steam with it. From all I can learn I think the *Columbia* has a cargo of arms and ammunition.

I am Sir, Your obedient Servant,
C. M. Allen, Consul

◩ Susan must have been greatly relieved to learn that her husband was taking a respite from his duties. Confirmation of Charles's character was etched in bold relief by his refusal to take a bribe that was, in fact, the equivalent of his salary for an entire year.

July 9, 1862

I could have pocketed $1,000 last week for a certain act if I had chosen which though not quite honorable no one would have been the wiser from, but I did not choose to do it though every effort that human ingenuity could invent was brought to bear. I send you a letter I received from the owners of the *Wheatland.* I am going to Hamilton to stop one week. I have a good place to stop there. I have so little society here, I shall get to be a perfect heathen if I don't get out soon.[45]

◩ Returning to his duties after a week's rest in Hamilton, Charles writes a long letter to Susan expressing once again his frustration and loneliness. Many of his friendships in Bermuda were, by necessity, temporary ones. Charles must have been cheered by the first visit of family members when his brothers, Anson and John, came to Bermuda for a brief visit. The uncharacteristically bitter tone of this letter is easily understood by the facts that he had been attacked in his office and on the street, his flagstaff had been cut down, and his closest friend in Bermuda had become incapacitated by drink.

July 15, 1862

I had my flag-staff cut down on 3rd July so could not hoist my flag on the 4th. Resolutions of a very complimentary nature to me were passed by the Board of Underwriters of New York & I received a high compliment from the State Department under the autograph of Mr. W. H. Seward and under the Board Seal.[46] The Underwriters wish me to make application to have my salary raised but I do not think it best at present; they say it would be done but I will wait awhile. Fraser is about 55 years of age & was for a long time in the Department at Washington.[47]

We do not have a great many vessels now to New York & have to wait a long time for news. I suppose before this McClellan has taken Richmond or he has got whipped.[48]

You complain of loneliness when you are surrounded by friends; what can you think of me in such a God-forsaken place as this with scarcely one friendly person to speak to? I have once been attacked in my office and once knocked down in the street within a few days; the general sentiment is "It's good enough for him; he's a damn Yankee." I got along fairly well last winter as there were a number of Americans here & some of them with me a part of the time. Anson and John were here but they are gone now & there is no one person here to my knowledge of Union sympathy—even old Capt. Dick Higgs is gone.[49] When I got particularly "blue" I could run in & see him; he is a good-hearted man.

The Devil has full possession of James, he is drunk all the time. He has just sent me a note written in a trembling hand asking me to lend him $2. I have returned the note with the reply that I have no money to lend, the sooner he is dead the better. I would gladly help him if he would quit drink but that I fear he will never do.[50]

The *Lodona* departs and the *Keronese* arrives with yellow fever aboard. Yellow fever was an ever-present threat during the summer months. Vessels often arrived in Bermuda carrying the fever and those stricken were routinely quarantined to halt the spread of this and other then untreatable diseases.

No. 30
Consulate of the United States at Bermuda
July 29th 1862

The Secretary of State
Washington, D.C.

Sir

I have the honor to inform you the Steamer *Lodona* left here on the 16th inst. having cleared for Nassau. There was landed from her here 23 tons saltpetre, which was shipped to New York. She had on board when she left 100 Bbls sulphur, which appeared on her manifest as drugs.

The British side wheel steamer *Anglia* of Liverpool from Bristol via Fayal, arrived here on the 20th inst. reports bound to Nassau, in want of coal. She is top-sail Schr. rigged, 37 tons burden, has two smoke stacks, and draws 10 feet of water.

The British Screw Steamer *Keronese* of London from Cardiff via Nassau, with coals to J. T. Bourne, Southern Agt., arrived here on the 21st inst. with sickness on board. She was sent to quarantine where she now remains, three of his crew and the Capt wife and daughter having died with Yellow Fever.

The British Screw Steamer *Phoebe* of London arrived here on the 27th inst., reports to be bound to Nassau, in want of coal. She is barque rigged about 550 tons burden.

Both the *Anglia* and *Phoebe* have on board a large quantity of powder and were ordered to leave the visual anchorage for one more remote from town. There is stored here 16 cases rifles, and 25 cases cartridges, landed from the Steamer *Adela.*

I am Sir, Your obedient servant,
C. M. Allen, Consul

▨ Charles tells Susan that with "little business doing" in St. George's, he is once again in Hamilton, where prices, to his dismay, are double those of St. George's. His mention of "Richardson" may refer to their longtime friend and neighbor in Belmont, Silas Richardson. The "Causeway," which would connect St. George's to the main island, would not to be completed until 1871.

August 2, 1862

The weather is pretty warm here now, there is but little business doing; Southern steamers are more plenty than ever; 4 in port now: the *Peterhoff, Keronese, Phoebe,* and *Anglia,* with powder enough on board to blow up a Nation. The *Keronese* has the Yellow Fever on board, 5 having died with it, no cases on shore.

The *Columbia, Adela,* and *Lodona* I see have been caught. See if they can catch the *Peterhoff, Phoebe, Gladiator,* or *Harriet Pinckney*—they are all here. I think this place is as bad as Nassau; some of the vessels have been painted light-colored & no doubt they are bound for the South direct.[51]

I came into Hamilton last week but I shall not stay here long; I have to pay $1.44 a day for board, while in St. George's it cost me but 60 cents. There is to be a Causeway built from Longbird Island to the Mainland; there is not over 4 ft water at high tide at any one place; the distance is about one mile with shoals & islands most all the way.[52] I think they will pay from 50 to 60 thousand dollars hard money. If Richardson was to come here, I think he could take the job & make a large pile out of it. Proposals are to be received till October 1st; there is but one person that will propose here & his offer will be very high. I have no doubt later than October will answer. One American looked it over last year & said he could do it easily for $30,000.[53]

◼ Never knowing the extent of available storage facilities in Bermuda, many blockade-runners were forced to remain at anchor in St. George's harbor with their combustible cargoes.

No. 35
Consulate of the United States of America at Bermuda,
August 9th, 1862

The Secretary of State
Washington, D.C.

Sir
The British Steamer *Peterhoff* of Hull, arrived here on the 30th inst. with a cargo said to be bound to Nassau. She has a supply of coal. I am unable to ascertain the cause of her remaining here so long.

The *Anglia* has landed a large quantity of powder which is stored in the government magazine. She has steam up now and will leave today, having cleared for Nassau.

The *Phoebe* has powder said to be eighty tons which they have tried to get storage for, but have been unable to do so. They seem undecided what to do and appear to dislike to proceed farther with it on board.

I am, Sir, Your obedient servant,
C. M. Allen, Consul

◼ Charles writes to Susan, with great satisfaction, when he learns of the capture of the *Memphis*.

St. George
August 19th 1862

The steamer *Memphis* which we captured near Charleston was coming here. I am thankful they got her. It knocks the arrangements of the secesh into a cocked hat. Two steamers have been waiting for her for three weeks.[54]

◫ Allen suggests a U.S. naval presence near Bermuda, seeing an opportunity to apprehend blockade-runners as they depart for Confederate ports.

No. 36
Consulate of the United States of America at Bermuda
August 19th 1862

Hon. W. H. Seward, Secretary of State,
Washington, D.C.

Sir

The Steamer *Phoebe* is discharging her cargo here—her powder has gone into a whale house on a distant part of the island. The *Peterhoff* is still in port. I learn they have been waiting for the steamer *Memphis,* which vessel was bound here when captured.

A Mr. Colton, said to be one of the firm of Z. C. Pierson & Co., has been here for some time past, and from all I gather, I think it is their intention to send their merchandise direct from here to the Southern States instead of going to Nassau as heretofore. A steamer called the *Merrimac,* with a southern cargo is hourly expected here from England, also some vessels from the Southern States.[55]

I beg to suggest that it might be of advantage, for some of our war vessels to come off these islands and send a boat on shore at the port of St. George's. Her Majesty's ship *Melpomene,* fifty one guns, received orders on the 16th inst. to proceed to the vicinity of Nassau and left the next day.

I am Sir, your obedient servant,
C. M. Allen

◫ Because the Confederate states had very few powder works, they were greatly dependent on securing powder from overseas. It must have been discouraging for Allen to see such large quantities of powder arriving in Bermuda with such frequency.

No. 38
United States Consulate at Bermuda
August 28th 1862

Hon. Wm. H. Seward
Secretary of State, Washington, D.C.

Sir

The British steamer *Gladiator* arrived here on the 23 inst. and the British Screw Steamer *Harriet Pinckney* 16 days from London arrived on the 27th. They report they are bound to Nassau with general cargoes. The *Gladiator* was not allowed to anchor at the usual anchorage as she had powder on board.

The *Phoebe* is still here. She has landed 500 packages of powder, a few cases of guns, and some liquors, but has most of her inward cargo on board. She is a vessel in all respects very much like the *Lodona,* has been painted a light lead color since she came here. They have an abundant supply of coal here at present.

I am, Sir, Your obedient servant,
C. M. Allen

🔲 Allen reiterates his belief that U.S. warships should be stationed near Bermuda and submits a long list of vessels in St. George's waiting to supply blockade-runners.

No. 39
United States Consulate at Bermuda
Sept 5th 1862

Hon. Wm. H. Seward
Secretary of State, Washington, D.C.

Sir

The British Steamer *Merrimac* arrived here this morning. She appears to be a powerful side wheel boat, and is deeply laden said to have arms and ammunition.

The British steamer *Minho* arrived here on the 1st inst with six hundred bales of cotton, reports to have left Charleston at 8 o'clock A.M. of the 27th ult. She brings ten passengers. She was out of coal when she arrived here and had burned her spars to make steam. She was twelve hours off these islands in sight. The U.S. Ship *Ino* arrived here on the 29th ult. and left next day. Had she remained here thirty six hours longer, the *Minho* would have been an easy prize. It appears to me to be of great importance to have some of our gunboats in these waters.

There is now in port here beside the two above named steamers *Gladiator, Harriet Pinckney,* and *Phoebe.* Also the Schr. *Jane* of Halifax, Brig *M. A. Horton* of Windsor, Ship *Drogheda* of Liverpool, & Barque *Almona* of Searsport, Maine, all laden with coal for Southern steamers. The Master of the *Almona* supposed he was bringing coal for the British government until he arrived here. I think the *Phoebe* is waiting here for the *Anglia* to return from some Southern port. The *Minho* reports the arrival of the steamer *Scotia* at Charleston from Nassau a short time before she left.

I am Sir, Your Obedt. Servt.
C. M. Allen, Consul

▦ Allen observes from the increased activity at St. George's that blockade-runners are finding it easier to operate from Bermuda than from Nassau. He once again strongly urges a U.S. naval presence off Bermuda.

No. 40
U.S. Consulate at Bermuda
September 10, 1862

Hon. Wm. H. Seward
Secretary of State, Washington

Sir

From a conversation overheard last night between the master of the Steamer *Minho* recently from Charleston and the master of the Steamer *Phoebe* I learned the cargo of the *Minho* is to be discharged here and she is to take a cargo from the *Phoebe* and return to Charleston. It is their intention to be there between the 20th and 25th inst and go in the night as there will then be no moon. The *Minho* had this morning hauled to the wharf and commenced discharging. She is a screw steamer of about 300 tons painted light lead color. Her mainmast entirely gone. Fore and mizzen top masts with all spars gone. She draws when loaded about 9 1/2 feet of water.

I have communicated the above information to our consul at Halifax with a request that he forward it at the earliest possible moment.[56]

The *Gladiator* is discharging her powder here. Other steamers are expected here soon. I hope the Navy Department will consider the importance of keeping some watch about these islands or at least communicating with them as often as possible as it is evident the blockade breakers consider it less hazardous to come and go from Bermuda than Nassau.

I have the honor to be, Sir,
Your obedient servant,
C. M. Allen, Consul

Allen reports that four more blockade-runners are about to leave unimpeded for Charleston.

No. 41
United States Consulate at Bermuda
September 17th 1862

Hon. Wm. H. Seward
Secretary of State

Sir

I have the honor to inform you that the British Screw Steamer *Ouachita* 28 days from England via Madeira, arrived here on the 15th inst.

She is 73 tons burden, has two masts, is topsail schooner rigged, and draws about 6 1/2 feet of water. I am informed she will leave here this week for Charleston. They have this morning commenced painting her a lead color. The Steamer *Minho* having discharged her cargo of cotton is now alongside the *Phoebe* receiving a cargo and will probably leave for Charleston about the 20th inst.

The *Gladiator* is discharging her cargo here. It consists mostly of arms and ammunitions. The *Merrimac* is today coaling and it is supposed she will leave for Charleston soon.

I am Sir, Your obedient Servant,
C. M. Allen, Consul

■ Being preoccupied with the steady arrival and departure of blockade-runners at St. George's, the consul submits his third quarter report a few days later than usual.

No. 42
Consulate of the United States at Bermuda
October 16th 1862

Hon. Wm. H. Seward
Secretary of State, Washington, D.C.

Sir
    Herewith enclosed, I have the honor to hand you the following returns for the quarter ending the 30th September, 1862; viz.

Arrivals & Departures No. 1 and
Navigation & Commerce, at the port of St. George No. 2
Arrivals & Departures No. 3 and Navigation and Commerce at the Consular
    Agency at the Port of Hamilton No. 4
Also account of Fees received by the Consular Agent at the Port of Hamil-
    ton No. 5

I am Sir, Your Obedient Servant
C. M. Allen, Consul

■ Though the warships USS *Tioga* and USS *Sonoma* are stationed in Bermudian waters, they are unable to prevent the departure of two blockade-runners. Allen is heartened by news that the blockade at Charleston now appears to be more successful in halting Rebel traffic.

No. 44
Consulate of the United States of America at Bermuda
October 21, 1862
Hon. Wm. H. Seward
Secretary of State

Sir

The British Steamer *Ouachita* left here on the 10th inst. She went out through the reefs at the west end, and the *Minho* succeeded in getting out past the *Tioga* and *Sonoma* in the night of the 12th inst., after making two previous unsuccessful attempts. The *Tioga* and *Sonoma* left here on the 13th inst. having stayed as long as they could with the coal they had. The Steamer *Herald,* Coxetter, arrived here on the 17th inst., four days from Charleston with cotton. She brings twelve passengers among which is Lieut. Maury.[57] I understand the *Herald* is to return soon to Charleston. There is now here nearly 4000 tons of Cardiff coal for the use of the southern steamers.

The *Merrimac* and *Phoebe* have been seized here by orders from England, and probably cannot leave for some time. The master of the *Phoebe* has been in prison for some weeks. The cotton from the *Herald* has been seized by the custom house authorities for violation of the revenue laws.

The *Harriet Pinckney* is now in port here with her cargo on board. Coxetter advises them they cannot get into Charleston. A passenger from Charleston in the *Herald* informs me the British steamer *Hero* was the only steamer there when he left; she was loaded with cotton and had made several unsuccessful attempts to get out.

I have the honor to be Sir,
Your Obedient Servant,
C. M. Allen, U.S. Consul

Allen not only communicated with the Department of State and other consuls but also wrote to commanders of blockading ships with maritime intelligence as well as war news. An example is Allen's letter to Commander Wilkes.[58] Wilkes, the same officer whose actions in 1861 had precipitated the *Trent* affair, created a second diplomatic incident just a month before this dispatch was written. Warships were only allowed to remain in Bermudian waters for twenty-four hours. Wilkes stationed the USS *Tioga* and USS *Sonoma* outside of St. George's harbor for more than a week in an attempt to capture departing blockade-running vessels. Wilkes used every delaying tactic he could to lengthen his stay, which resulted in an acrimonious exchange of letters with the governor of Bermuda. Allen kept a low profile throughout this episode. Wilkes, however, was forced to enter into lengthy correspondence with the Department of the Navy in a vain attempt to justify his actions.

U.S. Consulate at Bermuda
October 21, 1862

Rear-Admiral Wilkes,
Commanding U.S. West India Squadron, West Indies

Sir

The brig *Urana* is now ready and is to leave today. The long delay has been caused by the east wind, which prevented her getting here for two weeks after you left. I hope she will arrive in time to meet your wants.[59] The steamer *Herald,* four days from Charleston, with cotton, arrived here on the 17th instant. She is under command of Coxetter. She brings a number of passengers, among which is Lieutenant Maury.

Our Army has gained a decided victory over Van Dorn and Price at Corinth.[60] There have several vessels arrived here with coal for the Southern steamers since you left. They have now about 3,000 tons.

I have the honor to be,
Your obedient servant,
C. M. Allen, U.S. Consul

▨ When Allen was publicly accused of being a spy, along with his friend Edward James, the artist took indignant exception to the accusations in his letter to the editor of the *Bermuda Royal Gazette* of October 21, 1862.

To the Editor of the Royal Gazette:

Sir,

Smollett's admirable story of the three black Crows seems destined to receive a remarkable exemplification in the case of the [?] individual who addresses you and who craves a [?] of your paper to make known his complaints. "However," says Dean Swift, men may "differ about the right to put a man on the rack, none ever denied him the right of hollowing as loud as he liked when he was there." Here then follow my groans from the rack of an exceedingly unfair and extremely ridiculous suspicion which some of my neighbours at St. George's have contrived to construct for me.

Until the last few weeks I was certainly under the impression that, having left London for New York in an American Liner some twelve months since, I was driven in here by stress of weather, and, whilst my fellow passengers continued their voyage in other vessels, was induced by the solicitations of new found friends and by prospects of employment—which by the way have been more than realized—to remain here, first for a couple of months and then to take up my abode here altogether, I was also under the impression that, by the invitation of my Captain, I remained on board our ship during her three months stay in St. George's harbour, and there had frequent opportunities of meeting the American Consul who was a constant visitor to his countrymen, and that the mutual esteem and friendship which thus sprung up between Mr. Allen and myself ended in a very kind offer on his part, whereby, on my leaving my ship, I became a lodger under the same roof with him, an arrangement to which I regret to think an end must now be put by the arrival of his family. Certainly I did seem to recollect that my time since my arrival here has been pretty fully occupied in making drawings of local scenery and of all sorts and sizes of vessels visiting the harbour of St. George's and in extracting sundry guineas from the pockets of British, French, American, Danish and other visitors by the process. Such, I say was only lately my own impression of the industrious and innocuous course of life pursued here by this 'shipwrecked mariner.'

But it appears, Sir, I have been all along, as Lord Foppinton says, 'in bed and dreaming'—my presence here is, I find, due to a deep laid and long standing scheme on the part of the Government of which one Abraham Lincoln is the head, that in the pay of that Government I have been—[?] some non-Bermudians—here for several years—where I have been living during the period I have hitherto been unable to discover, in one of the Walsingham Caves perhaps or up a cedar tree. My duties it appears must have been for a long time nil and then began by furnishing correct likenesses—please don't charge advertisement price for this—of all vessels about to run the blockade—this was my first black Crow, but

vires acquirit eundo

on the principle of the little fable I started by referring to, and my duties presently increased to supplying sketches and particulars of the forts here and their armaments, and thus was my second black Crow developed, while Crow No. 3 culminated in regular statistical information of the size, strength, etc., of all our men of war on this station, as well as concerning mysterious reefs and equally mysterious channels whereby invasion or evasion might be accomplished.

It appears furthermore that my residence under the same roof with Mr. Allen was also part of this deep-laid scheme, it being the deliberate opinion of the whole Washington Cabinet that the duties of a spy could be most efficiently performed by a gentleman to whom public attention would be necessary directed by his residing with the American Consul, and by his being seen in the broad eye of day constantly passing from the consulate on board all sorts of vessels in the harbour taking measurements and making sketches. A glorious specimen of 'Yankee' cuteness!—Furthermore it appears that the same Cabinet was unanimously of opinion that information about our Ships could be best obtained by the same gentlemen never going on board one of them, nor making sketches of any single one of them—with the sole exception of a distant sketch of the '*Racer*'—out of all that have been here during the last 12 months, and no doubt it was part of the same scheme to manage matters so that the gentleman in question should never receive an invitation on board from any British Naval Officer, whilst on the other hand the officers of the U.S. Navy asked him on board all their vessels, gave him free access to them whenever he pleased, furnished him with every information and permitted him to carry on shore with him not only any number of sketches but all sorts of particulars of measurements, armament, tonnage &c.—moreover I was instructed it seems not to enter any but two forts, one at the entrance of the harbour and that only once in my life, and the other at Ireland Island, and on both occasions to be careful to be seen and noticed, and above all to be accompanied by a British Officer on every occasion—another magnificent instance of Yankee intelligence!

Perhaps also is formed part of the same astute policy to instruct the officers of the U.S. Navy visiting the Islands to put not one single question to me touching the size, strength, armament or any other statistic of either ships or forts here, but to seek their information carefully from any other sources but that of their accredited agent.

Such seems to be the nature of the impeachment—you will permit me to affirm distinctly that I do not remember such a pretty mixture of ludicrous absurdity and willful mendacity advanced against any gentleman in the whole course of my life.

I would fain I confess look on the whole affair as a tour de force on the part of a well-known fondness of my St. George's neighbours for a practical joke. Could I however for a moment suppose that anything serious was intended, I should be most deeply obliged to any of your correspondents who would indicate to me—first—the specific acts of which I am accused, and secondly the name of the accuser—I leave to Mr. Bob Sawyer the vulgar and common place remedies of "punching heads" and "pulling noses," but I am an English gentleman of [hitherto] unimpeached loyalty and of sensitive instincts and I know how to deal with any scoundrel who dares to try and fasten on me by implication or otherwise the name of "spy" or "traitor."

Meanwhile I will venture to add, that, whatever may be the object of the fabrications in question, I shall be so far from allowing them, or a thousand times their weight in malice and virulence, to alter the footing on which I stand with the first man in these Islands who extended to a shipwrecked stranger the rites of a really cordial hospitality—and that whilst my own countrymen fought shy of the "waif"—that it is my firm intention to continue to cultivate with him a sincere friendship, of which I am justly proud, to the last moment of my life.

I am Sir, Your obedient Servant,
Edward James
St. George's, 14th Oct., 1862

P.S.—I have made no allusion to my public status, simply because I entertain a very sincere respect and admiration for the quarter from which my appointment came, and would not for a moment entertain the thought of offering in that direction the insult of supposing even an approach to a belief in the old wife's fable in question.[61]

🔲 By late 1862 Allen was settled in relative comfort, and it was therefore a desirable time for Susan to join her husband, if only for a short while.

The same issue of the *Gazette* that printed Edward James's letter also reported that "Mrs. C. M. Allen and daughter" arrived from New York aboard the *Eliza Barss*.[62] After being apart for almost a year, the Allens were reunited. It seems likely that Charles took time away from his duties to be with Susan and their daughter, as his next communication with the Department of State was not written until November 4. Susan's trip was doubtless a rough one, given an autumn passage.

No. 45
U.S. Consulate at Bermuda
November 4, 1862

Hon. Wm. H. Seward
Secretary of State, Washington, D.C.

Sir

I have the honor to inform you that the U.S. Steamers *Mohican* and *San Jacinto* arrived here on the 1st inst. The machinery of the *Mohican* is considerably damaged and will require about a week to repair. They report very heavy weather. The *San Jacinto* will leave today.

The Steamer *Herald* left here, supposed for Charleston, on the 26 ult.

I am Sir, Your Obedt. Servt.
C. M. Allen, U.S. Consul

▨ Blockade-runners continue to arrive even as winter approaches. Allen reports that the schooner *St. George* is departing for Turks Island to secure a cargo of salt for the Confederate states. With very few saltworks located in the Southern states, this commodity was in great demand. In an interesting twist of fate, the schooner *St. George* had been the ship that brought Allen to Bermuda.

No. 46
Consulate of the United States of America at Bermuda
December 8, 1862

Hon. Wm. H. Seward
Secretary of State

Sir

The British iron screw steamer *Justitia* of London, of the burden of about 800 tons, with a full cargo, arrived here on the 4th inst. She has on board a very small quantity of freight for the British Government. There is no doubt her cargo mostly is intended for the Southern States.

The side wheel steamer *Cornubia* of London, ten days from Madeira, arrived also on the 4th. She does not appear to have any cargo. She is a very fast boat and is intended I think to take the cargo of the *Harriet Pinckney* and *Justitia.* I am informed she belongs to the same owners of the two last named. She has had her color changed since she arrived here from black to a light lead color.

The schooner *St. George* of Bermuda formerly the *Crystal Palace* of Rock-land, Maine, has been purchased by the Southern agent here, on Southern account, and left last week for Turks Island to load with salt. The schooner *Charles Turner* of Nassau, left here on the 4th inst. laden with powder and cartridges. She cleared for Nassau.

It is reported here that the steamer *Merrimac,* now here, has recently been sold to the Confederate States government. I cannot ascertain that such is the fact, her cargo is all on board as when she first came here. The ship *Ella* of Liverpool left here on the 5th inst. with 625 bales cotton brought here in the *Herald* from Charleston.

I am Sir, Your Obedient Servant
C. M. Allen, Consul

▨ Allen's exequatur was formally received in Bermuda more than a year after his arrival.

The *Bermuda Royal Gazette* of November 25, 1862, printed the text of the exequatur, indicating that "under any ordinary circumstances such a mere matter of routine would require no observation but as the long delay in the transmission of the document in question has given occasion for some extraor-dinary malconstructions in the shape of whisperings that Mr. Allen's exequatur would be withheld in consequence of some underhanded representation and backstairs influence which it was confidently asserted would be brought to bear at head quarters, we have much pleasure in calling special attention to the circumstance." The article continued, stating that the only reason for the delay was "the thousands of documents yearly presented" to Her Majesty for signature and the "incessant demand for the Queen's pen."

The wording of the exequatur was again published in the December 2 and December 9 issues.

VICTORIA R.

VICTORIA, by the Grace of God, Queen of the United Kingdom of Great Britain and Ireland, Defender of the Faith, etc., etc., etc. To all and sin-gular our loving Subjects to whom these Presents shall come, Greetings.

Witness The President of the United States of America has by a Commission bearing date the Seventh day of August One Thousand Eight Hundred and Sixty-one, constituted MR. CHARLES M. ALLEN to be Consul at Bermuda; and for such other parts as shall be nearer thereto than to the United States; And We, having thereupon approved of the said CHARLES M. ALLEN as Consul for the said United States according to the Commission before mentioned—Our Will and Pleasure are, and We hereby require that you do receive, countenance, and, as there may be occasion, favorably assist him the said CHARLES M. ALLEN in the exercise of his Office, giving and allowing unto him all the Privileges, Immunities, and advantages thereunto belonging.

Given at One Court at Saint James, the Twenty-first day of October, One Thousand Eight Hundred and Sixty-two, in the Twenty-sixth Year of Our Reign.

By Her Majesty's Command,
RUSSELL.[63]

⊞ Allen discovers that a former U.S. consul is now engaged in blockade-running. His dispatch may refer to Edward C. Stiles, U.S. consul at Vienna before the Civil War. At the same time that Allen was appointed U.S. consul to replace Frederick B. Wells, Edward Stiles was recalled by President Lincoln and replaced with Theodore Carrisiur of Illinois.

No. 47
Consulate of the United States of America at Bermuda
December 13th 1862

Hon. Wm. H. Seward
Secretary of State, Washington, D.C.

Sir

The Steamer *Cornubia,* Captain Burroughs, left here today for Charleston with a cargo from the Steamer *Justitia,* reported as general merchandise.

She has as supercargo one Stiles, who represents himself as a native of South Carolina, and formerly U.S. Consul at Vienna, and at one time serving as an officer in the U.S. Navy.[64] He appears to have full control of both the Steamers *Justitia* and *Cornubia* and is reported as their owner, but his name does not appear on their registers. He claims to be familiar with the channels to the port of Charleston, and is the only person on board who can act as pilot there. They take with them from her a Bermuda pilot, promising to return him within four weeks. The *Cornubia* is a steamer well adapted to run the blockade, and undoubtedly faster than any vessel previously here. I think it is their intention to take from here the cargoes of the *Harriet Pinckney,* the *Justitia,* and another steamer which they are soon expecting.

I am Sir, Your Obedient Servant,
C. M. Allen, U.S. Consul

CHAPTER 4

"A great many blockade runners in the harbor now"

▣ The year 1863 did not begin on an auspicious note. Until this time, the hostility of the Southern sympathizers in St. George's had been directed toward Allen personally, but now the sovereignty of the consulate itself was violated. This incident did not auger well for the coming events of 1863.

No. 1
Consulate of the United States of America at Bermuda
January 6, 1863

Hon. Mr. W. H. Seward
Washington, D.C.

Sir:

Herewith enclosed I transmit the following returns for the quarter ending 31 December 1862 viz

1. Arrivals & Departures
2. Navigation & Commerce Port of St. George's
16. Navigation & Commerce Port of Hamilton
17. Report of Fees received at the Consular Agency at Hamilton, also the following accounts
3. For rent of wharf for coal, and for pilotage paid at the request of the commander of the *San Jacinto*
4. For postage for flag staff & flag

5. For office rent two quarters together with voucher numbers from 6 to 13 inclusive, and

18. certificate of exchange numbered 18. Also

14. list of official letters sent from and

15. received at the consulate during the year.

▣ The numbers 14 and 15 are not presumed to be perfectly correct as my office was entered during the night through a window and my official correspondence taken away. The expense for flag staff was incurred by some evil disposed person having cut it down.

The order to pay pilotage is not sufficiently definite. It was sent to me by the pilot after the vessel had left. I have neglected to make a commercial report in conformity to the regulations as I could get no definite information to base it upon from the Custom House as their statistics are not made up till the first of January. I shall not draw for the amounts sent the State Department till I hear the accounts have been audited and allowed.

I am Sir, Your Obedient servant
C. M. Allen, Consul

▣ The year 1863 began with Allen's reporting no fewer than six blockade-runners in port at St. George's. One of these, the *Cornubia,* was to make frequent appearances over the next eleven months until the ship was finally captured in November of 1863 while attempting to run the blockade at Wilmington.

No. 2
Consulate of the United States of America, Bermuda
January 24, 1863

Sir.

The British steamer *Princess Royal* last from Halifax arrived here on the 17th inst, reports having experienced heavy weather and thrown overboard a portion of her cargo. She left yesterday for our Southern coast. From all I can learn I think she is a slow steamer.

The *Cornubia* returned here on the 19th inst. from Wilmington with 300 bales cotton and 80 Bbls rosin and turpentine, reports having left there at daylight on the morning of the 14th, was chased till 11 o'clock by a U.S.

Steamer. She has discharged and is now about one half loaded with arms and ammunition. Will probably leave here about Tuesday next. She has a pilot brought from Wilmington. She reports having attempted to get into Charleston but found it too dangerous and went into Wilmington without having any one acquainted with the waters there. Reports having left the steamer *Giraffe* in port. Could not get a full cargo out as it was not to be had. She brings as passenger a person reported to have letters of credit for $200,000 for the purpose of buying and fitting a steamer.

The steamer *Gipsy Queen* from Matamoros via Havana with 700 bales cotton and $225,000 in spices arrived here on the 10th inst and left on the 20th for Liverpool. The *Phoebe* has been sold and goes to Australia.

The *Justitia* having discharged left on the 17th inst. for home.

The *Harriet Pinckney* has discharged cargo and is now taking in the cargo of the *Cornubia* and will leave for Liverpool in a few days.

Capt. Hunter of the mail steamer *Delta* which arrived here today from St. Thomas, reports the *Alabama* 300 miles south of here on the 15th inst.

I have the honor to be, Sir,
Your Obedient Servant,
C. M. Allen, Consul

The steamer *Cornubia* leaves St. George's with a full cargo. Although the most vital war materiel to pass through Bermuda was arms and ammunition, the *Cornubia's* cargo of blankets, boots, shoes, and clothing were goods also necessary for the prosecution of the war.

No. 3
Consulate of the United States of America at Bermuda,
January 27, 1863

Hon. Wm. H. Seward,
Secretary of State, Washington D.C.

Sir,

The steamer *Cornubia* left here last night. I was misinformed when I stated in my No. 2 that she was partly loaded with arms, ammunition. She has a cargo consisting of Blankets, Boots and Shoes, clothing, etc. She takes a Bermuda pilot and will undoubtedly return here if successful.

I am Sir, Your
Obedient Servant,
C. M. Allen, Consul

▨ Allen reports that an American citizen in Bermuda has entered into blockade-running. A little-known aspect of blockade-running is the fact that some Northerners, putting profits before patriotism, also engaged in this traffic. In this dispatch, Allen's reference to an "American residing in Bermuda" may refer to this activity.

No. 4
Consulate of the United States of America at Bermuda
February 3, 1863

Hon. Wm. H. Seward,
Secretary of State, Washington D.C.

Sir

The British steamer *Miriam* of and from London, arrived here on the 30th ultim. She purports to be bound to Nassau in want of coals. She has a quantity of powder on board. I infer it is their intention to go direct to one of our Southern ports. She is an iron boat of about 500 tons, has three masts, and a propeller. Apparently is not a fast vessel.

The schooner *Alma* of Bermuda of about 70 tons has been recently purchased by an American citizen residing here for the ostensible purpose of sending to Beaufort, N.C., for lumber. There is but little doubt she is intended to run the blockade.

The steamer *Merrimac* which has been lying here since last summer has a new master, has recently been painted and appearances indicate she will not remain here much longer. They are trying to get a place to store their powder as they wish to take other cargo instead.

I am Sir, Your obedient servant
C. M. Allen, Consul

▨ The normally punctilious consul discovers that no quarterly reports regarding fees collected at Hamilton have been submitted. Allen's lapse in this matter is perhaps understandable, given the almost continuous stream of blockade-runners on which he reported.

No. 5
Consulate of the United States of America at Bermuda,
February 3, 1863

Hon. Wm. H. Seward,
Secretary of State, Washington, D.C.

Sir,
   Herewith I hand you return of Fees received at the Consular Agency at Hamilton during each quarter of the year 1862 which I omitted to send at the proper time.

I am Sir, Your obedient servant
C. M. Allen, Consul

▨ Allen reports that the *Cornubia* has once again successfully run the blockade.

No. 6
Consulate of the United States of America at Bermuda,
February 19, 1863

Hon. Wm. H. Seward,
Secretary of State, Washington, D.C.

Sir
   The steamer *Cornubia* arrived here at daylight this morning with 300 bales cotton, reports having made the passage from Wilmington, N.C., in 71 hours. She is now discharging and I am informed will return again with all possible dispatch.

I am Sir, Your obedient servant
C. M. Allen, Consul

◈ The *Cornubia* continues to run the blockade with great regularity.

No. 7
Consulate of the United States of America at Bermuda,
February 25, 1863

Hon. Wm. H. Seward,
Washington, D.C.

Sir

The steamer *Cornubia* having discharged and taken in cargo will leave here today for Wilmington. She has a large quantity of arms and ammunition on board. The master says he will be here again in three weeks.

I am Sir, Your obedient servant
C. M. Allen, Consul

◈ After two years of war, ships were still running the blockade from Bermuda with regular success. Allen's imaginative efforts at impeding this traffic now take a new direction. Allen's friend Edward James had vigorously protested in the columns of the *Bermuda Royal Gazette* the assertion that he was a spy in the employ of the U.S. consul, sketching blockade-runners for the government. Five months later, Allen offers to supply sketches of blockade-runners, perhaps the work of James. The offer was accepted with alacrity.[1]

Although there is no conclusive proof that James supplied the "portraits" Allen sent to the government with his dispatches, for Allen also mentioned that he liked to paint, but it is most probable that James was the artist. It was not likely that the U.S. consul would have stood at the wharf sketching blockade-runners.

Allen had trouble enough contending with British and Bermudian blockade-runners. It must have been doubly disheartening for him to inform his government of unscrupulous New York merchants, such as "Porter said to belong to New York," who were channeling arms and munitions through Bermuda to the Confederate states.

No. 8
Consulate of the United States of America at Bermuda
23 March 1863

Hon. Wm. H. Seward,
Secretary of State, Washington, D.C.

Sir

I have the honor to report the arrival here on the 21st instant of the Brig *Dashing Wave* from London with a cargo for the Southern States consigned to J. T. Bourne, agent for southern steamers here.

The schooner *St. George* of Bermuda formerly the *Crystal Palace* of Rockland is now on the rocks at the north of these Islands with a cargo of cotton reported to be from Charleston. She probably will be a total loss.

The steamer *Cornubia* arrived here yesterday from Wilmington which place she left on the 18th inst. She has a full cargo of cotton which is now being discharged. She will not probably be here more than one week.

The steamer *Merrimac* has been thoroughly overhauled, her masts taken out, except the foremast, bottom cleaned and hull and upper works painted lead color. It is reported she will leave for Charleston or Wilmington in about two weeks.

She is in charge of a person by the name of Porter said to belong to New York and formerly an officer in the U.S. Navy. He claims to be a relative of Com. Porter, U.S.N., report says he is the person who took the *Alabama* or *290* from Liverpool to Fayal.[2]

I enclose herewith a portrait which is a correct likeness of her as she is now. I will take, and forward, a like sketch of all the Rebel Steamers that come here, if it would be of any service.

The Schooner *Alma* of Bermuda left here on the 20th instant with a cargo of salt and liquor. She cleared for Beaufort, N.C., but intends to run the blockade.

A person called Major Watson or Walker said to be from Richmond, Va., has been here about 4 weeks, he claims to be an agent of the Confederate States of America and is said to hold a commission from Jefferson Davis.[3]

The reception the *Cornubia* received on her return here yesterday must have been very gratifying to her officers. As she came into the harbor, the shores and wharves were lined with the inhabitants who greeted her with cheer after cheer.

I am Sir, Your obedient servant
C. M. Allen, Consul

▦ Allen's job was made more difficult by the arrival of Confederate major Norman S. Walker, chief disbursing agent at Bermuda, who was responsible for the transshipment of goods. Walker's office was at the historic Globe Hotel, practically in sight of the U.S. consulate. Walker's wife, Georgina Ghoulson Walker, became known as "The First Lady of Confederate Bermuda." Confederate officers and dignitaries were often lavishly entertained at the Walker home, "Banana Manor," in St. George's.

No. 9
Consulate of the United States of America at Bermuda
24th March, 1863

Hon. Wm. H. Seward,
Secretary of State, Washington, D.C.

Sir

The steamer *Genl. Beauregard,* late the *Havelock,* Coxetter Master of and from Charleston, came into port here at 5 o'clock last night under the Confederate flag. She brings 1030 bales of cotton. They report having left Charleston at 4 P.M. on the 19th inst.

The engineer of the *Cornubia* who has left her here informed me she is owned by the Confederate Government and is not allowed to carry any goods for merchants. He says they were chased nine hours by a U.S. steamer when attempting to enter Wilmington and threw overboard $20,000 worth of goods to lighten the vessel. He further informed me she will return again to Wilmington, and will attempt to get in through New Inlet. There was four steamers loading there when they left, and one, the *Britannia,* came in the day before they left.

Major Walker, the Confederate agent here, seems to have charge of the *Cornubia,* his wife and family came with him.[4]

I am Sir, Your obedient servant
C. M. Allen, Consul

▦ The consul sees a dramatic increase in the number of Southerners arriving at St. George's. By the spring of 1863, the sleepy little village had become something of a boomtown. St. George's proved adept at providing all the necessary vices for the glut of blockade-runners anxious to part with their profits.

No. 10
Consulate of the United States of America at Bermuda,
April 3, 1863

Hon. Wm. H. Seward,
Secretary of State, Washington, D.C.

Sir

I have the honor to inform you that the steamer *Cornubia* left here for Wilmington on the 28th ult with a full cargo, mostly arms and ammunition. She takes a Bermuda pilot.

The steamer *Genl. Beauregard* has her outward cargo all on board consisting of Enfield rifles, 1 battery of six guns complete, 500 bags of salt-petre, Blankets, etc. She is consigned to the house of Fraser & Co., Charleston, and will not leave here till next week.[5] She draws 12 feet 6 in. with 200 tons coal in.

The schooner *St. George* was from Wilmington and not from Charleston as I reported. She is now in port undergoing repairs. She has a portion of a cargo of salt engaged and will leave again as soon as they can get away.

The islands here are filled with Southerners. They seem to have plenty of money and have purchased largely from the merchants here.

I am Sir, Your Obedient Servant
C. M. Allen, Consul

⊞ The consul's returns for the second quarter of 1863 are submitted.

No. 11
Consulate of the United States of America at Bermuda
April 6, 1863

Hon. Wm. H. Seward,
Secretary of State, Washington, D.C.

Sir,

I have the honor to enclose herewith the following returns for the quarter ending March 31, 1863 for the port of Saint George viz

Arrivals and Departures of American Vessels, No. 1
Navigation and Commerce of the United States, No. 2

Also the following returns by J. T. Darrell, Consular Agent, at the port of Hamilton

Arrivals & Departures of American vessels, No. 3
Navigation & Commerce of the United States, No. 4
Quarterly Statement of fees on account of vessels, No. 5
Account of fees received, No. 6
Account of fees for certificates etc., No. 7

I am Sir, Your Obedient Servant
C. M. Allen, Consul

Bureaucracy never seemed to have agitated Allen. While both he and the government at Washington were faced with matters of national survival, there was still someone in the Department of State insisting on uniformity in the numbering of dispatches.

No. 12
Consulate of the United States of America at Bermuda,
9th April 1863

Hon. Wm. H. Seward,
Secretary of State, Washington, D.C.

Sir
Your letter of the 9th Feb'y was received yesterday in which you direct my attention to Section 325–331 of the Consular Manual in regard to numbering and endorsement of despatches.

In commencing a new series of numbers at the beginning of the year, I was guided by Section 88 of Consular Regulations. Shall I renumber the copies of despatches sent this year, commencing from the number at the close of last year?

Your Obedient Servant
C. M. Allen, Consul

◈ Not only slaves but free people of color were often compelled to labor for the Confederate army. Allen explains that eight "free people of color" and two slaves had requested his assistance in securing passage to a Northern port. It is interesting to note that these individuals arrived in Bermuda, having "stowed themselves away till after they had passed the blockade." They were fortunate, for many outbound blockade-runners were routinely fumigated before leaving port to expose such stowaways.[6]

No. 13
Consulate of the United States of America at Bermuda
April 18, 1863

Hon. Wm. H. Seward,
Secretary of State, Washington, D.C.

Sir

The Rebel steamer *Genl. Beauregard* left here on the 14th instant, and the steamer *Robert E. Lee,* of Wilmington, three days from there, arrived here on the 16th instant, with 600 bales cotton, turpentine, tobacco & rosin. She was formerly the *Giraffe,* but is now under the Confederate flag.

The steamer *Merrimac* left yesterday for Wilmington.

The *Cornubia* is expected tomorrow, as she was to leave Wilmington last Wednesday night. This is the fourth time she has been there from here, and makes her trips as regular as the Mail steamer to Halifax, having occupied in her former trip three weeks and three days each.

I have sent to New York, at my own expense, three men from the *Cornubia,* and five from the *Robt. E. Lee* and have two contrabands on hand.[7] The men sent to New York were free people of color who shipped in the south to escape being compelled to work on the fortifications, and did not wish to return. The Contrabands stowed themselves away till after they had passed the blockade.

Your Obedient Servant
C. M. Allen, Consul

◈ Allen continues to alert the Department of State that the *Cornubia* once again has eluded capture.

No. 14
Consulate of the United States of America at Bermuda
April 21, 1863

Hon. Wm. H. Seward,
Secretary of State, Washington, D.C.

Sir

I have the honor to inform you that the steamer *Cornubia* arrived here at 6 A.M. yesterday, 66 hours from Wilmington, having been about three weeks and two days.

The steamer *Robert E. Lee* will leave here for Wilmington in about 8 days with a cargo mostly of arms and ammunition.

The *Cornubia* if not caught will probably be back here again in about four weeks.

Your Obedient Servant
C. M. Allen, Consul

▨ The consul once again diplomatically urges a U.S. naval presence at Bermuda, explaining in detail where ships could best be put to use.

No. 67[8]
Consulate of the United States of America at Bermuda,
May 19, 1863

Sir

I have the honor to report the arrival here on the 7th instant of the British steamer *Eugenie* from England via Madeira in ballast. She is a side wheel boat of about 350 tons and is undoubtedly very fast. Captain Halpin, formerly of the steamer *Harriet Pinckney,* which vessel discharged a cargo here last winter and returned to London, is her master. She is now receiving a coat of light blue paint, also her cargo consisting so far entirely of cases of rifles or muskets. It is expected she will leave here about the middle of next week.

The steamer *Cornubia* left here today for Wilmington having been detained by the desertion of her engineers and a portion of her crew.

I am well informed there is some four or five steamers expected here from

England some of which if not all are now on the way. The merchants are importing large quantities of merchandise for the Southern trade—goods from New York are being shipped in considerable quantities on board the Southern steamers.[9]

I beg to suggest in view of the increasing traffic between these Islands and the Southern ports and as the season for severe storms has past that the presence in these waters of one or two fast gunboats would be a great detriment to the very profitable business that is now being carried on here, with a prospect of its being largely increased.

On account of the reefs which extend around the North and west of the islands, the blockade runners most invariably make the land from the southwest and are compelled to come into the south to get into port—a gunboat lying off in that direction would keep them from approaching the last, and if fast enough, would be most sure to capture them.

I have the honor to be Your Obedient Servant
C. M. Allen, Consul

◈ Charles's sister Sarah Elizabeth died in February 1863. They were very close, and the news of her death must have affected him deeply. After eighteen months in Bermuda, he began to prepare for his first leave of absence.

No. 68
Consulate of the United States at Bermuda,
18 May 1863

Hon. Wm. H. Seward,
Secretary of State, Washington, D.C.

Sir

On account of recent death in my family and my health being poor, I would like to go home for a short time during the coming warm weather.

If the Department should think it consistent for me to do so, I would recommend Mr. William C. J. Hyland for Vice Consul.[10] He is a British subject, a person of high standing and unmistakable union sympathies.

There is no American citizen here I could recommend.

I have the honor to be Sir, Your Obedient Servant
C. M. Allen, Consul

◼ Allen describes the methods and operations of Northern blockade-runners to the collector at the port of New York City in an attempt to halt this traffic at its source.

No. 69
Consulate of the United States of America at Bermuda
6 June 1863

Hon. Wm. H. Seward
Secretary of State, Washington, D.C.

Sir

I have the honor to report the arrival here on the 22 ultim of the steamer *Robt. E. Lee* from Wilmington with 600 bales cotton, turpentine, rosin & tobacco. She left here yesterday for Wilmington with a cargo consisting of salt provisions, potatoes, onions, 300 boxes rifles, shot, shell cartridges and liquors.

The steamers *Eugenie* and *Cornubia* came in on the 28 ultim from Wilmington on the 25th with full cargoes of cotton.

The *Cornubia* left yesterday for the same port with a cargo as follows viz, 41 packages and 72 boxes dry goods, 201 boxes cartridges, 100 boxes minne rifles, 100 barrels salt provisions, 50 boxes tin, 50 pigs lead and six carboys acid.

Heavy mails and a large number of passengers are passing through here by these boats.

The steamers *Genl. Beauregard, Merrimac,* and *Emma,* are hourly expected here from Wilmington.

The *Eugenie* is now loading and will leave soon.

Vessels from New York come here, land their cargoes, and immediately take them on board, or transfer them to citizens here without discharging and clear for Nassau or Matamoros. I have advised the collector of New York of the facts in relation to their movements here.

I have the honor to be Sir,
Your Obedient Servant
C. M. Allen, Consul

◼ The consul reports on the ever increasing blockade-running traffic at Bermuda. Two new vessels, the *Venus* and the *Harkaway,* make their first appearance at St. George's.

No. 70
Consulate of the United States of America at Bermuda
12 June 1863

Hon. Wm. H. Seward,
Secretary of State, Washington, D.C.

Sir

The steamer *Eugenie* left here yesterday for Wilmington with a large quantity of salt provisions, rifles and sabres.

The steamer *Venus* of London with the full cargo, last from Madeira, arrived here on the 10th instant. She is a sidewheel vessel of about 700 tons, has two masts, and square sails. Will draw about nine feet of water with coal on board, she has been painted white since she came here.

The screw steamer *Emma* from Wilmington arrived here the same day with 350 bales of cotton, 400 boxes tobacco, and a quantity of spirits turpentine.

I learned the steamer *Merrimac* was to leave Wilmington the night of the 10th for this place.

The schooner *Harkaway* of Bermuda of the burden of about 65 tons left here yesterday with assorted cargo, her master made application at the custom house for clearance for Port Royal, S.C., but could not get it and cleared for Nassau.

She flew the rebel flag a portion of the time while in port here.

I have the honor to be Sir,
Your obedient servant,
C. M. Allen, Consul

▣ Allen continues to report that Northern war profiteers are sending a steady stream of goods from New York to Bermuda for transshipment to the South.

No. 71
Consulate of the United States of America at Bermuda
17 June 1863

Hon. Wm. H. Seward,
Secretary of State, Washington, D.C.

Sir,

I beg to apprise you that large quantities of merchandise are shipped from New York to these islands and here transferred on board steamers for the blockaded ports.

There is no doubt Maj. Walker, who styles himself Confederate states agent, is receiving goods from New York by most every vessel, under various marks.

A large portion of the goods shipped from here to Wilmington are from New York.

I am Sir, Your obedient servant
C. M. Allen, Consul

The *Lord Clyde* of Dublin brings a full cargo from Cardiff destined for the Confederate states.

No. 72
Consulate of the United States of America at Bermuda
17 June 1863

Hon. Wm. H. Seward,
Secretary of State, Washington, D.C.

Sir,

I have the honor to report the arrival here on the 14th instant of the British side wheel steamer *Lord Clyde* of Dublin reported 15 days from Cardiff with a full cargo. She has been painted a light color since she came in here and will probably leave tomorrow for Charleston. It is their intention to return here.

The steamer *Venus* left on the 14th, previous to leaving they took down the topmasts and all the yards.

I am Sir, your obedient servant,
C. M. Allen, Consul

Northern war critic Clement L. Vallandigham arrives in Bermuda. Vallandigham was an Ohio Democrat. He was a bitter critic of the Lincoln administration and eventually was banished to the Confederate states. He objected vociferously to President Davis and was ejected from the Confederacy as well.[11]

Edward Everett Hale's *The Man without a Country* is thought to have been inspired by the life of Vallandigham.

Allen wrote this dispatch on his forty-first birthday.

No. 73
Consulate of the United States of America at Bermuda
22 June 1863

Hon. Wm. H. Seward,
Secretary of State, Washington, D.C.

Sir,

I have the honor to report the arrival here on the 20th instant of the steamer *Jeff Davis* [*Lady Davis*] of and from Wilmington on the 17th instant. She was formerly the British steamer *Cornubia* but now under the Confederate flag.

She brings as passenger Mr. C. L. Vallandigham. I learned he will go from here to Halifax by the first opportunity. I am informed the *Jeff Davis* [*Lady Davis*] brings dispatches for the Confederate steamer *Virginia,* that she is soon expected here, that Semmes of the *Alabama* is to take charge of her—of the truth of these reports I cannot ascertain. They are believed by those who have a better opportunity to know than I have she brings no freight except 17 bales of cotton. The Master reports having left Wilmington in company with two steamers and two brigs, all of which escaped the blockade, that they left eight steamers in port waiting for cotton—that all the cotton there had been destroyed by fire.

The steamer *Harriet Pinckney* from England has just come into port here. She flies a pennant and I am informed she is chartered to take home some soldiers by the British government but brings a cargo for the Confederate States.

The *Lord Clyde* is now leaving port, having been detained for the want of a pilot.

The *Emma* is waiting for an arrival from New York to complete her cargo.

I am Sir, Your obedient servant,
C. M. Allen, Consul

▩ There is some confusion as to the date of the following letter. The Edith Wistowe Allen transcript dated this letter July 7, 1862. As it includes incidents relating to the Vicksburg campaign of 1863, and also as Patricia Allen Chaplin cited a date of June 24, 1863, for portions of this letter, we will assume this letter to Susan was written sometime in the summer of 1863 after Charles had moved into the home of William C. J. Hyland in June. This was just prior to his taking a leave of absence.

June 24, 1863

A great many blockade-runners in the harbor now, more than ever before—3 or 4 a day sometimes but few get caught. They are making a great deal of money. The rebel steamer *Florida* came in yesterday and left at night; she has burned one or two vessels near land and has blockaded the port for nearly two weeks; neither the Authorities nor the papers do not find one word of fault; it is all right when it is on that side; if one of our vessels should do so there would be a "howling."

The winter is quite warm, some Yellow Fever among the shippers; one death on shore; whether there is any more or not it is difficult to tell as the Authorities are apparently disposed to keep it dark for fear of hurting the business of the place.[12]

Ben Higgs and I have had a row; when the *Belmont* was ready to leave I wanted $1,000 to pay my portion; I had the money loaned but told the parties I would give them 10 days notice. As the money was going to H & H I thought it would make little difference with them if they waited 10 days.[13] I went to Higgs and told him the case stood thus & asked him to take my note for 10 days as I should have the money then to pay it; after all I have done for them, what do you think he said? He would do it for 5%. At the same time all their Consular business since I came back last Fall has not been paid for; all the money I have had from them is $20; they do not owe me less than $400 now. I gave him my mind pretty freely. Since then one vessel's bills amounting to $260 he sent for. I sent it without being receipted; he returned it, asking me to receipt it and he would give me their note. I told him that I would receipt it for his Note at 10 days with a good endorser and 5% added. I gave him pretty decidedly to understand I asked no favor of him & did not wish him to ask any of me. As soon as Hyland comes home, I shall have a settlement. I think hereafter they will learn that they cannot use me for nothing as they like. Hyland means well but never finishes a thing.

Since I have been writing, Mr. James has had a fit & came near dying. I have just been in to see him.

I have just had a call from young Crowell of the hotel who says there is a man there who wants to see me & if he can arrange with me, I can make a few thousands as well as not; he has the money and wants me in my official capacity. As near as I can make out, it is a blockade-running enterprise from New York. I shall see him tomorrow & shall look favorably upon his plans until I get all the information I can.

The girls at Hylands are frightened out of their wits tonight & say the house is haunted as they hear unearthly sounds from the cellar; it is haunted with 'Red Coats.' Someone tried to get in night before last but did not succeed as I heard them.

Everything is high here in the Provision line. Beef 36 cents per lb.; Mutton 40, Eggs 40 a dozen, Chickens 30 cents live weight and every thing else in proportion. Cause: No beef allowed to leave New York & great demand by blockade-runners. Steamers go from here to Wilmington apparently with as much safety as they would go to New York & every week adds new ones to the already large fleet from here. Well, they even take Vicksburg's Southern reports, say Pemberton is alright & Johnston will use up Grant.[14]

I have lots of bouquets sent to me, some are very beautiful but the hot weather is too much for them & if there is no rain soon, there will be no flowers. Peaches are ripe and quite plenty; I wish I could send some to you.

Allen submits his report for the second quarter of 1863.

No. 74
Consulate of the United States of America at Bermuda
June 30, 1863

Hon. Wm. H. Seward, Secretary of State,
Washington, D.C.

Sir,

I have the honor to enclose herewith the following returns for the port of Saint George's for the quarter ending this day viz

Arrivals and departures of American vessels, No. 1
Navigation and commerce, No. 2

also the following at the Consular agency at the port of Hamilton viz

Arrivals and departures of American vessels, No. 3
Navigation and commerce, No. 4
Fees received on account of vessels, No. 5
Transcript of fee book, No. 6
Extract from transcripts of fee book, No. 7

I am Sir, Your obedient servant,
C. M. Allen, Consul

🔲 Men from American vessels destroyed by the *Florida,* under the command of Captain Maffitt, are assisted by the consul in returning to the United States.

No. 75
Consulate of
the United States of America at Bermuda,
July 7, 1863

Hon. Wm. H. Seward, Secretary of State,
Washington, D.C.

Sir,

The whaling schooner *V. H. Hill* of Provincetown, Freeman, Master, arrived here on the fourth instant with 54 seamen put on board on the 27th ultimate by the rebel steamer *Florida.* They report they belonged to the following ships destroyed by Capt. Maffitt:[15] *Southern Cross,* Howes, Master, of Boston from the Pacific side of Mexico bound to Boston, burned June 6, in Lat 1, 15 south, Long 36 West; *Red Gauntlet,* Lucas, master, of and from Boston bound to Hong Kong, laden with coal, burned June 15th in Lat 7, 34; *Benjamin F. Hoxie,* Crarey, Master, of Mystic from Mazatlan, Mexico, for Falmouth, England laden with logwood, hides, 30 tons of silver ore, and about $500,000 in silver bars, and $7,000 to $8,000 in gold, burned June 16th Lat 12N, Long 20.

As there is but two vessels in the port here not engaged in the southern trade, and one of them not to be obtained except at extravagant prices, it has left me no alternative but to make the best bargain I could with the master of

View of St. George's Harbor, St. George's, Bermuda. Painting by Edward James (Courtesy of St. George's Historical Society, St. George's, Bermuda)

the other, and send the men home at once or keep them here, at an expense of about $40 per day for an indefinite period of time, I have therefore agreed with Capt. Doe of the British Brig *Henrietta* to take the men to New York for the sum of $770 payable in gold, he agreeing to pay their expenses after tomorrow morning, as he may not be able to leave for some days.

I have the honor to be, Sir,
Your obedient servant,
C. M. Allen, Consul

▨ After eighteen months at his post, the consul was finally able to take a leave of absence to go home to his wife and family in Belmont, New York. The Allen family was reunited for the first time since the war commenced. Although Susan and one of their daughters had visited Bermuda the previous October, Charles had not seen the other children for more than a year and a half.

It was fortunate for Allen that he left St. George's on the eve of what was to become known as the disorderly summer of 1863. By July 1863 the living conditions in the town of St. George's had become unbearable. The town was overcrowded with underpaid dock workers and crews from blockade-running vessels. Sanitary conditions, which had never been good, became dramatically worse. The fetid claustrophobic little town with its strong undercurrents of violence had sixty-seven licensed drinking establishments as well as many unlicensed ones.[16] All of this contributed to an increase in civil unrest. A dock workers' strike brought even more people into the tiny village looking to replace the strikers. Tempers escalated and a climax was reached when a suspicious fire broke out on Penno's Wharf that destroyed more than three thousand bales of cotton. That same night, an assassination attempt was made on William Tudor Tucker, who had been involved in strike negotiations. The unrest did not subside until mid-August.

No. 76

Consulate of the United States of America at Bermuda

9 July 1863

Hon. Wm. H. Seward, Secretary of State,

Washington, D.C.

Sir,

It is my intention to leave here today for New York.

The official bond of Mr. W. C. J. Hyland has been transmitted to the Secretary of the Treasury.

I have the honor to be Sir, Your obedient servant,

C. M. Allen, Consul

⬚ The U.S. government was regularly informed during Consul Allen's leave by the capable Mr. William C. J. Hyland, who wrote weekly to the secretary of state, reporting on blockade-runners and related maritime matters. Hyland also served as police magistrate in St. George's during the disorderly summer of 1863.[17] He was one of the few individuals in Bermuda who favored the cause of the Union.

No. 78

Consulate of the United States of America

Bermuda, 15th July 1863

Sir

I have the honor to acknowledge your dispatches No. 31, 32, and 33.

In reply to No. 32 for the information of the Navy Department, the English Commanders of Bermuda cleanse the bottoms of iron vessels by the use of the Diving Bell, and also by the services of a submarine Diver in armor. This latter course is preferred and is very effectual.

The steamer *Robt. E. Lee* under the flag of the so called Confederate States arrived at this port on the 9th inst. from Wilmington with Cotton and Turpentine and is now taking in cargo from Warehouse for a return voyage.

I am, Sir, with much respect, Your most obedient Servant

W. C. J. Hyland, Vice Consul

◩ While the CSS *Florida* was in port, Capt. John Maffitt, with a flair for the dramatic and ironic, engineered a salute to the Confederate flag by British forces at St. George's. When Maffitt asked if his salute to the Union Jack would be returned, British forces informed him that it would be returned gun for gun. The exchange of salutes duly took place on July 17, 1863. This is perhaps the only such salute accorded to a vessel of the Confederate navy.[18]

No. 79
Consulate of the United States of America
Bermuda, 21 July 1863

Sir

I have the honor to inform you of the arrival at this port on this 6th inst. of the armed steamship *Florida* under the flag of the rebel States of America.

Eight men composing the crew of the Brig *Wm. B. Nash,* of Cherryfield, Me, which vessel was boarded and burned by the *Florida* on the 8th inst. at 40' N. Long, 70' W. while on a voyage from New York to Marseilles, have been landed, and sought the protection of this Consulate.

Capt. Coffin also reports the burning by same vessel on the evening of the same day of a Whaling Schooner from Province Town (name unknown). She had been abandoned by her crew who had witnessed the burning of the foreign vessel. At the time of boarding these vessels she was in pursuit of a Steamer with four funnels, supposed to have been the [USS] *Ericsson.*

The *Florida* salutes the British flag on the 17th Inst. which was acknowledged from a Battery onshore. She is now undergoing repairs to hull and machinery, and is in want of coal which has been refused her by the Naval Department at these Islands. She is now alongside the *Robert E. Lee* transshipping silver bars, chronometers, etc. for Wilmington. The Steamer *Harriet Pinckney* is momently expected from Halifax with coal for rebel steamers.

The paddle wheel steamer *Hansa* from England, *Ella* and *Spaulding,* beam engines from St. John, N. B. for Nassau, *Venus* and *Gladiator* (screw) with cotton, etc. from Wilmington have all arrived within the past week, the latter this morning.

I am, Sir, with much respect, Your most obedient servant
W. C. J. Hyland, Vice Consul

◼ The British brig *Eagle* departs Bermuda carrying cotton and a portion of the silver captured by the CSS *Florida* a month earlier. When it was discovered that the silver rightfully belonged to a British firm, John Tory Bourne had it shipped to its rightful owner, narrowly avoiding an embarrassing incident.[19]

No. 80
Consulate of the United States of America
Bermuda, 25th July 1863

Sir

I have the honor to inform you that the British Brig *Eagle,* Capt. Norfolk, sailed from this port on the 22nd instant for Liverpool, G.B., with a cargo of cotton, taken from warehouse here, and a large portion of bar silver from the rebel steamship *Florida,* the whole value at 50,000 pounds. The silver has been transferred by bill of sale to John T. Bourne, the agent of the rebel states.

The steamship *Gladiator* will sail for Liverpool in a couple of days with her inboard cargo of 1000 bales cotton.

The schooner *Harkaway,* Capt. Frith, will sail tomorrow for Nassau in ballast. She has taken something from the *Florida* but cannot ascertain in time for this communication of what it consists.

I am, Sir, with much respect,
Your most obedient Servant
W. C. J. Hyland, Vice Consul

◼ This detailed dispatch of vessels in port was written while Hyland was serving not only as vice consul but also as police magistrate. It is faintly surprising that he managed to write at all during this time of civil unrest at St. George's.

No. 81
Consulate of the United States of America
Bermuda, 27 July 1863

Sir

The British iron screw steamer *Miriam* arrived at this port on the 25th instant in 17 days from Liverpool with a full cargo of merchandise, much of which I learned consists of arms for the rebel states and will be warehoused in stores hired by their agents here.

The steamship *Florida* also sailed on the evening of the same day after caulking and repairing vessel and taking a full supply of best Cardiff coal brought here from Halifax by steamer *Harriet Pinckney*.

I have also to report the arrival yesterday of the British paddle steamer *Lord Clyde* and *Banshee* and Confederate steamer *Lady Davis* formerly the *Cornubia* and this morning steamer *Eugenie* all from Wilmington with cotton.

The schooner *Harkaway* reported on 25th instant has been chartered by rebel agent to go to Nassau for coal and I have every reason to believe that the steamer *Harriet Pinckney* will leave in a few days for Halifax for a similar purpose. No coal can be procured here and there are nine steamers requiring it.

I am, Sir, with much respect, Your most obedient servant
W. C. J. Hyland, Vice Consul

▨ As this dispatch indicates, the need for coal to fuel the blockade-runners was both ongoing and enormous. A blockade-running vessel required about 200 tons of coal for a run between Bermuda and Wilmington, North Carolina.[20]

Written at the top of this dispatch: Copy sent to Adm. Lee[21]

No. 82
Consulate of the United States of America
Bermuda, 7th Aug. 1863

Sir

I have the honor to report the following arrivals at this port. On the 30th July steamer *Mail* from Cork bound for Nassau was supplied with coal and proceeded on her voyage on the fourth instant, Brig *Sevant* and Bark *Harkaway* from Liverpool with provisions and merchandise for agents of the rebel states. On the 3rd instant Steamer *Juno* with cargo of merchandize and hardware for the same. Steamer *Fanny & Jessie* from Halifax, N.S., for Nassau is repairing machinery and will sail in a few days. Steamer *Don* from London with merchandize for merchants here, and also for rebel agents. The steamer *Gibraltar* late *Sumter* from Liverpool with hardware, lead, shot, and shell, arrived on the 1st inst, and is transferring her cargo or a portion of it, to other steamers. She is bark-rigged and has all the appearance of a gunboat. On the 4th instant the British screw steamer *Florida* with 1,000 tons of coal from Nassau arrived and is supplying the other steamers, and yesterday a large bark from

Wales also arrived with a similar cargo for Confederate Agents. There are at this moment nine steamers loading and will sail in a few days for Wilmington. Other agents from the Southern States are establishing themselves here and making preparation for an extensive import and export business.

I am, Sir, with much respect, Your most obedient Servant
W. C. J. Hyland, Vice Consul

▦ Replenished with coal from Nassau, fifteen blockade-runners are fueled and ready to depart for the Southern states. Hyland echoes Consul Allen's belief that the presence of a U.S. cruiser near Bermuda would be able to capture blockade-runners as they left the island.

No. 83
Consulate of the United States of America
Bermuda, 19th August 1863

Sir

I have the honor to acknowledge your No. 1.

Since my last communication of the 4th inst. the *Gibraltar* and several other of the steamers employed in running the Blockade have sailed for Wilmington. These vessels have all cleared for Nassau and St. John with cargoes of arms, ammunition, and provisions. The former carried two very heavy guns, destined for the works at Charleston. Abundance of coal has been brought up from Nassau for the use of these vessels and other is momently expected from England. The *R. E. Lee* arrived yesterday from Wilmington and reports having been chased by USS *Vanderbilt* for 14 hours, and escaped only by throwing overboard cargo and the darkness of night. A United States cruiser in the vicinity of these Islands to the southwest could not fail of good results.

The steamers usually running to Nassau have altered their route to these islands, and no less than fifteen were in this harbor last week. The want of opportunity to the United States prevents information being forwarded of earlier dates.

I am, Sir, with much respect, Your most obedient Servant,
W. C. J. Hyland, Vice Consul

◙ Learning of the presence of a U.S. naval vessel near Bermuda, some block-ade-runners shift their operations to Nassau. This is Hyland's last dispatch before the return of Consul Allen.

No. 84
Consulate of the United States of America
Bermuda, 12th September 1863

Sir
I have the honor to acknowledge your dispatches No. 2 and 3. The USS *Fort Jackson,* Captn Aldin, reported at this Consulate on the 10th inst. and after receiving all necessary information immediately proceeded on a cruise. The presence of these vessels has created alarm among the Blockade runners and as several steamers are momently expected from Wilmington, I am san-guine they cannot all escape the *Fort Jackson.*

Since this vessel has made her appearance in these waters, I understand the route of several of the "Runners" has been altered for Nassau.

The rebel steamer *Lady Davis* arrived on the morning of the 10th inst. bring-ing as passengers on their way to Europe Commodore Barron and Professor Benslow.[22]
I am Sir, with much respect, Your most obedient Servant
W. C. J. Hyland, Vice Consul

◙ While Charles was spending the summer with his family at Belmont, he was visited by Alex V. Fraser of the New York Board of Underwriters. Their friendship had begun the previous year during the *Wheatland* affair. While the consul often earned the sometimes begrudging respect of the British and Bermudian officials with whom he contended, Fraser's letter to Susan illustrates how Charles's personal qualities engendered loyal and true friendships.

As from Brooklyn, Sept 13, 1863.

Mrs C. M. Allen,
Belmont, Alleghany Co. N.Y.

Dear Madam:
I send by Adams Express a box containing some trifles for the children, marked to each distinctly. I trust they may be received as a slight testimonial

of the regard and friendship I entertain for your husband and for your hospitality to myself and my son during our visit. With regard to Mr Allen, I regard him as one of those friends who is at all times entitled not only to my friendship but to the utmost confidence of the Government & as such shall have my best services at Washington and those of my friends. If I can in any manner serve your interest, please command me. Accept the assurances of the friendship of my family & believe me, very faithfully yours,

Alexander V. Fraser[23]

After three months with his family at Belmont, Allen returned to his post in Bermuda, retracing the route he had taken two years earlier as a newly appointed consul. Allen's dispatches were written in a clear and legible hand. The first dispatches written after his return exhibit a somewhat perfunctory style and a strained orthography. This may be explained by the lingering effects of his long illness, which began even prior to his departure for New York.[24]

No. 85
Consulate of the United States at Bermuda
October 26th 1863

Hon. Wm. H. Seward, Secretary of State,
Washington, D.C.

Sir,
   I have the honor to enclose herewith the following returns for the quarter ending September 30th 1863 viz.:

1. Arrivals and departures of American Vessels
2. Navigation and commerce account of fees received at the consular agency at the Port of Hamilton
3. Account for fees as per form No. 45 at Consular agency.
4. Account for fees as per form No. 44 at the Consular agency.

   Having been sick for some time past I have been compelled to defer making the returns for the last quarter till now.

I am Sir, Your obedient servant
C. M. Allen, Consul

◈ Obviously still quite ill, Charles writes a poignant letter to Susan as blockade-runners continue to fill the harbor of St. George's.

October 26, 1863:

Mr. James has done all for me he could and is the only one who has shewn me any friendship. The Harbor is so full of vessels there is scarcely a chance for one to anchor—all secesh.[25]

◈ Late in the year Allen reports on the number of ships filled with Southerners arriving at St. George's. As the blockade became more effective, and as it became more difficult for the blockade-runners to reach Wilmington, the Southern presence in Bermuda increased dramatically.

No. 86
Consulate of the United States at Bermuda
October 31st 1863

Hon Wm. H. Seward, Secretary of State,
Washington D.C.

Sir,
I have the honor to report the following blockade-running steamers in port here at the present time viz.:
Flora, Dee, A. D. Vance, Ella, Ella & Anna, Cornubia/Lee, and *Boston* all of which with the exception of the *Boston* will probably leave for Wilmington within 10 days.
The *Boston* came in leaky some weeks since from Halifax and is not yet repaired. Her cargo was badly damaged.
About twenty five sailing vessels are in port here now with Cargoes for the confederates. I am preparing as full a statement as it is possible for me to obtain of rebel commerce at these Islands since the commencement of the rebellion and hope to be able to forward it soon.[26]

I am Sir, Your most obedient servant
C. M. Allen, Consul

◨ Allen notes that one of the blockade-runners was departing for Florida to secure cotton. Because the Bermuda-Wilmington run was becoming more dangerous for the blockade-runners, other more lightly guarded ports were favored.

No. 87
Consulate of the United States at Bermuda,
November 10, 1863

Hon Wm. H. Seward, Secretary of State,
Washington, D.C.

Sir,

Since my No. 86 of October 30 the following steamers have arrived here to be employed in running the blockade, viz:

November 2, *Heroine*, [?] from Glasgow is top sail rigged, side wheels and draws but four feet of water. Has capacity of 300 bales of cotton. It is reported she is to go to Indian River, Florida.

November 5 *Powerful,* Lenin [?], from Quebec is a small side wheel river boat with wheels well aft about 150 tons burden.

November 8th *Ceres* from London screw boat of about 300 tons is discharging a portion of her cargo and receiving a coat of light paint.

November 9, *City of Petersburgh* from the Clyde, a fine powerful paddle boat with capacity for 1300 bales of cotton.

The following steamers have left here, viz.: *Dee, A. D. Vance, Flora, Ella & Anna,* & *Ella* on the 3 instant, on the 4th, *Cornubia/ R. E. Lee* and *Powerful,* all having cleared for Nassau.

In addition to the above, several sailing vessels have arrived from England consigned to Rebel agents here.

I am Sir, Your most obedient servant
C. M. Allen, Consul

◨ Allen is finally able to report tangible results from the blockading squadrons.

No. 88
Consulate of the United States at Bermuda
November 20th 1863

Hon Wm. H. Seward, Secretary of State,
Washington, D.C.

Sir,

I have the honor to report the arrival at these Islands, yesterday, of the British iron screw steamer *Coquette* of Liverpool, twelve days from Cork, with a general cargo, and steam machinery. She is about 300 tons register three masts, with fore and aft sails and draws ten feet of water. I am informed she will attempt to go in to Wilmington.

The steamer *Gibraltar* late the rebel steamer *Sumter,* now under the British flag, arrived here from Wilmington on the 15th instant, with 350 bales of cotton. She will proceed to England.

The steamer *Flora,* under the British flag, arrived here on the 18th instant from Wilmington with a cargo of cotton and a large number of passengers.

The blockade runners here are in much trouble having recently sustained heavy losses, they report the blockade of Wilmington very strong. The general opinion among them is the addition to the blockading fleet was caused by the *Gibraltar* being in port but as she has escaped it will soon be reduced so as to be no more effectual than heretofore. The steamers *Heroine* and *Ceres* are still in port here, several other steamers have been purchased in England and are soon expected here.

I am Sir, Your most obedient servant,
C. M. Allen, Consul

▨ Allen reports that ships in Bermuda are hesitant to run the blockade. Few ships are arriving at Bermuda from blockaded ports.

No. 89
Consulate of the United States of America at Bermuda
11 December 1863

Hon Wm. H. Seward, Secretary of State,
Washington D.C.

Sir,

Since my No. 88 the following blockade-running steamers have left here. Steamer *Denbigh* on the 2 instant, *Flora* on the 3rd and *Ceres* on the 4th. The *Coquette* and *Heroine* are still in port with Cargoes on board, were ready to leave some days since but are afraid to go. The *Coquette* is high out of water, the danger of her being captured is considered great, her voyage may be abandoned.

British steamer *Denbigh* from England arrived in the 22 ultim consigned to a southern house here, paddle boat with capacity for about 350 bales cotton. British steamer *Ranger* from Plymouth arrived on the 9th instant, paddle boat, in appearance very much like the *R. E. Lee* but not quite as large.

There has been no arrivals from blockaded ports for some days, the *A. D. Vance* and *Dee* were expected ten days ago.

The top sails schooner *G. O. Bigelow* left the port of Hamilton a few days since with a cargo of salt. I think she will attempt to run the blockade.

I am sir, Your most obedient servant
C. M. Allen, Consul

▓ Finding a stronger U.S. presence off Wilmington, blockade-runners continue to experience difficulties in reaching that port.

No. 90
Consulate of the United States of America at Bermuda
December 21, 1863

Hon Wm. H. Seward, Secretary of State,
Washington D.C.

Sir,

The steamers *Coquette* and *Heroine* of which I spoke in my last left here on the 12 instant, the *Coquette* returned on the 19th reports having been among the blockading fleet off Wilmington, but could not get in.

The steamer *Ranger* left on the 14th with a full cargo, and returned here today, not having been into port.

Steamer *Flora,* from Wilmington with cotton, arrived here on the 16th instant when off these islands they saw the British Mail steamer and supposing her to be an American war vessel in pursuit, they made for the land with all speed and run her on to the reefs, and knocked a hole in her bottom. It is doubtful if she can be repaired here. Steamer *The Dare,* of and from Glasgow, came in on the 16 instant, she is a new paddle boat, of about 300 tons, draws five feet of water, has been painted white.

Steamer *Presto* arrived today from England. She is in appearance very much like *The Dare.*

I am Sir, Your most obedient servant
C. M. Allen, Consul

■ Consul Allen reports that a large number of Confederates in Bermuda are planning "some piratical scheme."

No. 91
Consulate of the United States of America at Bermuda
December 22, 1863

Hon Wm. H. Seward, Secretary of State,
Washington, D.C.

Sir,

I beg to inform you that the crews and many of the officers of captured blockade runners are arriving here by most every vessel from the states and shipping again for the same purpose. Were it not for them, it would be difficult for the blockade-running steamers to get crews.

There is at these Islands at present time a large number of desperate men from the Southern states, some fifty having arrived from Halifax last week, one of which report says is John H. Morgan.[27] About one hundred have been here for some time, their board is paid by Confederate Agents. Some piratical scheme is evidently contemplated by them. I shall endeavor to obtain all the information possible and if such is the case, do all in my power to prevent the accomplishment of their designs.

I am Sir, Your most obedient servant
C. M. Allen, Consul

◈ The consul reports that an attempt is to be made by the blockade-runners to reach Charleston.

No. 92
Consulate of the United States of America at Bermuda
December 22, 1863

Hon Wm. H. Seward, Secretary of State,
Washington, D.C.

Sir,
   I have just learned from a source I think to be reliable that the blockade runners here will attempt to run into Charleston instead of Wilmington.

I am Sir, Your most obedient servant,
C. M. Allen, Consul

◈ Allen alerts the Department of State of the estimated times of departure and arrival of at least nine blockade-running vessels. Attempts to run the blockade were invariably made on moonless nights that further camouflaged a vessel's presence.
   As the year 1863 closed, Secretary of the Navy Gideon P. Welles noted in his diary: "The year closes more satisfactorily than it commenced. . . . The War has been waged with success, although there have been in some instances errors and misfortunes. But the heart of the nation is sounder and its hopes brighter."[28]

No. 93
Consulate of the United States of America at Bermuda
December 29, 1863

Hon Wm. H. Seward, Secretary of State,
Washington, D.C.

Sir,
   Since my last the British steamers *Will o' the Wisp* from Glasgow and *Vesta* from Plymouth have arrived here. The *Vesta* is a twin boat to the *Ceres*. *Will o'*

the Wisp is a paddle boat of about 120 tons. There is now in this port of Saint George nine blockade-running steamers, seven of which will probably leave for the Southern States about the end of this week, so as to be on the coast when there is no moon.

I am Sir, Your most obedient servant
C. M. Allen, Consul

CHAPTER 5

"I have used my utmost endeavors"

■ Consul Allen submits his returns for the fourth quarter of 1863. With the great number of people in wartime St. George's, real estate values and rents dramatically increased. With lodgings and office space at a premium, Allen had no choice but to accept the escalating rent for the consulate.

No. 94
Consulate of the United States at Bermuda
January 1, 1864

Hon. Wm. H. Seward
Secretary of State, Washington, D.C.

Sir,

I have the honor to enclose herewith the following returns and accounts for the year and quarter ending December 31, 1863:

Navigation & Commerce, No. 2
Arrival & Departure of American Vessels, No. 1
Account for office rent for six months with vouchers, No. 3
Account for postage, No. 4
Account of official letters sent from and received for the year 1863, No. 5 & 6
Names of persons employed at this consulate during the year 1863, No. 7
Also returns from the U.S. Consulate Agency at Hamilton numbered 8 to 13

I have been compelled to pay an increased price for office rent and have been notified of a further increase at the end of six months. I can get no other place.

I am sir, your obedient servant,
C. M. Allen, Consul

⧈ Ships unfamiliar with Bermudian waters could easily suffer irreparable damage on the northern reefs that extended several miles out from shore. When blockade-runners arrived in need of major repairs, which could not be provided in Bermuda, their only recourse was to try to reach Halifax, Nova Scotia.

No. 95
Consulate of the United States at Bermuda
January 18, 1864

Hon. Wm. H. Seward,
Secretary of State, Washington

Sir

The steamer *Will o' the Wisp* left here for Halifax on the 3 instant, she came here with the intention of going to Wilmington but proving leaky was sent away for repairs.

Steamers *The Dare,* Capt. Skinner, and *Vesta,* Capt. Eustice, left on the 3 instant for Wilmington with 408 packages merchandise.

Steamer *Nola* from London with a full cargo mostly dry goods ran onto the rocks off these Islands and went down, vessel and cargo nearly a total loss. She was a good vessel and recently cost 31,000 pounds sterling. Was a sister ship to the *City of Petersburgh.* Both the last named ships were owned by Confederates. Steamer *Flora* before reported as having been on the rocks off these islands, after undergoing temporary repairs, left on the 7th instant for Halifax, sprung a leak and went down the next day about 60 miles from land.

Steamer *Dee,* Captain Beers, from Wilmington with 465 bales cotton, arrived on the 11th instant, screw boat, 216 tons register.

Steamer *City of Petersburgh,* Captain Fuller, from Wilmington with 789 bales cotton arrived on the 12th instant and left for the same port on the 15th. Steamer *Nutfield,* Captain Hawks, from London arrived on the 18th instant, is a paddle boat, 402 tons. Has a bowsprit, two masts, one smoke stack and draws 8 feet of water when laden. Has since her arrival been painted light color. She is to be commanded by Capt. Horner, formerly in the *Flora*. Steamer *Don,* Capt. Roberts, from Wilmington with 561 bales cotton, came in on the 14th instant, screw boat 233 tons.[1]

Steamer *Index* from London arrived today, is very much like the *Nutfield* in appearance.

Several other steamers are expected here soon from England. The Steamer *Syren,* formerly belonging to the British Government and used here for some years past by her Majesty's officers, has recently been sold to Southern parties.

I am informed she is to be sent to the Confederacy for a dispatch boat. She is about 60 tons burden, 3 masts, one smoke stack, bowsprit and figure head, is a very rakish trim looking craft, will not steam over 9 miles per hour in smooth water.

I am Sir, Your most obedient servant
C. M. Allen, Consul

For three years, Allen's efforts to stem Confederate blockade-running through Bermuda had been frustrated by his geographic isolation. His dispatches often reached the Washington authorities only after the fact. As 1864 began, there were hopeful signs that the U.S. government was about to counter Confederate blockade-running with clandestine operations. This became apparent to Allen when a Frenchman named Peyrusset arrived in Bermuda on a ship loaded with Confederate supplies. The Frenchman came to Allen with an introduction from Charles Francis Adams, U.S. minister to Great Britain. Peyrusset asked Allen's financial assistance in getting to Washington as quickly as possible.

At the same time, a man claiming to be a U.S. detective from Baltimore also arrived in Bermuda informing Allen that he was attempting to reach Cuba in order to foil a Confederate plot. As Allen's dispatch demonstrates, he had his doubts about the bona fides of both of these individuals until he was assured by another undercover agent and the Department of State that both men were, in fact, known to the Department, which vouched for the authenticity of their credentials.

No. 96
U.S. Consulate at Bermuda
January 22, 1864

Hon. Wm. H. Seward,
Secretary of State

Sir,

A Frenchman calling himself Peyrusset arrived here in the British barque *Agrippina* on the 10th instant from London.[2] He brings Hon. C. F. Adams' card with the following written over the printed name "Mr. Allen, receive the bearer, M. Peyrusset, he will make known his business and you can act as you see fit. London Nov. 12/63." He appears much disappointed that he found no letter or instructions here. The *Agrippina* has on board 50 tons of coal, about 100 tons of powder, 70 tons cartridges and a large quantity of rifles. Is now in this port of St. George's. Mr. P informed me he went on board the same vessel at London with the sanction of Mr. Adams and Consul Morse, who paid him ten pounds, says from the information he then had he believes the *Agrippina* was to supply the *Alabama* or some other Rebel Privateer. Says they cruised about 14 miles southwest of the Azores from the 5th to the 10th of December but spoke no vessel. The Captain (McQueen) came here in irons and the evidence before the Police Court proves his statement that they delayed off the Azores to be correct. The man has every appearance of being honest. He is here destitute. I have let him have $25 and in the absence of any instruction am at a loss to know what to do. He wants to leave here today for Washington via Halifax; wants me to let him have $80 to pay his passage, which request I have not complied with.

A person calling himself Major M. Somers, claiming to be a U.S. Detective from Baltimore, called upon me on the 12th instant. Said he had followed a Rebel Lieut. here who took a part in the capture of the *Chesapeake* and wanted me to have him arrested at once.[3] From the information I have I was satisfied one of the principal actors in that capture was here, but in the absence of all proof of a positive nature I did not think it advisable to make any move for his arrest. I stated all the circumstances connected with this man which had come to my knowledge to the Governor. While he was willing to assist me in any way he could, he thought it injudicious to try to stop him.

The man Somers said he must be in Havana as soon as it was possible for him to get there as there was a plot on foot to capture one of the New Orleans steamers. He left the next day in steamer from St. Thomas. Said he was nearly destitute of money and wanted me to supply him and take his draft on the War Department. The papers he presented to me satisfied me. He was in May last employed as a U.S. Detective or he had stolen his papers from some other person. As there was some suspicious circumstances connected with this man, I declined to let him have money and hope I was not wrong in doing so.

I am Sir, your obedient servant,
C. M. Allen, Consul

▨ A note in a different hand was included with this dispatch. It was written by someone in the secretary of state's office.

Write to this man confidentially that the D[epartment] has no doubt that the men herein referred to were as they represent themselves, but that though for obvious reasons they could not be officially recognized. He will be reimbursed for any reasonable advances which he may make for them.

Tell him also to send us a [scheduled?] account in his own name for their expenses with his voucher, his [draft?] to be drawn payable [in coin?].

▨ At this time Allen was continuing his own intelligence gathering by involving himself in St. George's social affairs. On two occasions in January 1864 he attended the Masonic Lodge St. George's No. 200 as a prospective member, and on one occasion Monsieur Peyrusset was also in attendance. Masonic records of the meetings of January 15, 1864, and February 18, 1864, which Allen attended, make it clear that the Lodge St. George's was attended by visitors and fellow Masons from the Confederate states.[4] On December 7, 1864, Allen was raised to the sublime degree of Master Mason.[5] In this dispatch, having refused assistance to the Baltimore detective, Allen provides the assistance that the Frenchman, Peyrusset, was seeking.

No. 97
January 23, 1864

Hon. Wm. H. Seward
Secretary of State, Washington

Sir:

Since writing my No. 96 yesterday, I have received some papers from Capt. Squire in regard to Mons. Peyrusset and a letter advising me to send him to New York by steamer today.[6] I will do so, giving him one hundred dollars in addition to the $25 before paid him. He will require it all to pay his bills here and get there. Do I act wisely or not?

I am sir, your obedient servant
C. M. Allen, Consul

Allen asks for clarification over the complex issue of bonds for merchant ships arriving in Bermuda. This dispatch is one of the few that Allen misnumbered.

No. 96
Consulate of the United States of America at Bermuda
February 3, 1864

Hon. Wm. H. Seward
Secretary of State, Washington, D.C.

Sir.

I have the honor to enclose herewith form of affidavit and certificate (No. 1) used by me for the purpose of canceling bonds given in New York for merchandise shipped to these Islands. I have been in some doubt as to the exact intent of the bond and have written several times to the Collector of Customs at New York in relation to them but have been unable to get any information.

It is a well known fact that a large portion of the merchandise imported from New York goes if not direct, indirectly, into the hands of persons employed in running the blockade.[7] There is not a merchant here that does not sell more or less to Southern parties and in cases where I have reason to believe they were imported to sell without special intent to supply that trade, I have attached the endorsed form of oath and certificate. In some cases, I have afterward become satisfied they were intended to be sold to Southern parties or to be sent to blockaded ports. In all such instances I have promptly informed the Collector of Customs at New York.

Circulars have been sent from New York houses to their correspondents here informing them the certificate attached by me is not sufficient to get their bonds canceled and asking them to get a different one. I am at a loss to know what different one I can give as this one seems to be all the circumstances of the case will admit.

If it is the intent of the bond to prevent a merchant here in the regular course of trade to sell any article imported from New York to a person or persons engaged in running the blockade or to Southern parties, I can readily see this certificate and affidavit are insufficient.

I have supposed the bonds were intended to prevent parties from importing goods here with the intent of supplying those engaged in running the blockade or with the intent of shipping them to blockaded ports. As I would like to know fully what is intended that I may be able to perform my duty understandingly, will you please instruct me?

There is no doubt the bonds have had the effect to stop the heavy shipments from New York here on rebel account, but I have reason to believe they still get large quantities of mdse from New York via Halifax and in some cases which have come to my knowledge, merchandise in considerable quantities has arrived here from New York without being cleared there consequently without coming under bonds, as in the case of the *Georgiana* of which I informed the Collector of Customs at New York.

I am Sir, Your obedient servant,
C. M. Allen, Consul

UNITED STATES CONSULATE

AT BERMUDA, ———————————— 186———————

I, C. M. ALLEN, Consul of the United States of America for the Islands of Bermuda, do hereby certify that the Goods and Property mentioned and described in the Affidavit and Schedule hereunto annexed have been landed at the port of ————————, Bermuda, and entered at the Custom House here, and the duties thereon paid at the said Custom House, as appears by the Affidavit hereunto annexed.

I do further certify that in my opinion the said Goods were imported for sale and consumption in Bermuda and are intended to be sold to any one who chooses to purchase, without reference to person or place.

Given unto my hand and seal of office, the day and year above written.

United Stated Consul

_____ being duly sworn, says he is the importer hereinafter named, that the annexed Schedule contains a list of all the Goods and Property shipped from _____ to said _____ by and in the ship or vessel called the _____ on or about the _____ day of _____, 186__: that the said merchandise has been landed at the port of _____, Bermuda and entered at the Custom House there, and the duties thereon paid at said Custom House; that the said Merchandise has not been, nor is it intended to be sold or used to aid or comfort any person, state or country in rebellion against the Government of the United States of America.

Sworn to before me at Bermuda, this ___ day of _____, 186_____

United States Consul

🔲 Consul Allen repeatedly urged a U.S. naval presence near Bermuda and at other ports such as Halifax, Nova Scotia, which were often blockade-running destinations but well outside the limits of the blockade.

No. 98
Consulate of the United States of America at Bermuda
February 15, 1864

Hon. Wm. H. Seward
Secretary of State, Washington, D.C.

Sir

I have the honor to report the arrival here on the 9th instant of the steamer *Will o' the Wisp* from Halifax where she had been for repairs. She took in a cargo of ordnance stores and left on the 13th for Wilmington.

Steamer *Harriet Pinckney* from England arrived on the 11th instant. I am informed she is to be employed, together with another steamer about her size, both of which are said to be owned by the "Confederate Government" in running regularly between here and England.

Confed. steamer *A. D. Vance* from Wilmington arrived on the 11th instant with a cargo of cotton, a large portion of which was burned on the wharf the first night after being landed. She left again for Wilmington the evening of the 13th.

Steamers *Emily* and *Caledonia* left on the 6th for Wilmington. Steamer *Minnie* has a cargo on board but cannot leave for want of a Wilmington pilot and expects to remain during this moon.

The Confederate steamer *Eugenie* will probably go to Halifax for repairs in two or three weeks. I am in hopes to ascertain the day she will leave in time to inform the Consul there by the mail steamer the last of this week.

If we have any war vessel in those waters they may capture her as her machinery is out of order and she cannot make much speed.

Marshal Kane and about twenty Confederates arrived in the mail steamer from Halifax last week.[8]

I am Sir, your obedient servant,
C. M. Allen, Consul

⊠ As the Southeast Blockading Squadron's efforts grow more effective, Allen reports that Nassau blockade-runners are now operating from Bermuda.

No. 99
Consulate of the United States of America at Bermuda
February 20th 1864

Hon. Wm. H. Seward
Secretary of State, Washington, D.C.

Sir,

I have the honor to report the following blockade running steamers now in this port of Saint George, viz: *Boston, Minnie, Coquette, Hansa, Eugenie, Index, City of Petersburgh, Flora, Thistle,* and *Syren.* The *Hansa* came in from Wilmington last Monday with 540 bales of cotton, the *City of Petersburgh* the day following with 750 bales and the *Index* with 500 bales and one hundred passengers.

The *Flora* arrived yesterday from England. She brings as passenger Capt. Maffit, formerly in command of the Confederate privateer *Florida.*

The *Thistle* arrived this morning from England, has some machine for the *Coquette,* her machinery having broken down in her last attempt to run the blockade.

All of the above with the exception of the *Eugenie* (which is out of repair and will go to Halifax) will probably attempt to run the blockade during the last quarter of this moon or the first quarter of the next.

The *Boston* has been sold to Southern parties and is fitting for sea. The *Coquette* will be ready in one week.

The *Nutfield* and cargo, reported totally destroyed, cost more than one million of dollars and was the most valuable cargo they have ever sent from here to attempt to run the blockade.

I am informed most of the blockade running steamers will for the present come here instead of going to Nassau. Several of the steamers from England are expected here in time to go to Wilmington during the coming dark nights.

I am Sir, your obedient servant,
C. M. Allen, Consul

⬛ The consul again suggests strategically placed gunboats to intercept blockade-running vessels.

No. 100
Consulate of the United States of America at Bermuda
March 1, 1864

Hon. Wm. H. Seward
Secretary of State, Washington, D.C.

Sir,

Captain Maffitt, late of the privateer *Florida,* intends to leave here tomorrow as Master of the steamer *Flora.*

A correspondent who is in a better position to obtain information than I am says it is his intention to come out from Wilmington or Charleston with an iron clad, that the guns are now here for her. He also says all the vessels from Wilmington bring these Islands to bear east one half south distant thirty miles and that a gun boat stationed there cannot fail to fall in with some of them. Steamer *City of Petersburgh* left here yesterday for Wilmington. She is under the command of one Fuller, the same person who supplied the *Nashville* with coals in February, 1862 when in port here.

Several other steamers will leave here for Wilmington in a few days.

I am Sir, your obedient servant,
C. M. Allen, Consul

◙ Admiral Milne, acting in compliance with the Act of British Neutrality, refuses to let blockade-runners undertake repairs at the naval dockyard in Bermuda.

No. 101
United States Consulate at Bermuda
10 March 1864

Hon. Wm. H. Seward
Secretary of State, Washington, D.C.

Sir,

The steamer *Flora* under the British flag left here on the same inst for Wilmington under command of Capt. Maffitt and returned on the 4th leaking badly. She cannot be repaired here as Admiral Milne will not allow her or any other blockade runner to receive any repairs at the Naval Dockyard.

Steamer *Caledonia* arrived on the 6th from Wilmington with 308 bales of cotton. Was five days making the passage. She cannot steam over six knots per hour.

Steamers *Index* and *Coquette* left on the 3rd instant for Wilmington.

Brig *Carl Emile* from Liverpool, barque *Enterprise* from Newport, and ships *Storm King* and *Gambia* from Cardiff, have arrived during the past week with cargoes for the Confederates. The *Gambia* went onto the rock near the entrance of this port (St. George's). Vessel and cargo nearly a total loss.

I am Sir, your obedient servant
C. M. Allen, Consul

◙ While Allen was often frustrated by half-hearted cooperation from British and Bermudian officials, it is clear that he was constantly searching for new and creative ways to protect the interests of his country and its commerce. When, in the early spring of 1864, Southerners were taking passage on New York–bound vessels, Allen, alert to the possibilities of sabotage, proposes sending lists of suspicious passengers to the U.S. marshal at New York.

No. 103
Consulate of the United States of America at Bermuda
19 March 1864

Hon. Wm. H. Seward
Secretary of State, Washington, D.C.

Sir,

I am informed by a correspondent here that most every vessel from here to the States or British provinces carry as passengers Southern men, part of a gang organized here for the purpose of shipping on board some of our steamers and capturing them if an opportunity offers or of working themselves into the favor of parties whereby they may be able to destroy government and other property. Some go today by the mail steamer to Halifax. I shall inform the consul there and send a photograph of one of the leaders.[9]

Would it not be well to not allow any passengers to land at New York from vessels arriving there from here till an officer permits them to do so and in all cases where I have any knowledge of any suspicious persons being on board there will be a package of letters directed to the Post-Office at New York, under the seal of this consulate, containing one directed to the U.S. Marshal giving all the information I can obtain.

I am Sir, your obedient servant,
C. M. Allen, Consul

Allen's informants came both from St. George's residents sympathetic to the cause of the Union and from disaffected crew members of blockade-running vessels. On occasion, however, his informants gathered intelligence from within the Confederacy itself. The most important of these efforts in the spring of 1864 was the acquisition of the pilot's signals used to guide the blockade-runners in entering and leaving Wilmington.

No. 104
U.S. Consulate at Bermuda
19 March 1864

Hon. Wm. H. Seward
Secretary of State, Washington, D.C.

Sir,

I enclose herewith a paper this moment received. It will explain itself. I also have obtained the signals used for vessels coming out of Wilmington and as the *Shenandoah* is now under weigh coming from the Dock Yard bound to sea, I will board her and communicate with Captain Ridgley.[10]

I am Sir, your obedient servant,
C. M. Allen, Consul

▩ This enclosure, from one of Allen's informants, was written on four pages. The top or first line is missing on each page due to poor microfilming of the original.

. . . Yesterday I gave Richards a letter for you and I told him there the pilots of these vessels were very dissatisfied with General Whiting's last instructions in regards of them which were that they were to pilot any steamer in and out for 300 dollars per month and if they stay out of Wilmington over 6 weeks unless captured they are to be conscripted.[11] This I got from Mr. Grissan, the pilot of the *Index,* whose father is now in Lafayette and he told me that it would not be long before some one of the pilots will be conscripted. . . .[12]

. . . so it would be a good [illegible] for Wilmington for then he said that he would not be surprised if one of the pilots did not go over to the Yankees and if so there would be an end of Wilmington blockading for either of the pilots could place 2 or 3 gun boats off the bar so that nothing could come out without being seen and last night another pilot by the name of Jefferson came to me complaining about how they are treating him I told him what Mr. Grissan had told me and he confirmed it for he says all the Yankees . . .

. . . want to know is the blockade signals and then they would know when we are coming out as well as we know ourselves but we might get in and not be seen as our signals are not set untill we get in to the port but coming out they would [be] shure to catch us. Now I will try and find out what those signals are, no one knows but the Captn. & Pilots and I hope to be able to do it. And now I must tell you the rate of speed of the boats here about to leave which I got from the pilots and engineers. First the *Caledonia* now going to W not over 6 knots, *Index* 7 ½

. . . *City of Petersburgh* [illegible], *North Heath* Now 8, *Minnie* 8 ½, *Greyhound* probably for Nassau. Good 9 knots so that I hope the *Shenandoah* may stand a chance for some of them when they start and now for some more men that leaves here tomorrow by the *Excelsior*. There are three, their names are D. Bell from Baltimore but in C.S.A., Mr. Wm. Adams, a Wilmington man and Charles Benson, a German by birth but has been in the C.S.A. and for the last year on Blockade. There is also a Captn. [Everest?] here came on the *Petersburgh,* a bearer of dispatches and I think will go to Halifax in said *Petersburgh.*
more [anon?]

🔲 The consul reports on Captain Maffitt in Bermuda and Captain Beers, "king" of blockade-runners, who was actually Lt. George Henry Bier, Confederate navy, master of the *Greyhound*.

No. 105
Consulate of the United States of America at Bermuda
March 31, 1864

Hon. Wm. H. Seward
Secretary of State, Washington

Sir

The following steamers have left here for Wilmington during the past few days, viz: Steamer *A. D. Vance,* Captain Wiley, a southern man left of the 26th. Steamer *Minnie,* Gilpin, an Englishman who has twice been captured left on the 27th.

The *North Heath* and *Caledonia* left yesterday, Captain Burroughs, formerly in the *Cornubia* is in the *North Heath*. Captain Wiley a southern man is in charge of the *Caledonia*. The steamer *Index* leaves today for Wilmington and the *Greyhound* under Captain Beers, late of the *Dee,* is to leave tomorrow for Nassau.

Captain Beers was formerly in our Navy. He is called the Admiral here and is considered the King of blockade runners. If captured he will claim to be an Englishman and will, I am informed, disguise himself at Nassau.

Steamer *Syren* is to leave next Saturday.

There has been no arrival of blockade runners since my last.

Captain Maffit is still here waiting for a steamer. He is drunk the greater part of the time.

I am, Sir, your obedient Servant
C. M. Allen, Consul

▩ Numerous blockade-running vessels arrive in Bermuda in need of repair.

No. 106
Consulate of the United States at Bermuda
7 April 1864

Hon. Wm. H. Seward
Secretary of State, Washington

Sir:

Since my No. 105 of March 31 the British steamers *Edith* and *Ellen* have arrived here from England. *Edith,* double screw, two straight tall stacks abreast, straight stem, two masts, 420 tons, a new vessel. *Ellen,* side wheel, two stacks fore and aft, 320 tons, a fine new vessel cost 40,000 pounds sterling, is a sister ship to the *North Heath.*

The *North Heath* and *Caledonia* which left here on the 31 ultimo have returned to port. *North Heath* is badly strained. They were compelled to run her aground to keep her from sinking. Her cargo is badly damaged. She cannot be repaired here. The *Caledonia* I am informed will soon leave again for Wilmington. She is reported as badly strained and unfit to go to sea.

The *Index* is supposed to have gone down at sea with all hands.

Steamer *Syren,* now called the *Lady of Lyon,* left here yesterday. She now has but two masts, her mizzen mast having been taken out.

Confederate Steamer *Eugenie* leaves today for London to undergo repairs. Steamer *Lady of Lyon* is now coming into port, report says she is leaking. I am informed the *Ellen* which arrived yesterday is leaking badly.

I am sir, your obedient servant
C. M. Allen, Consul

◈ Allen requests advice on the disposition of personal property from a U.S. vessel.

No. 107
Consulate of the United States at Bermuda
April 7, 1864

Hon. Wm. H. Seward
Secretary of State, Washington

Sir:

From a vessel wrecked off these Islands I have possession of some property of no great value evidently belonging to George W. Hollins, late of the U.S. Navy consisting of a U.S. Naval uniform coat, some towels, shirts and other linen, a writing desk containing seals, coat of arms, and with some correspondence of no public importance. The vessel from which the above was received was the *Sarah E. Chapman* from New York.

Will you please inform me what disposition I shall make of the above.

I am sir, your obedient servant,
C. M. Allen, Consul

◈ Allen concludes his financial arrangements in the matter of M. Peyrusset. This dispatch is not in Allen's handwriting.

No. 108
U.S. Consulate at Bermuda
April 12, 1864

Hon. Wm. H. Seward
Secretary of State, Washington, D.C.

Sir:

I have the honor to enclose herewith accounts for money paid A. Peyrusset (No. 1). The circumstance of the case will be understood by referring to my dispatch No. 96.

I have made a draft for the amount and sent it to Mrs. C. M. Allen, Belmont, New York, who will forward the same after she is informed the claim has been audited and allowed. If allowed you will please inform her.

I am, Sir, Your obedient servant,
C. M. Allen, Consul

Consul Allen's expenses in St. George's inevitably exceeded his income, especially given the fact that he was supporting himself in Bermuda as well as his family in Belmont, New York. He also often extended his hospitality to visiting Americans. His situation had clearly reached a critical point by the spring of 1864 when he petitioned the Department of State for an increase in his salary. This situation clearly called for great tact and persuasion. While not conclusive, the British spelling and style of this dispatch indicates that it may have been written in collaboration with Allen's witty and urbane friend, Edward James. The style is substantially different from all of Allen's other dispatches and it bears strong similarity to Edward James's letter to the editor of the *Bermuda Royal Gazette* in November 1862.

U.S. Consul at Bermuda
12 April 1864

Hon. Wm. H. Seward,
Secretary of State, Washington

Sir:

I beg to call your attention to the following statements of facts as connected with this Consulate, and if I trouble you with the relation of some things already well known to you, I do so merely because they are necessary to the completeness and elucidation of my statements.

On my arrival in Bermuda in the month of November, 1861, I found a tolerably steady trade being carried on at the two principal ports, Saint George's and Hamilton, as regards imports, principally in the nature of supplies for the Colony itself, and for shipping activity, etc. as regards exports, almost exclusively in the nature of the vegetable products of the Islands. The extent of this trade may be gathered from the statistical facts that the value of the imports for the year 1862 was $1,194,660.00 and of the exports $222,078.00. Commerce with the United States entering into the above amounts to the extent of no less than $717,160.00 of the imports, or considerably more than one half of the whole trade of the Colony.

I found, moreover, that a very considerable part of the business of the Islands generally, but especially of Saint George's, was due to the necessities of vessels in distress and that a large number of these belonged to the United States; such was the general state of trade when I arrived. Soon after my arrival, however, a totally new line of business sprang into existence, in addition to and not by way of substitution for the regular trade of the place, and has since continued to expand and develop itself to an extraordinary extent.

This trade began with an occasional visit of a steam vessel about to endeavour to run the blockade of the Southern Ports, and has resulted in the port of Saint George's becoming a regular place of rendezvous for vessels engaged in this trade. Coal, munitions of war, provisions, clothing, medicines, etc. etc. are brought here, and reshipped on board of steamers to the blockaded ports, and on their return bring cotton which is here reshipped for the other continents.

This development has been accompanied not only, as of course, with a large increase in the profits of the local merchants, owners of wharves, and others, but with a vast influx as well of newcomers of all classes, merchants, agents, clerks, tradesmen, and laborers.

The natural consequence has been a corresponding increase in the price of all the necessaries of life; board has risen from $7.00 per week to $17.50, and as regards house room, there is difficulty amounting almost to an impossibility in obtaining accommodations at any price; some are living in tents, which a large portion of the laborers take their meals on the wharves and lodge on veranders or wherever they can. Houses, which three years ago would not rent for more than $150 per annum, are now bid for at $1,000. It will thus be seen, while on the one hand, the vast increase in trade of the place, and its peculiar nature, calls for increased vigilance and exertion on the part of the U.S. Consul, all the expenses, on the other hand, are very heavily increased.

Fully alive to the importance of maintaining friendly relations with the local

Government officials, I have considered it a part of my duty, while firmly insisting on all matters of rights, to cultivate so far as I consistently can, their good will as well as of the inhabitants, and I may, I think, be allowed to say I am on the very best of terms with officials here from the Governor downwards, and this in spite of a very strenuous effort made at some time since by certain interested persons in a matter of local commercial interest to bring about a different result, and I take some pride in thinking there is not one person on these Islands, official or other, who can point out one instance in which, though sometimes under difficulties and serious provocations, I have ever displayed any ill temper.

I may also mention that since the closing of the Southern ports, these Islands have been much resorted to by invalids from the United States. These visitors usually make their first call on the Consul, and I feel bound to afford them what assistance and hospitality lie in my power; on many occasions when the difficulty of obtaining lodgings has amounted to an impossibility, I have been glad to offer them an apartment in my house, and to entertain them at a heavy expense to myself. The hospitalities thus rendered during the last four months amounts to nearly forty weeks board for one individual. I am well aware that my official duties do not require the above expenditure, but under the peculiar circumstances I could hardly do less, neither have I felt at liberty to accept any remuneration which would gladly have been given.

I should mention that so many of our vessels have changed their flag that comparatively few belonging to the U.S. have for some time put in here in distress, consequently the Consular fees at the agency at the port of Hamilton of late have exceeded the amounts received here (at St. George's) and it might be worth considering whether it would not be advisable for me to take charge of the Consular work there as well as here, as I could arrange to be so many days in each week at the one place, and so many at the other, and am of the opinion, I can do all the business without detriment to anyone, and thereby return to the Government over $1,000 more in fees.

Since at present, provided they continue the same rules as the last two quarters, my own expenses at the same time would be somewhat increased, but not the amount saved to the Government. But in any case, I shall have soon to pay for my office here $50 per annum more than the Government limit; for this there is no help, as there is not another office to be had in the place, or a shelter of any kind that I can obtain.

Had I been at liberty to engage in business here, as my predecessor was, greatly to his pecuniary advantage, I am able to say from offers which were made me, I could have realized at least $6,000 the first winter I was here. The underwriters and ship owners of New York, and other commercial Cities in the United States, will I am sure agree with me, that it is largely at the expense of our commerce that the large profits realized here by Merchants, agents and Consuls have been made.

I should have no desire to engage in the business alluded to were I at liberty to do so and refer to the above merely to show you that in a pecuniary point of view, a salary as at present, with restrictions, is not as advantageous as heretofore with fees merely. I have endeavoured to lay before you a fair and just statement of the peculiarities of my position here, and having done so prefer to leave the matter in your hands entirely, rather than make any specific application or suggestion myself.

If my conduct here has been deemed satisfactory to the Government, I have no wish or intention to resign, but I must frankly say that if some considerable increase of salary not be accorded me I shall be compelled to retire at once into comparative seclusion and relinquish all hospitality for the future. My expenditures here for the past quarter have exceeded my salary nearly one hundred dollars in spite of the utmost carefulness. I take the liberty of urging upon your consideration the foregoing statements, and I have respectfully to submit that the case is one, which under the present existing circumstance, may favorably call for some increase of remuneration.

I am sir, Your obedient servant,
C. M. Allen, Consul

▨ Allen reports on a great number of incoming and outgoing blockade-running vessels.

No. 110
Consulate of the United States at Bermuda
20 April 1864

Hon. Wm. H. Seward
Secretary of State, Washington

Sir:
    I have the honor to report the arrival here of the following blockade running steamers viz,

April 12th, *Pevensey,* Hawk, from London with an assorted cargo, side wheel, two smoke stacks, 455 tons, draws nine feet when laden. She is a good and apparently a fast vessel.

April 15th, *Minnie,* 253 tons, Gilpin Master, from Wilmington with 733 bales cotton, and 333 boxes tobacco.

April 18th, *Constance,* Stewart, from Greenock, side wheel, two stacks, 163 tons, draws six feet, is now painted white.

April 18th, *Atalanta,* 11 days from England, is a double screw of great power, has two masts, two stacks, a straight stern, draws when laden eight feet of water; this vessel is undoubtedly faster than any heretofore here. She is to be under the command of Captain Horner, formerly of the *Flora,* and recently in the *Index.* He is an Englishman by birth, but a naturalized citizen of the United States, and has resided for many years in Charleston, S.C.

Steamer *Eugenie,* Porter, left here on the 14th for England for repairs. The following steamers are now in the port of St. Georges, viz:

Lady of Lyon, disabled and undergoing repairs, will leave during the old of the moon, *Pevensey, Constance, Ellen, Minnie,* and *Atalanta.* The *North Heath* is now afloat and yesterday went on a trial trip, report says she leaks some but will take a cargo for Wilmington. *Caledonia* is leaky, it is not yet known what will be done with her. I think she will leave for Wilmington in the condition she now is. *Boston,* having been twice sold, is now in litigation, and may be kept here for some months. *Harriet Pinckney* is taking in a cargo of cotton.

By the arrival of the *Minnie* it is reported the steamer *Juno* from Wilmington for Nassau broke in two and all hands were lost. Several new steamers from England are expected here daily among which are the *Badger, Fox, Let Her B,* and *Let Her Rip.*

Captain Maffitt is still here, he stays most of the time on board the ship *Storm King* anchored outside, and of late is seldom seen on shore.

I am Sir, Your obedient servant,
C. M. Allen, Consul

🔳 In the shadowy world of espionage, Allen had become a shrewd judge of character and motive. When asked to confirm his intelligence, Allen reassures Washington as to the reliability of his informants. The plots referred to in Allen's "No. 103" were to be borne out by future events.

Hand to Sec. of War for his consideration

No. 112
Consulate of the United States at Bermuda
May 3rd 1864

Hon. Wm. H. Seward
Secretary of State, Washington, D.C.

Sir:

Your No. 53 has been received, in which I am requested to furnish the Department with further information as regards the subject of my No. 103. The person upon whom I mostly relied for information was soon after taken sick and has been confined to his room till within a few days, consequently I have been unable to communicate with or obtain any other information from him.

Another party acting entirely independent of the person above alluded to, and without thus far receiving any pecuniary benefit, fully confirmed the information furnished me and forwarded in my No. 103.

The last named party left about the first of April for Wilmington, thinking by thus doing he could be of more benefit to our cause than to remain here, in which opinion I fully concurred with him, not knowing then the person first spoken of was sick, consequently I have been from that time to the present without any reliable information as regards their movements or doings.

I am of the opinion there has but few, if any, of the class of persons alluded to, left here of late directly for the states. A large number of passengers, mostly Southerners, have recently gone from here to Halifax, and other places in the British Provinces. Many are still here without any ostensible business, their expenses being paid by Major Walker, the Confederate Agent.

I have reason to believe the person spoken of as having left here for Wilmington was on board the steamer *Helen,* reported by me as the *Ellen,* which vessel went down at sea with nearly all on board. Should he return I think I could use him to advantage as he appears to have the utmost confidence of the blockade runners, and although he is well aware I have looked upon him with suspicion and have been very cautious in my intercourse with him, I believe he has always been truthful and reliable.

I am Sir, Your obedient servant,
C. M. Allen, Consul

⊕ Large quantities of coal were being stockpiled by the Confederates in St. George's. As the Confederacy began to be worn down by the industrial might of the North, the need for war materiel dramatically increased, and Bermuda consequently saw a great increase in the number of blockade-running vessels. During the summer of 1864 Allen's dispatches to the Department of State consist almost entirely of a frustratingly long list of ships in the harbor.

No. 113
Consulate of the United States at Bermuda
May 7th 1864

Hon. Wm. H. Seward
Secretary of State, Washington, D.C.

Sir:

The steamer *Index*, before reported by me as supposed to have been lost at sea arrived here on the third instant from Wilmington with 770 bales cotton. She now has her outward cargo on board and will leave here today. She has some large guns on board.

Steamer *Pevensey* left this morning for Wilmington or Charleston. Captain Burroughs formerly of the *Cornubia* is in command of her.

Steamer *Georgiana McCaw* arrived today from England, has been twelve hours on the rocks outside. I learn nothing of her as yet except she is a new side wheel boat, and is intended to run the blockade.

Steamer *Harriet Pinckney* will, I am informed, leave here for London about the 25th of this month with a cargo of cotton and a large number of passengers.

Some twenty vessels laden with coal are now afloat here, and there is now landed at this port of Saint George's some thirty to thirty five thousand tons of coal for the use of the Confederates and blockade runners. There is no doubt they expect to do a large business here the coming summer. Eight vessels with coal have from Cardiff arrived during the past week, report says from fifty to sixty more are on the passage here now.

I am sir, your obedient servant
C. M. Allen, Consul

⊕ The Confederate vessel *Florida* makes a brief appearance in Bermuda. The *Florida*, one of the most successful of commerce raiders, was captured three months after leaving Bermuda at Bahia, Brazil, by the USS *Wachusett*. Having been taken to Hampton Roads, Virginia, then under U.S. control, the ship was rammed and sunk on November 19, 1864.

No. 114
Consulate of the United States at Bermuda
May 14, 1864

Hon. Wm. H. Seward
Secretary of State, Washington

Sir:

The rebel steamer *Florida* came to anchor off the port of St. George's last Thursday at one o'clock P.M., reported last from Martinique. She left at 6 P.M. same day after landing one of her officers sick. I am unable to ascertain her destination. She received no supplies. I am not aware that any of her officers came on shore except the sick one. Reports ship *Avon* of Boston the last vessel destroyed.

The following steamers from England have arrived since my last report:

May 10, *Lynx,* Reid, Master last of the *Gibraltar.* Says he will go into Wilmington without waiting for a dark night.

May 12, *Rouen* and *Fox,* the two last are consigned to a new man here by the name of Sweeney, seems to be an agent of the house of Fraser, Trenholm & Co. These three vessels are all very much alike in appearance, seem to be made of steel and reported fast. They have two stacks, two masts, draw about 8 feet of water and have capacity for 600 to 700 bales cotton. They are now undergoing a change of color.

Steamer *Thistle* arrived from Wilmington on the 10th inst. with 700 bales cotton and the *Atalanta* on the 12th from same port, report having been hard chased by a U.S. steamer to the westward of these Islands and only escaped by darkness. The *Minnie* and *Greyhound* reported left Wilmington same time for here but have not arrived.

I am sir, your obedient servant
C. M. Allen, Consul

▩ The consul reports that a million British-made cartridges arrived in the Confederate states via Mexico. As it became increasingly difficult to penetrate the Atlantic blockading squadrons, the route to the South through Mexican ports became more attractive to the blockade-runners.

No. 115
Consulate of the United States at Bermuda
May 20, 1864

Hon. Wm. H. Seward
Secretary of State, Washington

Sir:

The British steamer *Mary Celestia* from London or Liverpool arrived here on the 17th, side wheel, two stacks fore and aft, two masts, about 250 tons, is now painted white, and taking in cargo.

Steamer *Lilian* from England arrived this P.M., said to be owned by Capt. Maffitt and named after a daughter of his. It is understood he will attempt to take her into Wilmington.

Steamer *City of Petersburgh* from Halifax arrived on the 11th at Hamilton and left the next day for Wilmington.

Steamer *Helen* came in on the 17th from Wilmington with cotton. She brings a letter to a person here calling himself Major Rawlins (formerly from New York), agent for Adams Co., New Oxford Street, London, manufacturers of arms, informing him that one million cartridges shipped by them via Matamoros had arrived at Richmond.

I think some eight steamers will leave here during the next ten days for Wilmington.

The *Harriet Pinckney* left yesterday for London.

I am sir, Your obedient servant,
C. M. Allen, Consul

🌐 Allen reveals the true identity of a Bermudian blockade-runner. He continues to provide the Department of State with sketches of blockade-running vessels.

No. 116
Consulate of the United States of America at Bermuda
May 30, 1864

Hon. Wm. H. Seward
Secretary of State, Washington, D.C.

Sir:

The following steamers have left here to run the blockade, probably for Wilmington since my No. 115 viz:

May 2. *Fox,* Ramsbeck master
May 24. *Atalanta,* Horner
May 24. *Lynx,* Reed, formerly of the *Gibraltar*
May 24. *Mary Celestia,* Usina, Master
May 25. *Caledonia,* Nelson, ditto
May 29. *Hester,* Hora, ditto

The *Lady of Lyon,* late the *Syren,* purchased from government here now under the command of Capt. Peniston, a native of these Islands for many years previous to the rebellion, sailing as master of American vessels out of Boston under the assumed name of Fisher, have [illegible] up to leave on the 28th for Wilmington, but could not clear as her papers cannot be found. Supposed to have been stolen.

I am informed the Str. *Lilian,* Captain Maffitt, and the *Flora* (I herewith enclose a correct likeness) will leave here tomorrow for the same destination.

The *Thistle* and *North Heath* are expected to leave soon. Also the *Rouen.*

Steamer *Pevensey,* Capt. Burroughs (an old offender), has just come into port from Wilmington with 1000 bales of cotton.

I am sir, your obedient servant
C. M. Allen, Consul

John Newland Maffitt, one of the South's leading sea captains, seems to have become overly fond of drink during his long stay in Bermuda, according to Consul Allen. Allen's comments seem to reflect something of his own temperate nature and steady habits.

No. 118
Consulate of the United States of America, Bermuda
June 4, 1864

Hon. Wm. H. Seward
Secretary of State, Washington, D.C.

Sir

I have the honor to report the following movement of blockade running steamers at the port of St. George's since my No. 116, viz departures May 30, *Lady of Lyon,* Peniston master, May 1, *Lilian,* Maffitt, Capt. Locke of *Chesapeake* fame is first officer. Maffitt is of but little account as he is drunk most of the time. *Flora,* McDougal, master (a new man) and *Thistle* left the same day, all the above supposed to be bound to Wilmington.

The *North Heath,* Capt. Burroughs, last of the *Pevensey,* has steam and is ready to leave port. She takes little or no cargo as she is in an unseaworthy condition. I learn she is to go to Wilmington for cotton. The *Pevensey,* now called the *Kangaroo,* is now leaving port. She has a new master, an Englishman by the name of Crispin.

Steamer *Lynx* arrived today from Wilmington with 600 bales cotton, having been chased by a U.S. gunboat and having thrown overboard about 100 bales cotton. She left here eleven days since in company with the *Atalanta* on a trial of speed to Wilmington and beat her fine home. She is undoubtedly the fastest boat from these Islands. Reed, formerly of the *Sumter,* later the *Gibraltar,* is Captain.

Report by *Lynx* says twelve boats are waiting in Wilmington for cotton with very little there when they left. Steamer *Boston* is to be sold at auction on Tuesday next for the third time. She has been in port here since last August.

I am sir, your obedient servant,
C. M. Allen, Consul

P. S. I enclose herewith a correct portrait of Steamers *Lynx* and *Helen.* I shall take pleasure in forwarding more of these likenesses if they are of any benefit.

Allen

▣ Allen reports on the seizure of the *William C. Clark* by the CSS *Florida.*

No. 120
Consulate of the United States of America at Bermuda
June 20, 1864

Hon. Wm. H. Seward
Secretary of State, Washington, D.C.

Sir

The rebel steamer *Florida* returned here last Saturday, she came into the port of Saint George's yesterday morning. I am informed she will remain here a week or more, a large portion of her crew have left her this morning. She may be detained some time to get a crew; I am also informed they expect this week another armed vessel to arrive here.

The crew of the Brig *Wm. C. Clark,* burned on the 17th inst. by the *Florida,* are now here. I enclose herewith the Master's report.

An English vessel of war leaves tomorrow morning for Halifax. I have written to the Consul there hoping he may have some war vessel in those waters and requesting him to send information by telegraph at once.

I am sir, your obedient servant
C. M. Allen, Consul

▨ After two years of urging a more aggressive policy toward the blockade-runners, Allen must have taken great satisfaction from the news that "most all the steamers from Wilmington arriving here report having been chased by our gunboats."

No. 121
Consulate of the United States of America at Bermuda
June 20, 1864

Hon Wm. H. Seward
Secretary of State, Washington, D.C.

Sir

The following blockade running steamers are now in this port of St. George's, and intend to leave during the old of this moon for Wilmington. *Edith, Lynx* (had been on the coast of Wilmington and returned), *Boston, Old Dominion* (new), *Little Hettie* (new),[13] *Atalanta, City of Petersburgh* and *Mary Celestia.*

The *Edith* was last from Nassau, was chased off Wilmington and came here, is now in quarantine, will probably be released in a day or two. The *Old Dominion* is a sister ship to the *City of Petersburgh.*

Little Hettie is a very long side wheel boat with two stacks and straight rail.

It is thought here the *Lady of Lyon,* late the *Syren,* has foundered at sea, two weeks from the time she left here. She had not arrived at Wilmington. Most all the steamers from Wilmington arriving here report having been chased by our gunboats.

Steamer *Index* will leave soon for England as she is considered too slow to run the blockade.

I am sir, your obedient servant,
C. M. Allen, Consul

▣ Allen took great pains to corroborate intelligence provided by his informants. Here he reports specific and reliable information about a "piratical expedition" from two very different sources, Captain Squire, who had aided Allen in the past, and the anonymous "Blockade Runner." This is one of the few instances where Allen's accurate intelligence reached authorities far enough in advance where actions could have been taken to thwart this plot. It does not appear that any action was taken, and the plot proceeded precisely as Allen had described it.[14]

No. 122
Consulate of the United States of America at Bermuda
June 20, 1864

Hon. Wm. H. Seward
Secretary of State, Washington, D.C.

Sir

The British schooner *Resolution* of Liverpool, now in this port of Saint George's, has recently been sold to a person who goes by the name Johnson, no doubt he is the Lieut. Braine of *Chesapeake* notoriety. I am informed through an unknown source by a person who signs himself "Blockade Runner," that she is intended for some piratical expedition, and thinks she will go to Cuba with the intention of capturing some steamer. There is no doubt in my mind that a combination of desperate men have possession of this vessel, for the purpose of capturing some steamer. Capt. S., sent from New York, having spent some time with them, is of the same opinion as Blockade Runner. The *Resolution* is about 80 tons register, black hull, with deep blue house on deck.

She may not leave here for some time. Capt. S. thinks they are going from here to Havana. I shall watch her close, but it is difficult for me to get reliable information. I think she could be captured when she leaves port if one of our gunboats could be here.

I am sir, your obedient servant,
C. M. Allen, Consul

⊕ A few days after his forty-second birthday, a frustrated consul reports that despite all of his efforts to thwart the "piratical expedition" of the schooner *Resolution,* the ship has departed Bermuda.

No. 123
United States Consulate at Bermuda
June 28, 1864

Hon. Wm. H. Seward
Secretary of State, Washington, D.C.

Sir

I regret to have to inform you that the schooner *Resolution* of which I have before spoken left these islands last Saturday. She is, in fact, under the command of one Braine who assisted in the capture of the *Chesapeake.* Her registered master is McRae. She cleared for Harbor Island with coal and has on board some thirty desperate men whose object is, I think, to capture some of our steamers.

I have used my utmost endeavors to obtain sufficient evidence to detain this vessel here, and had some very strong proof of her character. I did not think she would leave as soon as she did and thought it best not to make any official representation to the authorities here until I had obtained all the information I could, confidently relying upon the promise of the assistant Receiver General, the principal Revenue Officer at this port, to inform me when she cleared, which he did not do, and I was not informed she had left until the following day.

I deeply regret that this vessel should have gone to sea from these islands under the circumstances she has, but am conscious it was on account of no lack of zeal on my part.

I repeat her description: fore and aft schooner, black hull with deep blue deck house, apparently about 80 tons but registers only about 60 British. I think she has gone to the West Indies.

I am sir, your obedient servant,
C. M. Allen, U.S. Consul

⬡ The CSS *Florida* received coal in Bermuda and lay in wait offshore, boarding all vessels. Allen was not content to observe blockade-runners only from harborside but, as this dispatch indicates, took advantage of the hills surrounding St. George's to sight vessels long before their arrival.

No. 124
United States Consulate at Bermuda
June 30, 1864

Hon. Wm. H. Seward
Secretary of State, Washington, D.C.

Sir

I have the honor to report the following movements of blockade running steamers from this port of Saint George's since my No. 121 of June 20, viz:

Sailed June 20th *Lynx, Mary Celestia* and *Atalanta* for Wilmington. The *Index* left the same day for London, being considered too slow to make another attempt to get in to Wilmington.

The *Edith* was released from quarantine on the 21st and sailed on the 23rd for Wilmington. *City of Petersburgh* and the *Old Dominion* sailed on the 25th.

The *Rouen* left on the 28th. My information leads me to think she will attempt to get into Charleston.

The *Little Hettie* sailed on the 29th. After leaving the harbor she struck on the rocks and stove a hole in her bow, filled forward and sunk. She will not run the blockade at present, if ever, as she cannot be fully repaired here and it is doubtful if she can be put in a fit state to go from here at all.

The *Boston* which has been in port here since last August, went to sea on the 29th but returned same day to port. I am informed she will leave in a day or two. She is now owned by W. C. Campbell, has been thoroughly overhauled and repainted. Side wheel, beam engine, one mast high out of the water, and in appearance like some of the North river boats.

The following steamers have arrived here during the past few days, viz:

June 26th, *North Heath,* Burroughs
June 27th, *Lilian,* Wallace
June 28th, *Florie,* DeHorsey, all from Wilmington with cotton.
June 29th, *Hawk,* from London. Is a fine vessel of 500 to 600 tons. Three masts, barque rigged, and heavy sparred. I enclose portrait. Her crew have all been discharged here. I am informed she is to have a new master (Runner says Locke of *Chesapeake* fame who is now here, having returned in the *Lilian*) that she will go to Wilmington, there get a Confederate register and come out armed. She is iron and propelled by a screw, is reported fast.

I learn that Maffitt remained in Wilmington in charge of an iron clad. The *Florida,* after remaining in port nine days, went to sea last Monday evening but has not been far from land. She is in sight today from the hills about six miles off. She boards all vessels approaching these islands. She received all the coal and supplies they wanted. The coal was taken from the ship *Storm King,* C. L. Holson of Richmond, agent.

I am sir, your obedient servant,
C. M. Allen, Consul

▣ Allen reports that a case of yellow fever has been diagnosed on shore.

No. 125
Consulate of the United States at Bermuda
July 1st, 1864

Hon. Wm. H. Seward
Secretary of State, Washington, D.C.

Sir,
There is sickness among the shipping near this port of Saint George's, supposed to be yellow fever. One person died yesterday on shore undoubtedly of the same disease. The circumstances connected with his sickness lead to the presumption that it will spread here.

I am sir, your obedient servant,
C. M. Allen, Consul

■ The consul's returns for the second quarter of 1864 show no American vessels arriving at Hamilton. At this time, commercial interests were almost completely centered in St. George's. This resulted in an almost total lack of arrivals at Hamilton even though it was the capital of the colony and possessed a fine harbor.

No. 126
Consulate of the United States at Bermuda
July 1st 1864

Hon. Wm. H. Seward
Secretary of State, Washington, D.C.

Sir

I have the honor to enclose herewith the following return for the quarter ending June 30th, 1864, viz

Arrival and departure of American vessels at the port of Saint George's, No. 1
Navigation and Commerce at the same port, No. 2
Transcript of fees received at the consular agency at the port of Hamilton, No. 3

There have been no arrivals or departures of American vessels at the port of Hamilton during the last quarter. You will perceive by the return of fees from the agency at Hamilton that during the last two or three quarters the fees have greatly increased particularly so during the quarter just ended. The increase I think is owing to the peculiar state of things existing here at present, this port of Saint George's being almost exclusively a Confederate port. If it is thought best to make any change, will you please advise me.

I am Sir, your obedient servant,
C. M. Allen, Consul

■ Allen reports little decrease in blockade-running activities, noting eight arrivals and nine departures within two weeks.

No. 127
Consulate of the United States of America at Bermuda
July 13, 1864

To the Hon. Wm. H. Seward
Secretary of State, Washington, D.C.

Sir

I have the honor to report the following movement of blockade running steamers from this port since my No. 124 of June 30, viz.

Arrived July 2nd, *Mary Celestia,* Greene
4th, *Lynx,* Reid
6th, *Helen,* Leslie, and *Atalanta,* Usina
7th, *Alice,* Grant
8th, *Edith,* Murray
13th, *Lilian,* Martin, all from Wilmington with cotton.

Steamer *Falcon,* Fisher, arrived on the 4th from Glasgow, has three stacks, two masts, side wheel with two screws. She is commanded by a person who was formerly master of the *Don,* who then went by the name of Roberts. He is said to be an English naval officer, son of some nobleman, is an intimate friend of Governor Ord. If captured will try to pass himself off as a deck hand.

The following vessels have left this port for Wilmington, viz.

July 2, *Lilian,* Martin, *Boston,* Carrow
3rd, *North Heath,* Burroughs and *Florie,* Libbey
5th, *Little Hattie,* Horsey, was repaired with plank after being on the rocks, went to sea and returned on the 11th in distress having been chased two days.
6th, *Falcon,* Fisher
8th, *Mary Celestia,* Greene and *Lynx,* Reid. The *Lynx* returned to port this morning, having been chased off
11th, *Atalanta,* Usina

Steamer *Hawk* is still in port, has her yards all down. I can ascertain but little about her. Capt. Locke calls her his vessel. The *Little Hattie* when chased

Blockade-runner *Alice*. Painting by Edward James (Courtesy of Dr. Charles Peery, Charleston, S.C.)

run off her course and reported having spoken to the schr. *Resolution* on the 7th inst. with just sail enough to keep her steady in Lat 30, 30E, Long 76. My informant says they had apparently about forty men on deck, that when the Confederate flag was hoisted on the steamer, they gave three cheers.

The *Florida* was last seen from the land here on the 5th of July. While laying off here she burned a barque from Portland bound to the south side of Cuba laden with shooks and lumber, the officers and crew were put on board a vessel bound to Europe.

I am sir, your obedient servant
C. M. Allen, Consul

The detailed report which Allen submitted documenting blockade-running activities from 1862 to 1864 is all the more remarkable given the vast amount of correspondence and government forms that claimed his attention. In many ways, this document is the first draft of the history of blockade-running in Bermuda. Allen's "statement of the arrivals and departures of vessels employed in running the blockade" is reproduced in full in the appendix.

No. 129
Consulate of the United States of America at Bermuda
July 13, 1864

To the Hon. Wm. H. Seward
Secretary of State, Washington, D.C.

Sir

I enclose herewith a statement of the arrivals and departures of vessels employed in running the blockade of the Southern ports of the United States, and of those bringing merchandise here for that trade, from the first day of January 1862 to the 30 June 1864. I have delayed this report some time expecting to get some statistics from the Custom House here, but have not succeeded in doing so. It is not full, but as full as I have been able to make it, and may be of some use as a matter of reference hereafter. The number of steamers which have been employed, I find to be 86, 162 arrivals, 65 arrivals from blockaded ports, bringing about 40M bales cotton, a large quantity of tobacco and some spirits turpentine. 22 of these steamers have been captured or destroyed on their first trip from here, 19 captured or lost after making one or more trips, 8 have returned without attempting to run the blockade.

Some idea of the enormous profit made when successful may be had from the fact that the steamer *Flora* which went down at sea, after making three trips to Wilmington, had standing to her credit on the agent's books here one hundred seventy three thousand pounds sterling.

The warehouses here are all full, and arrangements are being made for some of these vessels to go to the port of Hamilton soon.

I am sir, your obedient servant,
C. M. Allen, Consul

▓ Allen reports a plot to liberate Confederate prisoners at Hatteras Inlet, North Carolina. The intended attack was to take place at Point Lookout Prison on the Chesapeake. This is an instance where Allen's informant was correct as to the nature of the conspiracy but incorrect as to its location.

No. 130
Consulate of the United States at Bermuda
July 19, 1864

Hon. Wm. H. Seward
Secretary of State, Washington, D.C.

Sir

I am informed the Steamer *Florie* has been detained by the rebel government at Wilmington for special service. The steamer *Little Hattie* now in port here is in the hands of rebel government agents and is being refitted. From all the information I can get, I think these vessels are to be used to carry parties to some place with the intention of releasing prisoners. One informant says they are intending to release prisoners confined in the vicinity of Lake Hatteras.

There is no doubt there is a conspiracy of some kind in process here. They are very close and it is difficult for me to get reliable information.

There is a quantity of seaman's uniforms here intended for the *Hawk,* blue trowsers, shirts and caps. The trowsers are like those used in our navy. The caps are of the style called Scotch with the word *Hawk* on the band in front. I will do all in my power to prevent these vessels leaving here for the purpose they are undoubtedly intended and have the assurance of the Lieut. Governor (who is now the acting Governor) that they shall not leave these islands for belligerent purposes if it is in his power to prevent it.[15]

I am sir, your
obedient servant,
C. M. Allen, Consul

▣ Allen reports the blockade-runners are fearful of the spreading yellow fever at Bermuda. He also notes that the plot to liberate Confederate prisoners apparently has been abandoned.

No. 131
Consulate of the United States of America at Bermuda,
July 29, 1864

Hon. Wm. H. Seward
Secretary of State, Washington

Sir,

Since my No. 130 of July 19th the following blockade running steamers have arrived here: 25, *Flamingo*, Atkinson, from London, three funnels, side wheel, sister to *Falcon*, has been painted white and left yesterday for Wilmington. 26, *Dieppe* from England, a sister ship to the *Old Dominion*, will probably leave tomorrow, has been painted white and has cargo on board. 27, *City of Petersburgh* and *Old Dominion*. 28, *Falcon* and *Mary Celestia*. 29, *North Heath* is leaking badly, will discharge cargo and go to Halifax for repairs. *Mary Celestia* was chased and threw overboard 150 bales cotton. The last five were all from Wilmington with cotton.

The *Edith* sailed on the 23, also *A. D. Vance*. The *Alice* on the 24th, *Flamingo* and *Lilian* on the 28th, all for Wilmington. I am informed the *Florie* has been released at Wilmington and the expedition to release prisoners has been abandoned. The *Atalanta* and one other screw boat has been taken by the rebel government for secret service.[16] *Little Hattie* has sickness on board and is in quarantine here.

The *Hawk* is in a distant part of the harbor and apparently nothing is being done on board. No one is allowed to visit her without the permission of Capt. Knox who has charge of her. Knox was master of the *Lee* when she was captured. There is but few men on board and they are rarely any of them on shore. I have used every means at my command to get some proof of her character but as yet have entirely failed. I am satisfied it was their intention to take her into Wilmington. I think that idea is now abandoned and that they are waiting for papers or instructions from Richmond. She is now light and draws eleven feet six inches.

The pilot of the captured steamer *Boston* returned here today from New York, says he disguised himself and passed as assistant cook. There is much talk among the blockade runners here of sending their steamers to Halifax on account of the prevalence of yellow fever at this port.

I am sir, your obedient servant,
C. M. Allen, Consul

▨ The consul reports the cessation of blockade-running activities in St. George's as the yellow fever spreads. Fully aware of the danger to which he is exposed, Allen nevertheless remains at his post.

No. 132
Consulate of the U.S. of America at Bermuda
August 5, 1864

Hon. Wm. H. Seward
Secretary of State, Washington, D.C.

Sir

I have the honor to inform you that the yellow fever is prevailing at this port of St. George's at the present time to an alarming extent. It has undoubtedly existed here for some weeks past in a mild form, but within a few days has assumed a most malignant nature. Many deaths are reported within the past twenty four hours.

From the indications today, I think the business of blockade runners is nearly at an end here for this season. Several cases are also reported in different parts of the islands. This whole colony is undoubtedly infected with this epidemic.

I am sir, your obedient servant
C. M. Allen, Consul

▦ During the yellow fever epidemic, Allen was visited by one Mr. Baylor of Georgia. Baylor claimed that he was representing the men of influence in his state who wished to sue for peace. Baylor asked Allen's assistance in getting to Washington. His credentials being somewhat suspect, Allen provided him only with the necessary passport and a letter of introduction to Allen's friend, Alex Fraser, in New York. Alex Fraser, as well as the government officials with whom Baylor met in Washington, D.C., were equally as cautious as Allen and nothing came of Baylor's purported peace overture.[17] This letter of introduction apparently was hand delivered by Mr. Baylor to the Secretary of State, as it does not appear with Allen's diplomatic dispatches.

No. 133 (not on microfilm)
Consulate of the United States of America at Bermuda
August 9, 1864

Hon. Wm. H. Seward,
Secretary of State

Sir:

C. G. Baylor, Esqr. of Georgia, having been in Bermuda for some time past and having on frequent occasions interviews with him, he has invariably expressed strong Union sentiments to me and also expressed a desire to go to Washington in an official capacity to do what he can for the restoration of the Union and to advise with you and others upon the mode of procedure, and having taken and subscribed an oath to support the constitution of the United States, I have granted him a passport conditioned that he proceed without delay on his arrival at New York to Washington. I may add Mr. Baylor placed in my hands for perusal a commission of a commercial nature signed by Governor Brown of Georgia under the seal of that State together with several other papers, that the said papers, together with any despatches, were stolen or lost from my carriage while coming from St. George's to Hamilton this morning.[18]

Mr. Baylor has been very closely watched here by Southern parties and they have on some occasions publicly insulted him.

I am sir, your obedient servant,
C. M. Allen, U.S. Consul

Even though Allen knew that the departure of the *Hawk* had been delayed by financial difficulties as well as by yellow fever on board, his vigilant efforts to stop the ship's departure continue.

No. 135
Consulate of the United States at Bermuda
Sept. 1st 1864

Hon. Wm. H. Seward,
Secretary of State, Washington

Sir

I beg to lay before you a statement of the following facts which have come to my knowledge in reference to the Steamer *Hawk,* now some weeks in the harbor of Saint George's: that the said steamer was originally built for a war vessel, that her lines and model were submitted to the Naval authorities at Richmond before she was built, that she is fitted with a double deck 3 ½ inches each in thickness bolted together so as to form one deck 7 inches thick. She is also fitted with ward and mess rooms for officers but few of her officers are here as yet, and those who are keep aloof from her with the exception of one Knox, said to hold a Lieutenant Commission in the rebel Navy and who has had charge of her since her arrival here to the present time. I am informed her Commander, E. C. Stiles, formerly of South Carolina, is expected to arrive here soon from England, that there has been some difficulty in liquidating claims upon the vessel in England which has detained him there and consequently detained the vessel here.

At present she is also detained by a considerable number of cases of yellow fever on board.

For more than two months past I have been in occasional communication with a man of the name of C. E. Donaldson who called on me representing himself as a native of Baltimore who had been imprisoned in the Southern States and having recently obtained his release had then just arrived here in one of the blockade runners from Wilmington. He claimed to be destitute and wished me to furnish him with means to get to Washington in order to communicate to the government his plan for the capture of Wilmington and also other information which it was important the government should be in possession of, but as he failed to satisfy me he could furnish any important information or that his plan could be of any benefit, I looked upon him with suspicion but informed him that any information important and available he could furnish me with would be paid for.

After repeated private interviews at which he communicated information invariably too late to be of any benefit, he applied for money. I then pointed out to him that what information he had so far rendered was of no use and declined to recognize it as giving him any claim for remuneration. From this man's intimacy with the officers of the *Florida* when they were here and some other information received, I was suspicious he knew more of some piratical movements here than he professed to. I asked him about the *Hawk*. He pretended to know nothing of her, but would inform himself and let me know. A few days later he informed me he had been on board and from all he could learn, she undoubtedly was intended for a blockade runner between Mobile and Havana. Thinking no benefit could be derived from any further intercourse with him, I informed him I did not care to communicate with him again.

Subsequently he called upon me, admitted that he had been deceiving me about the *Hawk,* on board of which vessel he held an appointment as acting master and added by way of accounting for his approaches to me that he had been badly treated in the South and wished for revenge. I requested to see his appointment which he produced. I enclose a copy numbered 1 and I may add, I have ascertained his name really is what he represented it to be, nor have I any doubt the notice of appointment is a genuine document.

I am well satisfied the *Hawk* was and probably now is intended for a piratical purpose, and that it is very possible to prove as much to the authorities here.

Donaldson would, of course, be the principle witness as well as agent in obtaining information and I am well convinced that money is what he wants and all he cares about, and if sufficient inducement is offered he will do all he can. He is a temperate man of considerable shrewdness and fair personal appearance.

I have pointed out to him by way of inducement that if this vessel should be condemned in consequence of information furnished by him, he may rely on being well remunerated.

It appears to me and I venture to submit that a good case can be made against the *Hawk,* that money will be needed to obtain the necessary evidence, and I would respectfully ask if it would not be advisable to send some gentleman here immediately, well versed in international law to assist in the matter.

There is no doubt the vessel must remain here for some time yet, if for no other reason because the fever is strong on board, and it appears to me the time has not yet arrived to lay the case before the authorities, nor is likely to arrive till I have had an opportunity of receiving your instructions.[19]
I have the honor to be sir, Your obedient servant,

C. M. Allen, Consul

▨ The Department of State provides the consulate with an official seal.

No. 136
Consulate of the United States at Bermuda
Sept. 1, 1864

Hon. Wm. H. Seward
Secretary of State, Washington

Sir
I have to acknowledge the receipt of five sets of "Diplomatic Correspondence 1863," also a seal for the use of the consulate.

The following blank forms are required for the use of this consulate, viz: numbers 8, 14, 33, 44, 45, 128, 138, also some letter paper, envelopes, and seals for certificates, etc.

I am, sir, Your obedient servant,
C. M. Allen, Consul

⊞ Blockade-runners continue to avoid Bermuda due to the yellow fever epidemic.

No. 137
Consulate of the United States at Bermuda
Sept. 1, 1864

Hon. Wm. H. Seward
Secretary of State, Washington

Sir,

I am informed from a source I think entirely reliable that the Steamer *Alexandra* (the same one that was last year detained by the British government), now called the *Mary,* touched off these islands on the 30th ultimo with the intention of coming into port here, but after communicating with the Confederate agent, left the same day on account of the prevailing epidemic.

My informant is the master of a schooner who was taken off his vessel at sea by the *Mary,* he having lost his crew by fever. He says she is owned by the Confederate government but does not meet their expectation as she is very slow, her speed being only about five knots per hour. He thinks she went from here for Halifax. I did not learn that she had any armament on board but destination is understood to be Charleston or Wilmington.

I am sir, your obedient servant
C. M. Allen, Consul

⊞ The yellow fever epidemic that swept through St. George's and much of Bermuda was the last major outbreak in the islands. Allen reported an almost total cessation of blockade-running activities during the height of the epidemic. By late September he reports, "Most of the non-residents have either left these islands or died." One of the few vessels to arrive in St. George's at this time was the *Mary Celestia.* When the ship ran aground and sank upon leaving Bermuda, Allen was accused of having paid the pilot to purposely wreck the ship. As Allen reports, "I am happy to say there is no evidence to substantiate their charge."

No. 138
Consulate of the United States of America at Bermuda
September 26, 1864

Hon. Wm. H. Seward
Secretary of State, Washington, D.C.

Sir

In consequence of the prevalence of yellow fever at these islands there has been but comparatively a small business done in blockade running for several weeks past. The only arrival from Wilmington since July was the steamer *Mary Celestia* belonging to Crenshaw Brothers. She lost several men by the epidemic while here, took in a cargo principally of canned meats and left for Wilmington, came onto a rock off these islands and sank in twenty fathoms in six minutes—vessel a total loss, cargo nearly so.

Much indignation has been manifested towards me on account of the loss of this vessel by southern parties and I am charged by them with having bought the pilot. I am happy to say there is no evidence to substantiate their charge. The pilot has been suspended for eighteen months.

Several steamers intended for blockade runners from England have touched off the islands but on account of the sickness here have left for other ports without coming into port. One, under the command of Capt. Gilpin, late of the *Minnie,* has for some days been anchored outside, has been painted white and will leave soon for Wilmington I am informed. She has a straight rail, two masts, two stacks and draws laden six and a half feet.

Steamer *Virginia* from England arrived yesterday and came into port. She is under the command of one Washburn, a resident of Boston. Several steamers of the "Blue Cross Line," from London have arrived off the islands and left for Halifax. One, the *Powerful,* came into the port of St. George's early in August, is still here having lost her master and twelve men.

The steamers of this line are consigned here to a southern man of the name of Phinnezy, late Phinnezy and Poole. They are sea going vessels and not intended to run the blockade, but to bring freight for the smaller steamers to take from here. I am informed that arrangements have been made to have one from London every two weeks.

Steamer *Hawk* is still in port, Knox left for Halifax.

Most of the non-residents have either left these islands or died. Business is consequently comparatively quiet. Crenshaw from Richmond is about the only prominent person engaged in the blockade running business here at present.

I am sir, your obedient servant,
C. M. Allen, Consul

🔳 The consul submits his regular quarterly returns.

No. 139
Consulate of the United States of America at Bermuda
October 6, 1864

Hon. Wm. H. Seward
Secretary of State, Washington, D.C.

Sir

I have the honor to enclose herewith returns as follows for the quarter ending September 30, 1864, viz:

Arrival and departure of American vessels at the port of St. George's, No. 1

Navigation and commerce at the same port, No. 2, together with arrivals and departure of American vessels.
Navigation and commerce transcript of fee book, extract from fee book and fees on account of American vessels at the consular agency at the port of Hamilton, numbered from three to seven inclusive.

I have the honor to be, sir,
your obedient servant,
C. M. Allen,
U.S. Consul

🔳 Perhaps one of Allen's greatest disappointments was the *Roanoke* affair, when the Confederate naval officer, John C. Braine, seized the U.S. mail steamer

Roanoke and burned the vessel off Bermuda in September 1864. Though the perpetrators were arrested by Bermudian authorities, they were held only briefly. It must have given Allen cold comfort to report on the destruction of the *Roanoke*. His dispatch of June 20, 1864, to the Department of State had accurately predicted how the plot would unfold.

No. 140
Consulate of the United States of America at Bermuda
October 17, 1864

Hon. Wm. H. Seward
Secretary of State, Washington

Sir

A steamer was reported off these islands on Tuesday the 4th instant, said to be the U.S. Steamer *Keystone State*. I was unable to learn anything definite about her till on the 6th. I received proof of men being shipped by the so called Confederate agent here for some vessel in the offing, supposed to be the *Edith,* escaped from Wilmington. Late on Saturday night of the 8th the first officer and purser of the steamship *Roanoke* of New York arrived at this consulate. From them I learned the said *Roanoke* had been captured on the night of the 29 September by the pirates that left here in the Schooner *Resolution* in June last, that the said *Roanoke* had been off the islands for some days, and had received men and supplies for here. Their affidavits setting forth the principal facts connected with the capture of the said ship were taken and sworn to before a Notary Public, and handed to the Lieut. Governor early on Sunday morning, with a request that he would take action in the matter. The vessel was that morning burned and both the captors and the captured came on shore at the town of St. George's. Braine and his party were immediately arrested and lodged in jail. After a three days examination, they were all set at liberty. I will forward all the correspondence and particulars by the next opportunity.

I think these pirates will go to Halifax with the intention of taking some vessel from Saint John's, New Brunswick. They most surely will continue their depredations unless their schemes are thwarted by the utmost vigilance of all interested.

I am sir, your obedient servant,
C. M. Allen, Consul

▣ Allen communicates that numerous blockade-runners are shifting operations to the Bahamas in order to avoid "the heavy expense of their business here."

No. 141
Consulate of the United States of America at Bermuda
October 24, 1864

Hon. Wm. H. Seward,
Secretary of State

Sir,

The following blockade running steamers are in port here at this time. *Wild Rover* and *Talisman* under the British flag from Wilmington with cotton. *Owl* and *Little Hattie* under the Rebel flag with cotton from Wilmington. The *Owl* received several shots coming out, wounding the Captain and some of the crew. The *Agnes E. Fry* and *Stormy Petrel* attempted to enter Wilmington but not succeeding returned here. The *Wild Rover* and *Agnes E. Fry* are to leave today for Wilmington. *Caroline* from Halifax loading to leave soon. *Dieppe* in port here for some weeks in difficulty about her ownership. The *Talisman* is under the command of Capt. Gilpin who has been captured three or four times.

I am informed that nearly all the blockade running steamers are to leave here on account of the heavy expense of their business here, some are to go to Nassau. Some eight that Cranshaw Bros. are agents for are to run to Green Turtle Key in the Bahamas.

The Blue Cross Line from London comprising six large steamers I am informed are no longer to come here but will run to Nassau.

I am sir, your obedient servant,
C. M. Allen, Consul

▣ The obligatory letter of acceptance is sent to the Department of State.

No. 142
Consulate of the United States of America at Bermuda
October 24, 1864

Hon. Wm. H. Seward,
Secretary of State, Washington

Sir

I have the honor to acknowledge the receipt of blank forms and stationery for the use of this consulate.

I am sir, your obedient servant,
C. M. Allen, Consul

🔲 The letters that Allen enclosed with this dispatch recount his efforts in the case of the *Roanoke*. Secretary of State Seward forwarded these letters to Charles Francis Adams, the U.S. minister at London, and instructed him to protest the legal proceedings in Bermuda to Her Majesty's government.[20]

No. 142
Consulate of the United States of America at Bermuda
October 28th 1864

Hon. Wm. H. Seward
Secretary of State, Washington

Sir,

I have the honor to enclose herewith copies of all the correspondence between myself and the authorities of these islands in relation to the *Roanoke* affair, numbered from one to five with copies of the enclosures they contained annexed.

It will I trust be obvious from this correspondence that all I could do under the circumstances was done to bring these men to justice.

The real facts of the case though no doubt known from the first to many in this town, were studiously concealed from me, and even after the arrest was made no official intimation was conveyed to me of the nature of the charge on which they had been arrested nor was I requested to attend the examination. I was thus left to get at the matter as best I could and under many disadvantages. It is however equally obvious that had I been in full possession of all the facts from the first and been able to make my application at an earlier stage of the proceedings, or to make any other kind or form of application, the result must have been precisely the same, as the decision come to by the authorities here was based not on any deficiency or error in the steps taken by me, but simply on the isolated ground that the acts proved did not in the opinion of the Law officer of the Crown amount to enough to establish the charge made and consequently could not come within the provisions of the treaty of August 9, 1842.

This is evident from the fact that the accused were liberated not on a decision of the magistrates, but on the withdrawal of the complaint by the Attorney General.

I am sir, Your obedient servant,
C. M. Allen, Consul

◉ Allen reports that seven steamers have left St. George's within the past few weeks, while only one has arrived from Wilmington.

No. 143
Consulate of the United States of America at Bermuda
November 7, 1864

Hon. Wm. H. Seward
Secretary of State, Washington

Sir

The following blockade running steamers have left this port for Wilmington since my No. 141 of October 25th viz : *Wild Rover* and *Agnes E. Fry* on the 25th; *Owl, Caroline, Little Hattie* on the 29th; *Stormy Petrel* and *Talisman* on the 4th of November.

The *Stormy Petrel* is under the command of Capt. Gordon who has made twenty nine voyages through the blockade. The *Virginia* arrived here from Wilmington with 1,000 bales of cotton on the 30th ultimo. She is a large new vessel and considered the most valuable of the fleet; is now in port here with an outward cargo on board. I enclose a portrait.

I am sir, your obedient servant,
C. M. Allen, Consul

◉ The ship that Allen refers to in this dispatch was actually the *Chickamauga*, its name having been changed two months before her arrival in Bermuda. The vessel was both a successful blockade-runner and a Confederate warship.

No. 144
Consulate of the United States of America at Bermuda
November 7th 1864

Hon. Wm. H. Seward,
Secretary of State, Washington

Sir

A Rebel war vessel has just come to anchor off these islands; reported to be the steamer *Edith,* ten days from Wilmington. Report further says she has destroyed six vessels.

I have the honor to be, sir,
Your obedient servant,
C. M. Allen, Consul

▣ The yellow fever season having passed, blockade-runners resume using Bermuda as a base of operations. Allen notes that there are more ships in St. George's than at any other time.

No. 145
Consulate of the United States of America at Bermuda
November 16, 1864

Hon. Wm. H. Seward,
Secretary of State, Washington

Sir

The following steamers have arrived at these islands from England during the past week, viz. *Vixen, Vulture, Emma Henry* and *Evelyn.*

The three first-named are in appearance very much alike, side wheels, two masts, two stacks, about 300 tons. *Evelyn* is a larger vessel with three stacks fore and aft, side wheel, with capacity for about 1,000 bales cotton. They all have been painted white since their arrival, have cargoes on board and will probably leave for Wilmington within a few days.

Steamer *Mary,* late *Alexandra,* arrived yesterday, reported eight days from Halifax for Nassau in want of coal. She is a very slow boat.

Virginia sailed yesterday for Wilmington.

Although it has been currently reported and generally believed that most of the blockade running steamers were to leave these islands not to return here, it appears from the large quantities of coal being received here that such is not the fact, as there is now landed and afloat in the harbor of St. George's more than at any previous time.

I am sir, your obedient servant,
C. M. Allen, Consul

◈ Obtaining intelligence from crew members of the *Chickamauga* during its brief stay at St. George's, Allen reports that the ship's intention had been to destroy lighthouses on Long Island.

No. 146
Consulate of the United States at Bermuda
November 16, 1864

Hon. Wm. H. Seward,
Secretary of State, Washington

Sir

The rebel arrived vessel reported in my No. 144 of Novr. 7 as having anchored off these islands, came into the port of St. George's the next day. She is called the *Chickamauga,* late the blockade running steamer *Edith.* Is now under the command of one Wilkinson who was master of the *R. E. Lee* at the time of her capture.[21] She had on board when she arrived here 171 men, about 70 of which deserted here, the authorities refusing to render any assistance in returning them.

The commander on his arrival has made application to his Excellency, the Lt. Governor, for time to make some repairs and also for permission to obtain a supply of coal. A survey was sent on board by order of his Excellency to examine the condition of the vessel and to ascertain the amount of coal required to take her to the nearest home port. Upon his report she was allowed one week to make repairs and also allowed to receive twenty five tons of coal. An officer was sent on board to see that she took no more than that amount. She had when she arrived here about 100 tons. When she left she had enough for about five days' consumption. Her commander wanted about 225 tons and offered a large price for a vessel to go outside and coal her, but I think did not succeed in getting any one to do so. She left here yesterday at noon.

I am informed by one of her officers who left her here that the next port she will go into will be Barbados (doubtful). I am also informed by several who deserted her here that it was their intention to destroy some of the Light-houses on Long Island and would have done so had not heavy weather come on and compelled them to keep away. The following vessels are reported to me as having been destroyed by this steamer: Barque *Mark L. Potter* of Bangor, Barque *Emma L. Hall,* and *Albion Lincoln* of New York, ship *Shooting Star* of New York and two schooners.

I am sir, your obedient servant,
C. M. Allen, Consul

■ Southern agents in St. George's continue to stockpile immense quantities of coal. The quantity of coal in St. George's at this time was large enough to fuel more than 150 blockade-runners.

No. 147
Consulate of the United States at Bermuda
November 28, 1864

Hon. Wm. H. Seward,
Secretary of State, Washington

Sir
I have the honor to report the following movement of blockade running steamers at these islands since my No. 145 of November 16, viz: arrived 20th, *Armstrong* from Wilmington with 750 bales cotton to Crenshaw Brothers. 23, *Talisman,* Knox master, with 450 bales cotton to James Thurrold, reports having been hard chased for two days, threw over her deck load. 24, *Ruby,* [and] 25, *Stag,* both from England via Madeira. The *Ruby* got short of coal and burned most of her woodwork. The *Stag* came in painted white.
Sailed Nov. 19 *Vulture,* 23rd *Evelyn,* 24th *Vulture, Armstrong,* and *Vixen.* 26th, *Emma Henry,* Reid master, late of the *Lynx,* all from Wilmington.
From the best information I can obtain I think there is at the present time nearly or quite forty thousand tons of steam coal in the hands of southern agents here.

I have the honor to be sir, your obedient servant,
C. M. Allen, Consul

⊠ The consul rarely let his emotions show in his correspondence with the Department of State. In this dispatch, however, his frustration is clearly evident given the Department's unresponsiveness to allegations about the *Hawk*. The obvious emotional strain under which this and the next dispatch were written were almost certainly caused by the news he received of the death of his brother, Jonathan Vaile Allen, who died in the battle of Cedar Creek, Virginia, on October 19, 1864.

No. 148
Consulate of the United States at Bermuda
November 28, 1864

Hon. Wm. H. Seward,
Secretary of State, Washington

Sir

By the arrival at this port of the steamer *Talisman* from Wilmington, I learn the *Chickamauga* late *Edith*, and the *Tallahassee*, late *Atalanta*, were in port there on the 20th instant. The *Tallahassee* had landed her guns and had on board a cargo of cotton. It was also understood at the time the *Talisman* left that the guns of the *Chickamauga* were to be landed and the vessel to be loaded with cotton.

Steamer *Mary*, late *Alexandra*, sailed from here on the 25th having cleared for Nassau. It is currently reported she is to be used for piratical purposes. She has been very closely watched here and I am sure she has received no armament at these islands. Steamer *Hawk* has been coaled, has her sails [bent?] and appears to be ready for sea. I am unable to obtain any reliable information in regard to her. No one seems to know who her master is or who her agents are or where she is bound.

I was much disappointed in not receiving a reply to my No. 135 of September 1st in regards to this vessel. The evidence therein intimated I was in honor bound not to use before the authorities here except upon certain conditions, which conditions it was not in my power to comply with. I have called the attention of the authorities here to the apparent character of this vessel and have reason to believe they have kept a watchful eye upon her.

I have the honor to be, sir, your obedient servant,
C. M. Allen, Consul

It must have provoked Allen almost beyond measure when the Department of State asked him to confirm his own version of events, which had occurred six months earlier. In verifying his account of supplies received by the *Florida,* Allen reiterates to the Department the obvious fact that "it is very difficult if not impossible for me to obtain positive proof in cases like this as most everyone here conceives it to be for his or their interest to countenance and aid the enemies of our Government by every means in their power, as almost the entire business of the place is at present dependent upon them."

No. 149
Consulate of the United States of America at Bermuda
December 16, 1864

Hon. Wm. H. Seward,
Secretary of State, Washington

Sir

I have the honor to acknowledge the receipt of your dispatch of October 11 numbered 75 with enclosures in reference to supplies furnished the rebel steamer *Florida,* and requesting me to furnish as soon as practicable a more explicit statement of the facts given in my No. 124 should my belief of them remain unchanged, together with whatever proof may conveniently be had in evidence of them.

In reply I would say that after careful inquiry I am fully convinced the statements made in regard to this vessel in my No. 124 were substantially correct and although doubtless restrictions were placed upon her receiving more than a specified amount of coal and supplies by the acting Governor, Col. Munroe.[22] I am informed by Mr. A. W. West, the ship carpenter who did the work on board the said vessel that no local officer was sent on board to see they did not exceed the limit. He further informs me that no repairs were absolutely necessary to be made and the most that was done was to make some extra spars which were not put to use while here. She lay for two days and nights at least alongside of the ship *Storm King,* receiving coal and with the large number of men they employed, there is little doubt they succeeded in getting all the coal they wished. There also is no doubt in my mind that a heavy gun was taken on board the said steamer under cover of the night from the said ship *Storm King.* It is very difficult if not impossible for me to obtain positive proof in cases like this as most everyone here conceives it to be for his or their interest to countenance and aid the enemies of our Government by every means in their power, as almost the entire business of the place is at present dependent upon them.

I am sir, your obedient servant,
C. M. Allen, Consul

The Confederate ship *Chickamauga,* under the command of John Wilkinson, arrived in Bermuda in November 1864. Though a great number of her crew deserted, others remained in Bermuda waiting to take passage on a New York–bound vessel. Allen secured details of the ship's intentions through conversations with one of these deserters. Concealing his identity and posing as a Southern sympathizer, Allen recounts portions of the dialogue and retells his experience in this dispatch.

No. 150
Consulate of the United States of America at Bermuda
December 16, 1864

Hon. Wm. H. Seward,
Secretary of State, Washington

Sir,

I have the honor to inform you of the arrival at these island of fifteen men late a part of the crew of the rebel steamer *Florida.* They were taken in charge by J. S. Black who acts as confederate agent here, and who is now paying their board. A portion of these men are now employed fitting out the British schooner *Isabella Maria* of Halifax recently purchased by Joseph Johnson, late Johnson & Crofts, who were agents for Braine in fitting out the *Resolution* in June last and who also did his business in the *Roanoke* case. It is generally understood here that Johnson purchased this schooner for, and in account of, the confederate agent Black and that she is to be under the command of some person holding a rebel commission. The *Isabella Maria* is a fore and aft schooner of seventy tons register with cabin and caboose on deck, draws eight feet of water and is not fast. Braine and one other of the *Roanoke* pirates are still here, all the others having left for parts unknown.

The men who claim to have deserted from the *Chickamauga*, numbering about 80, are mostly here, the board of a portion of them having been paid by J. S. Black. The most of these men represent themselves as belonging to the northern states and went on board the *Chickamauga* to escape from the South and being entirely destitute wished me to send them home. Driving to Hamilton a few days since, I overtook a person on the road and from his dress supposed him to be one of the deserters above alluded to. I asked him to ride and the following conversation took place:

You are one of the Chickamauga's men, are you not?
Yes, sir, I came in her.
You ran away from her, did you?
I came on shore and did not return.
Where do you belong?
In North Carolina.
You ought to be ashamed to run away. Our country needs every man she can get.
We can do more good by leaving than we could to remain.

After considerable conversation he informed me the Yankee Consul was going to send them all to New York, that a confederate officer would find employment for them there. From all the information I can obtain, I think the above conversation reveals the true policy of allowing these men to come on shore here.

Crenshaw Brothers formerly from Richmond, now engaged in running the blockade, made application to Capt. Touse of the British barque *Mary E. Purdy*, about to sail for New York, to take some of these men as passengers. He replied he would take them for $200 each in gold paid in advance and a pair of irons furnished him for each man. Some of them went on board.

It is my opinion the greater part of these men will go from here to the British provinces, perhaps in the *Isabella Maria*, but I think they will be more likely to go in other vessels, a few at a time.

I am sir, your obedient servant,
C. M. Allen, Consul

The year 1864 came to a close with little decrease in blockade-running activities and little respite for the resourceful Yankee consul.

No. 152
Consulate of the United States at Bermuda
December 30, 1864

Hon. Wm. H. Seward
Secretary of State, Washington

Sir,

I have to report the arrival at these Islands on the 23rd instant of the British steamer *Charlotte* from Wilmington with 1,015 bales cotton to W. P. Campbell. The *Charlotte* is under the command of one Cooke, formerly a British naval officer. Steamers *Owl,* Maffitt of the *Florida,* with 700 bales and the *Col. Lamb* with 1,764 bales of cotton arrived on the 24th from Wilmington. The last two named vessels are under the rebel flag.

The *Col. Lamb* will, I am informed, go from here to Havana for repairs. Steamer *Susan Beirne* left here on the 26th for Wilmington and returned on the 28th leaking badly, has been run on shore. It is thought she cannot be repaired here.

Steamer *Maude Campbell* from England consigned to W. P. Campbell arrived here yesterday.

The following blockade running steamers are now in the port of St. George's. *Dieppe* laid up, *Whisper* expected to leave today, *Charlotte* and *Owl* to leave soon, *Susan Beirne, Col. Lamb* and *Maude Campbell.*

I am sir, your obedient servant,
C. M. Allen, Consul

CHAPTER 6

"There could hardly have been greater consternation"

🔲 The consul submits his returns for the fourth quarter of 1864.

No. 153
Consulate of the United States of America at Bermuda
January 12, 1865

Hon. Wm. H. Seward
Secretary of State, Washington

Sir

I have the honor to herewith enclose returns from J. T. Darrell, Esq., consular agent at the port of Hamilton, for the quarter ending December 31, 1864 numbered from 1 to 4 inclusive, also aggregate return of fees at this Consulate and the agency at Hamilton for the year ending December 31, 1864, together with account for office rent for the year 1864. I have no arrival or departure of American vessels to report during the past quarter.

I am sir, your obedient servant,
C. M. Allen, Consul

🔲 In the past, Allen had helped escaping slaves and free people of color who made their way out of the Confederate states on Bermuda-bound blockade-runners. It is interesting to note that as the war entered its final phase Northern prisoners of war were also managing to escape from Confederate prisons and making their way to Bermuda by this same means.

No. 154
Consulate of the United States at Bermuda
January 12th 1865

Hon. Wm. H. Seward
Secretary of State, Washington

Sir,

It has come to my knowledge that several rebel conspirators left here last Saturday in the steamer *City of Petersburgh* for Halifax. The principal of the gang passed here by the name of Wood, his real name is Joseph E. Hunt, a resident of Savannah, Georgia. I have no doubt he took from here $22,000 in British gold to aid in carrying forward his schemes. I have sent his description so definitely that he cannot fail to be recognized to the Collector of Customs at New York. I also send by the same conveyance two men from the rebel states, one of whom I have no doubt is one of the conspirators under Hunt. He represents himself as a destitute refugee who wants to get to New York where he says he has friends. I have forwarded such information as will I think cause him to be arrested before he leaves the vessel. I think that important papers may be found in his possession and believe he has received money from the rebel agent here.

The other person sent, one Peters, I have reason to believe is honest and will do all in his power to detect Hunt and the others associated with him. As a precautionary measure, the master of the British barque *Zephyrena* in which vessel they take passage, has agreed to detain them on board till they are delivered into the custody of some officer duly authorized to receive them. I have failed to get any information of the precise mission Hunt goes on. My informant says he takes dispatches to one Richard Murray at the New York Hotel.

There is a large number of destitute refugees here from the rebel states who seek my aid. Almost every vessel that runs the blockade brings some, and not infrequently Union soldiers who have been captured and escaped come here by secreting themselves on board the blockade running steamers. Where I have evidence to believe they are not impostors, I have assisted them while here, and in many cases paid their passage to New York. My limited means will not allow me to render assistance to all whom I think honestly ask aid and need it. I would respectfully ask if some provision cannot be made to pay the passage of this class of persons upon their delivery to some proper official in New York.

I am sir, your obedient servant,
C. M. Allen, Consul

◨ On the day that Allen wrote this dispatch, the Northern amphibious assault on Fort Fisher began. The capture of the fort and of Wilmington dealt a fatal blow to blockade-runners at Bermuda. With Wilmington closed to them, the blockade-runners who were in Bermuda began to shift their activities to Nassau and Havana. From these places, they attempted to reach Gulf ports which had not yet fallen into Union hands.

No. 155
Consulate of the United States at Bermuda
January 13, 1865

Hon. Wm. H. Seward,
Secretary of State, Washington

Sir,

The rebel steamers *Stag* and *Chameleon* and the British steamer *City of Petersburgh* arrived here on the 30 ultimo from Wilmington with cotton.

The *Chameleon*, late the pirate *Tallahassee*, is under the command of Wilkinson who commanded the *Chickamauga*. The report from Wilmington by these vessels caused much despondency among blockade runners and depressed the business very much. Since the arrival of the Halifax mail last Tuesday, they have been very active. Some eight or ten steamers are now preparing to leave for Wilmington.

There arrived yesterday from England the *Florence*, *The Dare*, and *Eagle*. The *Rattlesnake* came in on the 9th. Steamer *Talisman* from Wilmington went down at sea. The crew was taken off by the schooner *Orville* of Bath and landed here on the first instant. Two of the principal rebel firms have gone from here to Nassau or some other West Indies port: Crenshaw Bros. and

J. H. Phinnizy. Should Wilmington be closed, they intend to run into some of the Gulf ports.

I am sir, your obedient servant
C. M. Allen, Consul

⊞ Blockade-running vessels return to Bermuda bringing news of the fall of Fort Fisher. As it became increasingly clear that the end of the conflict was growing near, Allen was at last able to report that "business was nearly suspended and had they known the Islands were to sink in twenty-four hours, there could hardly have been greater consternation."

No. 156
Consulate of the United States of America at Bermuda
January 23, 1865

Hon. Wm. H. Seward
Secretary of State, Washington

Sir,

The following blockade running steamers have left port here since my No. 155 of the 13th inst.

Owl, Maffitt, and *Charlotte,* Cocker, on the 14th; the *Rattlesnake,* Usina, on the 18th, and the *Chameleon,* Wilkinson, on the 19th, all for Wilmington.

The *Owl* returned on the morning of the 20th having on the night of Sunday the 15th communicated with Fort Caswell where they were informed Fort Fisher had been captured and they at Fort Caswell were to surrender the next day. Several other steamers were about to leave here when the *Owl* returned. Upon the receipt of the information by the *Owl,* business was nearly suspended and had they known the Islands were to sink in twenty-four hours, there could hardly have been greater consternation. The blockade runners and their aiders feel their doom is sealed, undoubtedly some of them will go from here to Havana thinking to run to Galveston. As yet I think they are undecided what to do.

The following steamers are in port here at this time: *Owl, Dieppe, Whisper, Virginia, Old Dominion, Maude Campbell, Stag, The Dare (No.2), Florence,* and *Almanderes,* the last named from Halifax.

I am sir, your obedient servant,
C. M. Allen, Consul

⊞ Allen reports the transfer of Confederate operations from Bermuda to Havana in hopes of entering Gulf ports.

No. 157
Consulate of the United States at Bermuda
Feby. 11th 1865

Hon. Wm. H. Seward
Secretary of State, Washington, D.C.

Sir,

Since my No. 156 all the Steamers then reported as in port here have left with the exception of the *Maude Campbell, Dieppe* and *Old Dominion.* They all cleared out for Nassau and Havana except the *Whisper* for Liverpool. Much of the merchandise and some of the coal on hand here at the time of the receipt of the information of the capture of Fort Fisher has been shipped to Havana and a general movement among blockade runners to settle up their business and get away. I think it has been their intention to go to Havana with the view of continuing their business from there.

Those remaining here are much encouraged to remain longer by the report received from Nassau yesterday that seven vessels had run the blockade of Charleston and two at Georgetown [South Carolina] since the capture of Fort Fisher. Report says two small vessels, a sloop and schooner, are now loading here for Saint Mark's.

I am sir, your obedient servant,
C. M. Allen, Consul

⊞ The consul reports that passengers may be arriving at U.S. ports without their required passports. To ensure passengers' legal entrance, Allen placed advertisements in local newspapers detailing the rules and regulations mentioned in this dispatch.[1]

No. 158
Consulate of the United States at Bermuda
Feby. 11th 1865

Hon. Wm. H. Seward,
Secretary of State, Washington, D.C.

Sir,

I have the honor to acknowledge the receipt of a package of blank passport forms and take this occasion to say the regulation in regard to passports is fully understood here by the community generally and particularly by the agent and master of every vessel leaving these islands for a port in the United States.

Although numerous applications have been made for passports to this Consulate none as yet have been granted, the parties either being unwilling to pay the fee required or unable to produce the requisite evidence of citizenship. I have reason to believe that numerous persons have left here recently without passports for New York and others are likely to continue to so leave as long as they are permitted to land without serious difficulty.

I am sir, your obedient servant,
C. M. Allen, Consul

▣ The prompt action of Bermuda's lieutenant governor prevented men who had served on the CSS *Florida* from embarking for the Confederate states. With the end of the war now clearly in sight, British officials in Bermuda were at long last providing the cooperation that Allen had so long sought.

No. 159
Consulate of the United States at Bermuda
March 1, 1865

Hon. W. H. Seward,
Secretary of State, Washington, D.C.

Sir,

Your dispatch No. 83 with enclosure is at hand.

Sixteen of the crew formerly belonging to the *Florida* with many other seamen are here under the charge of the Rebel Agent. Either the *Shenandoah*[2] or a rebel iron clad called the *Stonewall* are hourly expected here.[3]

The steamer *City of Richmond* under the British flag arrived here a few days since. One of her seamen informs me they took from Cherbourg sixty men which they put on board the *Stonewall* near Belle Isle, France. They also transferred a large quantity of arms and ammunition to the *Stonewall,* then under command of a Captain Page, formerly of the U.S. Navy.

The Authorities here are using their utmost vigilance to prevent the men of the late *Florida* going on board any rebel armed vessel. It having been supposed the *City of Richmond* would take these men from here, the Lieut. Governor ordered an Officer of the Customs to remain on board to prevent these men from leaving in her.

The U.S. steamer *Connecticut* came to anchor off these Islands on the evening of the 26th and left the next day.

I am sir, your obedient servant,
C. M. Allen, Consul

Reversing his stance, the lieutenant governor informs Allen that it would not be legally possible to prevent the men from the CSS *Florida* from leaving Bermuda on a Confederate vessel. But in the matter of the *Louisa Ann Fannie,* Allen and the lieutenant governor are in agreement that no munitions of war are to be provided.

No. 160
United States Consulate at Bermuda
March 6th 1865

Hon. W. H. Seward
Secretary of State, Washington

Sir,

I have the honor to inform you that a Steamer called the *Louisa Ann Fannie* under the British flag, arrived at these Islands on the 27th ultimo and came to anchor in the harbour of St. George's; from the appearance of the vessel and what little information I could obtain I came to the conclusion she was intended for a rebel privateer. On the 1st inst. I personally communicated with his Excellency, the Lieut. Governor, and made known to him my suspicions. On the following day, finding the said vessel had hauled to the wharf of the Confederate Agent, I addressed the Lieut. Governor a note (Enclosure No. 1). On the next day the Lt. Governor came from Mount Langton, eleven miles distant, and called upon me. Being absent at the moment I did not see him. On the 4th I received a reply to the note addressed to him on the 2nd inst (Enclosure No. 2). I am informed by an officer of the Customs that His Excellency has ordered that the Steamship above named be closely watched, and that she cannot receive anything of the nature of arms or ammunitions at this port without his knowledge and consent. I have just had an interview with the principal revenue officer at this port. He informs me her tonnage is 425 exclusive of engine room and that 58 men are on her crew list, several of which have been discharged today. The opinion of this official is as I believed honestly expressed to me, that this vessel came here for the purpose of receiving such aid as would enable her to leave this port and hoist the rebel flag, prepared to commence depredations upon our commerce. It is now his opinion as expressed to me that she will return to London. I do not think she can obtain arms or ammunition here, that she had them on board when she arrived here. I am unable to ascertain she had a cargo of some nature which is not to be discharged here.

Since writing the above I learn the *Louisa Ann Fannie* has a supply of arms and ammunition on board, but not having been allowed to receive such supplies as are wanted, the brig *H. G. Bagley* is loading by the rebel agent with the intent of supplying her at some other place.

I have also just learned from what I consider a reliable source that the Danish brig *Mathilde* has been for some days laden with coal in bags and is waiting to go out to supply a rebel [?] which is hourly expected here.

I shall at once go to the Governor and lay all the information I have before him hoping some immediate action may be taken to thwart their plans.

The men late of the *Florida* are still here. The Governor informs me that if it is proved, as he expects it will be, that as these men belonged to the Confederate service when they came here he has no power to prevent them going on board a Confederate vessel.

I herewith enclose a correct portrait of the *Louisa Ann Fannie* (Enclosure No. 3).

I am sir, your obedient servant,
C. M. Allen, Consul

⊠ A U.S. marshal, Capt. Richard Squire, was employed by the government as an undercover agent. He was an experienced sailor, and his work in Europe had resulted in the capture of several Confederate vessels. He had also been very helpful to Consul Allen for almost a year. Though Allen did the honorable thing in rendering financial aid to Squire, there appears to be no evidence that he was reimbursed.

No. 161
Consulate of the United States at Bermuda
March 6, 1865

Hon. W. H. Seward,
Secretary of State, Washington

Sir,

I have the honor to enclose herewith a copy of a letter handed me by Captain Richard Squire soon after his arrival in Bermuda in January 1864. He remained here until about 1st of November last. During the Spring he was confined to his room for some time by an injury to his leg and the necessary expense he was under left him with little means which during the summer became entirely exhausted. Later in the season he was attacked with the yellow fever and was confined to his room nearly six weeks. After recovering his health he obtained a situation as master of a barque chartered by a confederate house here to go to Nassau. After selling all his nautical instruments and everything beside he could part with, he found he was unable to pay his obligations here and his creditors would not let him leave without they were paid. He assured me he had received nothing from his employers since he came here and there were wages due him. I let him have one hundred and thirty one dollars which was the least amount absolutely necessary to keep him out of jail, for which he gave me his draft on Hon. Robert Murray. The said draft was returned to me protested for acceptance. In the meantime Capt. Squire had left the Island and I have not learned anything of him.

Believing Captain Squire by taking charge of the vessel alluded to would be in a better position to render service to the Government than by remaining here, I felt under the circumstances I could do no less than to aid him to the extent that he might be allowed to leave and believing also the recommendation from Marshal Murray would justify me in so doing, although it gave me no legal claim upon him or any other person except Capt. Squire.

I am sir, your obedient servant,
C. M. Allen, Consul

◈ With the departure from Bermuda of practically all blockade-runners and the departure of the Confederacy's chief disbursing agent, Major Walker, Allen must have felt, at long last, that the war was coming to an end.

No. 163
United States Consulate at Bermuda
March 20, 1865

Hon. Wm. H. Seward
Secretary of State, Washington, D.C.

Sir

I have the honor to inform you the steamer *Louisa Ann Fannie* left here on the 8th instant having cleared for Havana. Norman S. Walker, confederate financial agent at these Islands went in her. It is understood this vessel is to return here soon. The men late of the *Florida* are still here, no doubt they were expecting to go on board the *Stonewall.* The Danish brig *Mathilde,* which vessel I alluded to in my No. 160 as being laden with coal in bags to supply some vessel outside, has been discharged.

The brig *H. G. Bagley* having taken her cargo, the last named vessel is owned by the rebels and has other cargo in the nature of Naval supplies on board.

There is in port here at this time the following steamers belonging to the fleet formerly engaged in running the blockade: *Chameleon* (formerly *Tallahassee*), for England soon. *Whisper, Dieppe, Maude Campbell,* and *Hansa.*

I am sir, your obedient servant
C. M. Allen, Consul

◈ The blockade-running vessels are leaving Bermuda "but as they are all bound home their movements have excited but little interest."

No. 167
Consulate of the United States of America at Bermuda
April 4, 1865

Hon. W. H. Seward
Secretary of State, Washington, D.C.

Sir

The fifteen men to whom I have before referred as being a portion of the crew of the late rebel steamer *Florida* left here today for England in the British barque *Messina* after having been kept here for some months by the rebel agents at an expense of not less than $3,000.

British steamer *Ajax* which undoubtedly came here for the purpose of in some manner getting guns and war munitions with the intent to commit depredations on our Commerce is still in port. The action of Col. Hamley, acting Governor, in regard to this vessel is worthy of record. Had he not used the utmost vigilance and positively refused to allow any guns to be taken on board under any pretense, I believe she would have before this have proved herself a more dangerous vessel than either the *Florida* or the *Alabama*.

Steamer *Louisa Ann Fannie* arrived yesterday from Havana and has been sent to quarantine for fifteen days.

There are several of the late blockade running steamers in port, soon to leave for England. The arrivals and departures of this class of vessels have been frequent during the past few weeks, but as they are all bound home their movements have excited but little interest.

I am sir, your obedient servant,
C. M. Allen, Consul

▣ When Allen wrote his quarterly report on April 5, 1865, he could not have known that the last tragic episodes of the Civil War were unfolding.

No. 164
United States Consulate at Bermuda
April 5, 1865

Hon. Wm. H. Seward
Secretary of State, Washington, D.C.

Sir

I have the honor to enclose herewith the following reports for the quarter ending March 31st, 1865 on Arrival and Departures of American vessels at the port of St. George's, Navigation and Commerce with report of Fees received at the U.S. Consular Agency at Hamilton numbered from one to three in-

Blockade-runners *Maude Campbell* and *Hansa*. Painting by Edward James
(Courtesy of Bermuda National Trust Collection, Bermuda Archives, Hamilton, Bermuda)

clusive. There was no arrival or departure of American vessels at this port of Hamilton during the past quarter.

I am sir, your obedient servant,
C. M. Allen, Consul

On April 3 the capital of the Confederacy, Richmond, Virginia, had been taken by U.S. forces. On April 5 President Abraham Lincoln visited Richmond. When General Godfrey Weitzel, in charge of the occupation, asked the president's advice about the treatment of Richmond's citizens, Lincoln told him, "Be easy on them, Weitzel, be easy on them." Four days later, Gen. Robert E. Lee surrendered the Army of Northern Virginia to Gen. Ulysses S. Grant at Appomattox Court House, Virginia, where the war virtually came to an end. When Lincoln was assassinated on April 14, his policy of reconciliation with the Southern states also perished.

The military occupation of the Southern states and the rancorous politics of the Reconstruction era did not have a direct impact on the American Consul in Bermuda. Bereft of the immense profits from blockade-running, the isolated Atlantic island to which Charles Maxwell Allen had come in 1861 quietly slipped back into its prewar lassitude.

Mr. Lincoln's man in Bermuda was to further serve his country as U.S. consul at Bermuda through every succeeding administration until his death in 1888.

CHAPTER 7

"In the place where the tree falleth"

▣ Charles Maxwell Allen lived for nearly a quarter of a century after Appomattox. These years were to witness the rancorous politics of Reconstruction, the assassination of a second American president, the opulence of the Gilded Age, and the emergence of the United States as an international power.

But far removed from these events, life in Bermuda was peaceful for the Allen family. After the war, with his family reunited and firmly established in Bermuda, Charles was able to enjoy family life for the first time in four years. In 1865, he was forty-three years old and Susan was thirty-eight. Their five children, all under the age of sixteen, once again had a full-time father. As their children grew to honorable maturity, Charles and Susan established a notable and welcoming residence befitting their official position in British Bermuda.

These years also saw Charles, tempered by the vicissitudes of war, emerge as one of his country's most able and long-serving diplomats, but these years opened with a sinister plot and a great national calamity.

It was on the very day of Lincoln's assassination that Consul Allen uncovered a "diabolical scheme" to wage germ warfare against the Northern states. Allen's dispatch of April 14, 1865, to the Department of State is a masterpiece of explication.

No. 166
Consulate of the United States at Bermuda
April 14th 1865

Hon. Wm. H. Seward,
Secretary of State, Washington, D.C.

Sir,

During the prevalence of the yellow fever at these islands last September, a Dr. Blackburn formerly belonging to New Orleans, came here from Halifax for the ostensible purpose of aiding the physicians here.[1] He refused all offers of a pecuniary nature, either for his services while here, or for expenses incurred by his visit here, claiming to have had much experience in the treatment of said disease, and being desirous only of benefiting this community who had manifested so much sympathy for their "holy cause." While advocating his theory for the treatment of yellow fever, he never neglected on all possible occasions to advocate the cause of the rebels. After remaining here about one month, he returned to Halifax. Some three weeks since a person intimate in the Office of N. S. Walker, Confederate Agent here, sent me word he wished to see me confidentially as he had some information of importance to communicate.

I soon after had an interview with him when he informed me that Dr. Blackburn's expenses for his visit had been paid with funds from the Confederate Treasury, that the sole object of that visit was to collect clothing from the dead of yellow fever, to be sent to New York and other northern cities during the coming summer, that while here he, Blackburn, collected three large trunks full of such clothing which were then in these Islands in the care of a person employed by Blackburn, to take charge of them until next June, for which service he was to receive $150 per month, and in June he was to be paid $500 to take them to New York.[2] My informant refused to furnish any further information without I paid him for it, and demanded $500 for a full exposure as by so doing he would lose his position here and would be compelled to leave these islands. After repeated interviews finding I could get, by no other means than money, available information, I finally agreed to pay him the sum of $200 provided the trunks were found and circumstances proved to be as he had represented. He then informed in whose possession the trunks were, gave me a perfect description of them, and a minute detail of all the transaction connected with them.

After getting all necessary information, I made known the transaction to the health officer at this port (St. George's), who taking some other officers with him went to the house in which it was alleged the trunks were stored and demanded the trunks left there by Dr. Blackburn. The person in whose keep they were finding the facts had been revealed denied nothing, but acknowledged much and gave up the trunks, which were taken yesterday to the Quarantine Station, opened and found to contain wearing apparel and bedding, made up in small packages, decently clean, with dirty flannel drawers and shirts on the outside, all evidently taken from a sick bed, intermixed with these packages some poultices, and many other things which have been placed there for no legitimate purpose, were found, the whole of which were buried by direction of the health officer. From the evidence before me, I believe the facts in relation to these trunks and Dr. Blackburn's visit here were well understood by Confederate officers here, and that they have paid money to carry out the diabolical scheme.

I hope to get a thorough investigation of the matter and believe I am prepared to produce the necessary evidence to shew the affair in its true light. I shall use my utmost endeavours to have the contents of the trunks taken up at once and thoroughly destroyed as I believe there are parties here who would not hesitate to remove them if possible in order to carry out the original intent.

Trusting my action in this matter will be approved,
I remain, sir, your obedient servant,
C. M. Allen, Consul

◼ Both Americans and Bermudians were appalled by the discovery of the infamous "yellow fever plot." For many weeks, both American and Bermudian newspapers published details of the plot and Allen's part in uncovering it. Ultimately, Blackburn was arrested and tried in Canada; however, he was acquitted for lack of evidence.

Consul Allen's last Civil War dispatch was written on the day that President Lincoln was assassinated. The death of the first Republican president, whose party Allen had labored for since the early 1850s, did not affect him professionally, for the Republican Party continued in power and the Department of State continued under William H. Seward's leadership until 1869. To Charles Maxwell, however, the assassination of his president must have been profoundly disturbing.

It must have seemed ironic to him that the Bermudians, who had so recently been vociferous supporters of the Confederate states, now quickly extended their sympathy to the United States in florid terms in the columns of the Bermuda Royal Gazette.[3] The American consul also received ornate expressions of sympathy from many Bermudian government officials and civic organizations.[4] The war having brought an end to the "peculiar institution" of slavery, the letter of condolence that may have been most meaningful to Consul Allen was that which came from the colored citizens of St. George's.[5] The Lincoln assassination, the trial and execution of the conspirators, and the infamous "yellow fever plot" were sad postscripts to the American Civil War.

Charles Maxwell Allen's first four years in Bermuda had been incredibly busy, stressful, and dangerous. At the conclusion of the war, however, Bermuda was to enter into a long, steady decline. Allen must have realized that the full range of his finely honed diplomatic skills could not be exercised in the now quiet British colony.

Always conscious of the dignity of the office to which he had been appointed, the appearance in St. George's in July 1865 of the constantly inebriated U.S. consul from St. Thomas caused Consul Allen to report the incident to the Department of State.[6] In the consul's letter to the Department of State, he suggested that his talents might be better served at St. Thomas. Although Allen did not receive the appointment to St. Thomas, it must have given him a good deal of satisfaction to know that within six months the Department of State had replaced the offending consul. Allen never again expressed a desire to leave Bermuda.

The Allen family formed many lasting friendships in their adopted country as wartime passions cooled. These years were to witness a growing number of American visitors to Bermuda, escaping the cold New England winters to enjoy the island's temperate and salubrious air. American visitors to Bermuda invariably made it a point to visit the U.S. consul upon their arrival, and this custom continued for the remainder of Charles's and Susan's lives.

One of Allen's friends was an American who resided in Bermuda, the celebrated naturalist, John T. Bartram.[7] Bartram's diary provides an interesting and unexpected sidelight on Charles. In Bartram's diary, under the entry for February 14, 1866, he remarked: "This day there was shot at the east end of St. George harbour by Mr. Ellen [Allen] American Consul and sent to me for preserving a gull or Goeland length from tip of bill to end of tail is 23½ inches and exstent [sic] of wing is 4 foot 9 inches."

But these pleasant interludes came to a sudden end in May 1866 when the tranquility of the consul's days were shaken by a letter he received from his good friend, Ben Higgs, now living on Prince Edward Island. The letter communicated the news that Ben's nephew, Augustus Higgs, was seeking to have Allen removed as U.S. consul at Bermuda in the hopes of securing the position for himself. Augustus Higgs appears to have been a man of unsound character. He claimed that, with his uncle's assistance, he could prove that Consul Allen had been speculating in cotton during the Civil War. Higgs claimed to have the support of Generals Grant and Hooker and many members of Congress providing he could prove that the consul had engaged in trade.

Consul Allen's response to his friend's letters and Augustus Higgs's allegations were immediately forwarded to the Department of State with the following cover.

May 5, 1866

I take liberty to enclose herewith copies of a letter and its enclosure which has been shown me today by Mr. Hyland formerly of the firm Higgs & Hyland of this place. Mr. Hyland is now, and has been for the past eight years, Agent of the New York Underwriters resident here. Mr. B. Wilson Higgs was for some time a partner with Mr. Hyland in business here; is a native of Bermuda and has a wide reputation as an honorable and upright man; he removed to Prince Edward's Island about one year since. Mr. Henry E. Higgs, a brother of B. Wilson Higgs, and father of the young man who seeks to obtain this consulate, is also a native of Bermuda, but for some time a resident of the United States.

During the war he returned here, sought, and obtained employment, more or less, from firms engaged in running the blockade.

I am informed he has made arrangements with John T. Bourne formerly Rebel agent here to go into business when his son obtains the appointment that he is seeking, expecting through him as Consul to get the business of the distressed American vessels that put into this port.

I have no hesitation in saying that the reputation of Mr. Henry E. Higgs is not first rate here and any charges he, or any other person, may choose to make against me would be thankfully received and, I trust, satisfactorily answered.

▣ No further mention was made of this incident in any of Consul Allen's dispatches, and no action against him was ever taken by the Department of State. The conclusion of the Augustus Higgs affair found Allen secure in his consular position. Interestingly, at war's end, Bourne had written to Allen in the hopes of restoring cordial relations. The two adversaries died within a year of each other. It is not known if they ever reconciled.

Official business in Bermuda returned to a slower and more regular pattern. Dispatches from this period generally consist of routine quarterly reports, business connected with shipwrecks of American vessels, and informing his government of occasional appearances in Bermuda of former Confederates. Peacetime enabled Allen to take regular biennial leaves of absence to visit family and friends in the United States.

Bermuda's tranquil postwar years were occasionally intruded upon by events of international note. Such was the case when the British war steamer *Monarch* arrived in Bermuda in January 1870 bearing the body of the renowned American philanthropist, George Peabody. Consul Allen recounted the services he rendered during the *Monarch*'s brief stay in Bermuda.[8]

The *Monarch* remained about four miles to the East of the land where I visited her, and tendered my services, and received a small commission from her Commander who treated me with the utmost courtesy and consideration. As soon as I learned the *Monarch* was signaled off these Islands I hoisted my flag half mast and soon after all the flags of the shipping in port and at the various military stations also displayed in the same manner.

✸ In April 1871 Charles received the sad news that James, his older brother and former partner in the Orono Match Manufacturing Company, had died. James and brother Jonas, with their wives, had gone to California a few years after the death of their brother William Dennis to seek their fortunes. James did not prosper in California. Eventually he moved on to Blackfoot City, Montana, where he died at the age of fifty-one.

Within a month of receiving this news, Charles took the unusual step of requesting a leave of absence. Never absent from his post except for his regular biennial leaves, Charles's health broke in the spring of 1871, and he was forced to ask for an emergency thirty-day leave. While plagued with asthma all his life, only once before, in the summer of 1863, had Charles ever referred to his poor health in any of his dispatches.

The year 1872 was to bring great change to the Allen family, both professionally and personally. As the postwar fortunes of St. George's declined, so those of the capital city of Hamilton rose. Not only had the seat of government been located at Hamilton for many years, but also its growing commercial importance was indicated when the military headquarters moved from St. George's to Hamilton. The city was fast becoming the entrepreneurial center of Bermuda. Although St. George's remained the most accessible port in the islands, Hamilton was developing into the largest city in Bermuda. In 1871, consular fees received by Allen at St. George's amounted to less than $500, but the fees being collected by the consular agent at Hamilton amounted to almost $1,500 per annum. Allen's proposal that the consulate be moved to Hamilton not only made good sense due to that city's increasing importance but also would have the effect of nearly doubling his salary. The move was approved by the Department of State.

By 1872, Front Street was rapidly becoming the most important commercial and retail street in Hamilton. This east-west thoroughfare ran parallel to Hamilton Harbor and was intersected by Queen Street at the western edge of the business district. Just a few yards up Queen Street stood the Bermuda post office, and the corner of Queen and Front streets became one of the most important gathering places of Bermudians who had come to town to collect their mail and transact business. The intersection was often crowded with horses and carriages. Consul Allen moved the U.S. consulate to this important intersection.

The consul was asked by the Department of State to furnish a physical description of the consulate in 1885. In 1872, when the consulate was opened at this location, the rooms were probably not so elegantly appointed. Nevertheless, by 1885, in Charles's own words, "It was the best fitted, and the best located, office in the town."

No. 485
United States Consulate at Bermuda
September 17, 1885

Hon. James D. Porter
Assistant Secretary of State
Washington, D.C.

Sir:

I have the honor to report in compliance with the request in Department letter of the 31st ultimo as follows: The United States Consulate at Hamilton, Bermuda, is located at No. 12 Front Street, the principle business street in the town, and near the center of the business port of the street. It occupies the whole of the second floor of the building; the actual rental paid is $192.00 or L40 Sterling per annum and is paid quarterly without discount or drawback, in Sterling money, or by draft on the honorable Secretary of State to J. B. Heyl, the owner of the building, who occupies the lower floor.

There is no one on the premises when the building is closed; the building is of stone, and the windows are protected by folding wood blinds on the inside. The main office has two mahogany desks, two tables, chairs, a movable case of drawers, and a carpet. There is a stationary case across the side nearest the small rooms, extending from the hall to the door of the small front room and reaching from the ceiling to the floor, all of which are private property. The small room has a carpet, sofa, table and chairs. The visitors reading room has a long table, or desk and is supplied with the local papers, three files of New York daily papers, and various commercial publications.

The only articles of furniture belonging to the United States Government are one pine book case, open, shield or coat of arms, and seal press.

These rooms have been occupied by this Consulate from the time of its removal from St. Georges about 12 years ago. It is the best fitted, and the best located, office in the town those at the Public buildings only excepted; is convenient for business and pleasant for visitors.

The stairs leading to the street are of good width and convenient of access. The whole building is comparatively new and is kept in good repair. I enclose an outline sketch of the Consular floor and some photographic views of and from the buildings.

I am, Sir, Your obedient Servant,
Chas. M. Allen, Consul

▦ In March 1874, Charles and Susan became the parents of a daughter, Edith Wistowe, their sixth child and their only child born in Bermuda. Within two months of Edith's birth, Charles and Susan were preparing to leave for New York to celebrate the marriage of their daughter Mary Eva to Henry Whitney of Belmont. These happy events must have been tinged with some sadness, for before their departure for New York, news arrived of the death of Charles's father, James Allen, at the age of eighty-four. It was during this trip to the United States that Charles's youngest brother, Henry Seldon, a photographer, took the finest image of Charles that survives.

The removal of the consulate to Hamilton also made it desirable for the Allen family to live closer to Hamilton. The residence that would become the Allen family home in Bermuda is a two-story stone structure that was called Wistowe, located on Flatts Inlet, about six miles from Hamilton. The house is situated on a narrow neck of land with Flatts Inlet to the west and Harrington Sound to the east.

As a non-British national, Charles was not able to purchase Wistowe outright. After the Civil War, the house was purchased by Charles's good friend, James A. Atwood, and the Allen family resided there until early in the following century. Wistowe became the Allen family's first real home since Charles had left Belmont in 1861.

Wistowe, which still stands, was built before 1815. The east side of the house faces the road that connects St. George's to Hamilton, now known as the North Shore Road. The east or main entrance to Wistowe is clearly marked by two white pillars supporting a stone portico upon which is engraved the name "Wistowe." This entrance was used by the consul as the official entrance for visitors coming to his residential office.

There was a courtyard to the north that separated the east and west wings of the U-shaped house. In the courtyard Charles had placed a tall flagpole on which flew the Stars and Stripes, indicating that Wistowe was the home of the U.S. consul. The west side of the house leads down a small incline to Flatts Inlet. A reception room runs along the entire width of the second floor of the two-story house. This formal entertaining area opens onto a balcony that affords a fine view of Flatts Village.

The powerful tides that run from Harrington Sound below the Allen home and into Flatts Inlet inspired Charles to create a structure that would make Wistowe a splendid Bermuda attraction. On the south lawn he built a large and imposing fountain directly above an old canal that had been cut between the two bodies of water. Sixteen feet in diameter, cut into solid rock, the fountain held almost twenty tons of water and was powered by the tides nearly twenty-four hours a day. Stocked with fish, sea turtles, and other marine life and set on a lush green lawn surrounded by colorful flowers and foliage, the fountain would become a favorite gathering place for family and friends.

A photograph taken by Charles's friend James Heyl in about 1876 shows the family in the south garden of Wistowe Lodge.[9] The tall flagpole from which flies a large U.S. flag can be seen in the background. Charles's two daughters, Hettie and Genevieve, in pretty summer frocks, stand behind their mother in the garden. Charles, seated on the low wall between the house and the fountain, is elegantly attired in top hat and linen jacket. Susan, seated near her husband on the low wall, is wearing an attractive summer dress and gaily decorated straw hat. Their youngest daughter, Edith Wistowe, not yet two years old, is at her mother's knee. Young William Henry, in shirtsleeves, kneels at the fountain. This charming domestic scene is the only known family photograph of the Allens. Two family members are missing from the photograph: their son Charles Fletcher was in the United States, as was their daughter Mary Eva, now married and living with her husband in Bradford, Pennsylvania.

The now slow but steady rhythms of Charles's life were interrupted in February 1877 by the death of his oldest friend in Bermuda, Edward James. Surveyor-general of Bermuda, editor of the *Bermuda Chronicle,* talented, artistic, witty, well-read, a good and loyal friend—and much given to drink. These are the words that describe Edward James, the English artist who arrived in St. George's at almost the same time as Charles. Edward James died of apoplexy at the age of fifty-seven. His superb paintings of the blockade-runners are a unique visual record of the American Civil War in Bermuda. James's paintings are the perfect counterpoint to Charles's words in describing how the small island of Bermuda played such a large part in the events of 1861–65.

Charles lived to see a second American president assassinated. The death of President Garfield, shot four months earlier by an embittered attorney who

Wistowe, the postwar home of the Allen family in Bermuda
(From the editor's collection)

had sought a consular post, occurred on September 19, 1881. Consul Allen wrote to the Department of State "that the sorrow and sympathy manifested through the Colony by all classes on the receipt of the intelligence of the death of President Garfield was intense, deep and heartfelt."[10]

In February 1884, Charles received the sad news that his younger brother Anson Allen had died in Orono, Maine. Anson had become a noted naturalist, publishing a work still studied today, on seashells, some of which had been gathered in Bermuda when Anson had visited Charles in 1862.[11] With Anson's death, now only three of James and Sally Allen's eight children still lived: Charles, Amanda, and Jonas.[12]

Over the next three years, three more of Charles and Susan's children were married in the United States.[13] In 1880 Charles and Susan had only young William Henry, age nineteen, and Edith Wistowe, age six, at home.

The duties of the U.S. consul at Bermuda in the postwar years were certainly less dangerous than during the American Civil War but only slightly less hectic. Every letter received had to be logged in and answered. Every activity performed by the consul had to be documented on government forms, or more often on hand-drawn forms, and the activities compiled into the never-ending quarterly reports to the Department of State. Every American ship arriving and departing Bermuda had to be surveyed, with the appropriate forms approved by the consul. Almost every American arriving in Bermuda had one reason or another to stop in at the consul's office. Fees for services rendered had to be collected and accounted for in detail. Also during these years, there were many shipwrecks on the reefs of Bermuda. It was the consul's responsibility not only to report the facts of these cases but also, where necessary, to provide for the safe return of shipwrecked seamen and passengers to the United States. And, of course, now that Charles's family was at last with him in Bermuda, family duties also occupied more of his time.

With the recovery of Bermuda's economic fortunes, which had fallen upon hard times after the Civil War, the United States began to use its consul to facilitate trade between the United States and Bermuda. Consul Allen was required to report, again in detail, on Bermuda's imports, exports, and shipping. He was required to report, for instance, on the number and types of breeding cattle on the island, on the number of refrigerators in use (there were none), and on the fruit culture of Bermuda.

In October 1884, in response to an official request, Allen provided his government with a detailed report of the duties of the consul.

Bermuda, Charles M. Allen, Consul

In compliance with the request of the Department as stated in Circular dated August 21st 1884, I have respectfully to report that a large share of the business of this consulate is in certifying invoices, and the greater portion of the revenue is derived therefrom. Next in importance is the execution of debenture certificates, as a large part of the merchandise from Great Britain comes via New York in bond.

The export from the port of Hamilton to the United States during the year 1883 consisting principally of vegetables amounted to the sum of $540,008.00 as per invoices certified at this consulate. The whole amount of fees received at this consulate for the three quarters of the present year amounts to $1,962.00 of which $1,207.00 was for invoice certificates and $562.00 for the execution of debenture certificates.

Vegetables are shipped during the spring and early summer months and as the market value varies much, many times falling off or advancing in the same day, more than 25 percent as the supply comes freely or otherwise, to make up the cargo. There is a disposition among the shippers to invoice at the lowest rate and it is necessary one should carefully watch the market and by so doing and insisting upon the full market value, I feel sure there has been saved during the present year not less than $4,000.00 to the revenue of the United States.

A consul here requires some help during four months of the year, as on the days of the sailing of the New York steamer, there are from twenty to thirty invoices to be certified, all within three hours of the departure of the vessel and the triplicates to be prepared for transmission. The only way for one person to do his work would be to let the triplicates remain for transmission by the next vessel.

These islands have become a favorite resort for a large number of American invalids and others during the winter months, nearly, if not quite eight hundred having visited here during the last winter, and, while they are a source of revenue to the government of the United States, they are often a severe toll upon the consul, to whom they look for advice and required information, and as many bring letters from prominent citizens, they cannot be passed without some attention. As the hotel accommodation has been greatly extended this year, it is presumed this travel will increase, as many have heretofore been deterred from coming for want of accommodation on their arrival.

Chas. M. Allen, Consul
United States Consulate at Bermuda
October 6, 1884

In 1886, Charles was sixty-four years old, Susan was almost sixty, and they had been married for thirty-eight years. Charles could look back on twenty-five years of service to his country as consul at Bermuda. In this anniversary year, Charles and Susan held a Washington's birthday celebration on February 22 at the Whitney Institute in Flatts. A contemporary newspaper account described the festivities.[14]

Washington's Birthday in the Bermudas. A private letter from a Springfield tourist in the Bermudas gives this brief description of the way Washington's birthday was signaled in that bit of the Queen's dominion: First, a large merchant steamer laden with 550 bales of cotton and numberless bushels of corn went on the reefs just outside. She was en route from New Orleans to Bremen. This was at sunrise. In the afternoon, dingy, tub and sack races took place at or near the Princess hotel. In the evening, by invitation, tourists from the states were invited to a musical and theatrical entertainment at the Flatts, four miles from Hamilton. The entertainment was given by Mr. and Mrs. C. M. Allen in honor of the day. Mr. Allen has been American Consul, or rather consul from the United States, for 25 years. A fine engraving of Washington was placed conspicuously over the stage which was decorated with the United States and British flags. At the conclusion the guests—all Americans—were invited to partake of refreshments in a lower hall of the building.

🏵 In the summer of 1886, Charles took his first leave of absence in four years to visit family and friends in the United States. Also in this year the only known tribute to Consul Allen's twenty-five years of service was published in the *National Republican* newspaper.[15]

A Veteran Consul's Record.

Charles M. Allen, the Second Oldest Officer in the Service. C. M. Allen, United States consul at Bermuda, was appointed in November, 1861, and, with the exception of consul Sprague, at Gibraltar, is in point of service the oldest member of the consular corps. He has always displayed ability and energy in the discharge of his consular duties, and his reports have contained much of value to the exporters of the United States. Thus far he has been retained by the present administration, and should he remain in the service he will undoubtedly continue the excellent record he has made.

The portrait from which the accompanying cut was engraved was taken eleven years ago, Mr. Allen now being 64 years of age.[16]

Although the consular post at Bermuda is not rated as one of the highest class, yet, at the time of Mr. Allen's appointment in that place, it was one of the most important in the service. At the breaking out of the late war there were twenty appointments of consuls made who were known as "war consuls." They constituted a secret service of the government. Bermuda was a headquarters for blockade runners and agents of the confederacy. The consulate being at an English town, Mr. Allen's duties in looking after the interests of the United States were particularly delicate. His great ability was shown by the marked success which his efforts met. He was indefatigable in his exertions to serve the Union, and, at the same time, always continued on the most pleasant terms with the English authorities. During the four years of the war his post ranked next in importance to only Nassau.

Mr. Allen has never received a reprimand from the State Department during his long service. Having suffered from asthma for many years, and finding no climate to suit his health as well as that of Bermuda, he has never expressed a desire to change his post.

Mr. Allen antedates Mr. Adamson, now consul at Panama, whose appointment in the service was not made until four months later.

In March 1887, Charles's stepmother, Polly Vaile Allen, died at the age of seventy-seven. The last tie to his Vermont childhood was gone.

Also in 1887 Charles's son, Charles Fletcher, wrote a series of three articles titled "Blockade Running" for the *Pittsburgh Dispatch*. The articles included sketches from watercolor paintings by "E. J. Brooks, brother of Shirley Brooks, editor of Punch." E. J. Brooks was, in fact, Charles's friend, Edward James, whom many believed was the brother of Shirley Brooks. There is no conclusive evidence on this point. These colorful and anecdotal articles, which are quite interesting, contain many vignettes drawn from Charles Fletcher's impressionable youth in Bermuda and undoubtedly from the experiences of his father. Charles Fletcher and his wife lost their only son, Henry, the following year. Henry, age ten, who died of pneumonia on February 24, 1888, was the first grandchild of Charles and Susan.

The old patriot's years and labors were drawing to a close.

Consul Allen's last dispatch was written at the consulate at Hamilton on October 16, 1888. At that time, he was about to begin his twenty-seventh year as U.S. consul at Bermuda. Never tiring in his efforts to see his country well represented on distant shores, it is both appropriate and poignant that in his last letter he requested a new U.S. flag.

It was the sad duty of Charles Maxwell Allen's old friend, J. B. Heyl, to announce the death of the consul to the Department of State.

United States Consulate, Bermuda
December 24, 1888

Hon. T. F. Bayard,
Secretary of State
Washington

Sir:

It is my painful duty to inform you of the death of Consul C. M. Allen which took place this day 5 A.M. of congestion of the lungs. Mr. Allen has been a sufferer for many years.

Does the Government pay funeral expenses and when does Mr. Allen's pay cease.

I have the Honour to be,
Your obedient servant,
J. B. Heyl

◉ The *Bermuda Royal Gazette* paid touching tribute to Consul Allen, who had won the admiration and affection of the people who had greeted him with open hostility upon his arrival in Bermuda in 1861.[17]

The obsequies of the late C. M. Allen, United States consul at Bermuda, were largely attended on Christmas Day to Smith Parish Church from Wistowe. His Excellency the Governor, Lieutenant General Edward-Newdigate Newdigate, C.B. attended by Captain H. L. Gallway, A.D.C., and representatives from the Army and Navy, and the Civil service, were in attendance. Mr. Allen in his long and intimate intercourse with this community, won the respect and esteem of all classes, who sympathize with his family in their bereavement.

Upon the stately obelisk over his grave are inscribed the words[18]

CHARLES MAXWELL
ALLEN
U.S. CONSUL AT
BERMUDA
FROM 1861 TO 1888

Born at Heath, Mass., 1821
Died at Bermuda, 1888

In the place where
the tree falleth there
it shall lie.

Charles's wife of nearly forty years, Susan Elizabeth Richards Allen, lived on in Bermuda for another two decades. She died peacefully at her home, Wistowe, on April 1, 1909.

The veteran consul in his later years. Photograph by Henry Seldon Allen (Courtesy of Alice Ross de Kok)

Nearly a quarter of a century after the death of Charles Maxwell Allen, his son Charles Fletcher, who had become a published poet and author, wrote a book about the life of David Crockett, which now has become recommended reading for schoolchildren.

Charles Fletcher Allen's tribute to this great American patriot was perhaps also a fitting tribute to Charles Maxwell Allen.

It is hoped that this unpretentious volume may help to a better understanding of the life and motives of a man whose footsteps went into no dark places, and who died an honor to his race and his countrymen—a hero sans peur et sans reproche.[19]

Schedule of
Blockade-Running Vessels

On July 13, 1864, Consul Allen submitted "a statement of the arrivals and departures of vessels employed in running the blockade of the Southern ports of the United States, and of those bringing merchandise here for that trade, from the first of January 1862 to the 30 June 1864." His report consists of twelve handwritten pages with 302 arrivals listed.

Allen's report is presented in columnar form. It was prepared in arrival date order and consists of the following information:

Date of Arrival
Class
Name
Master
Tonnage
Where From
Where For
Cargo Inboard/Bales
Cargo Outboard/Bales
Agent
Date of Departure
Remarks

Allen undoubtedly used as his sources for developing this report not only his dispatches but also the *Bermuda Royal Gazette* and, where available, cargo manifests from the Custom House. He certainly did not have access to the papers of blockade-runners.

The information reported by Allen is often incomplete, particularly for the year 1862. His official records had been stolen early in 1863, and, as a result, for this period he relied principally on information in the *Bermuda Royal Gazette*. By mid-1863 it appears that Allen had some access to Custom House records, as he was more often able to obtain information on a vessel's tonnage and the number of bales of cotton arriving at and departing from St. George's.

In a very small number of instances, some blockade-runners were reported in Allen's dispatches but were not included in this report and vice versa. Allen's report includes a great number of vessels bringing coal to Bermuda, none of which were ever mentioned in his dispatches. Since these vessels did not run the blockade, he did not report them to the Department of State.

There are numerous discrepancies in arrival and departure dates of vessels between the dispatches and the report. There seems to be no discernable reason for this.

Once in Bermuda, Consul Allen quickly learned to differentiate between the classes of sailing vessels that called at St. George's. In his dispatches, as well as in this report, he identified each kind of vessel as it arrived in port as a barque, brig, schooner, steamer, or ship. The distinctions between each of these sailing vessels are described in the following list:

Barque: 3 or more masts
Brig: 2 masts, at least 1 square rigged
Paddle steamer: propelled by one or more paddle wheels driven by a steam engine
Schooner: fore and aft sails on two or more masts
Side wheel steamer: boats with paddle wheels on the sides driven by a steam engine
Steamer: driven by a steam engine

It is remarkable that Allen was able to create as accurate and detailed a report as he did. He compiled this report during what was the busiest period of blockade-running through Bermuda, when his time was almost fully occupied in investigating and reporting on blockade-running activities to the Department of State. It is ironic that the information requested by the Department was already in their hands in the form of Allen's regular and meticulous dispatches.

As noted previously, this report is the first draft of the history of blockade-running in Bermuda. It is of additional significance because it was compiled by an eyewitness to these events. In Allen's own words, it "may be of some use as a matter of reference hereafter."

Date Of Arrival	Class	Name	Master	Tonnage	Where From	Where For	Cargo Inboard	Bales	Cargo Outboard	Bales	Agent	Date Of Departure	Remarks
1862 Feb 17	Schr	Pearl	Beneridge		Beaufort, NC		Turpentine				J. T. Gilbert		Wrecked off the Islands
1862 Feb 20	Str	Nashville	Peagram		Southampton						J. T. Bourne	Apr 24	C. S. Privateer
1862 Feb 28	Str	Economist			Liverpool	Nassau	General				J. T. Bourne	Mar 5	
1862 Mar 20	Str	Bermuda	Westendoff		Liverpool	Nassau	General		General		J. T. Bourne	Apr 22	
1862 Mar 20	Str	Southwick	Starkes		London	Nassau	General		General		J. T. Bourne	Mar 25	
1862 Mar 31	Ship	Ella	Carter		Liverpool	Nassau	General		Part of inward		J. T. Bourne	May 15	
1862 Mar 31	Str	Herald	Tate		London	Nassau	General		Inward		J. T. Bourne	Jun 11	
1862 Apr 19	Barque	Rosetta	Jenkins		Cardiff	Nassau	Coal				J. T. Bourne		
1862 Apr 19	Str	Economist	Burge		Nassau	Liverpool	Cotton etc.	650	Cotton etc.	650		Apr 28	
1862 Apr 19	Str	Stettin	Johnson		Falmouth	Nassau	General				J. T. Bourne	Apr 22	
1862 May 1	Str	Southwick	Starkes		Nassau	Liverpool	Cotton		Inward		J. T. Bourne	May 5	
1862 May 6	Str	Gladiator	Hord	467	Nassau	Liverpool	Cotton		Inward		J. T. Bourne	May 8	
1862 Jun 6	Schr	Anna E. Berry	Gaskill		Wilmington	Liverpool	Cotton		Inward		R. S. Musson		In Port

Date Of Arrival	Class	Name	Master	Tonnage	Where From	Where For	Cargo Inboard	Bales	Cargo Outboard	Bales	Agent	Date Of Departure	Remarks
1862 Jun 11	Str	Stanley	Haste		Liverpool	Nassau	General		General		J. T. Bourne	Jun 26	
1862 Jun 13	Str	Leopard	Kaisbeck		Cardiff	Nassau	Ballast		Ballast		J. T. Bourne	Jun 13	
1862 Jun 19	Str	Adela	Walker		England	Nassau	Arms		Ballast		J. T. Bourne	Jul 3	
1862 Jun 30	Str	Lodona	Luckie		Hull	Nassau	General		Inward		J. T. Bourne	Jul 12	
1862 Jul 1	Str	Columbia	Leslie		Hamburg	Nassau	Arms, etc.		Inward		J. T. Fisher	Jul 9	
1862 Jul 20	Str	Anglia	Newlands		Bristol	Nassau	General		Inward		J. T. Bourne	Aug 8	
1862 Jul 21	Str	Keronese	Abbott		Nassau	New York	Coal				J. T. Bourne	Aug 12	
1862 Jul 28	Str	Phoebe	Johns		London		General		Inward		J. T. Bourne		
1862 Aug 2	Str	Peterhoff	Higlaly?		Hull	Nassau	General		Inward		J. T. Bourne	Aug 13	
1862 Aug 7	Str	Julia	Cope [?]		Sidney		Coal				J. T. Bourne		
1862 Aug 12	Schr	Luna	O'Brian		Halifax		Coal				J. T. Bourne		
1862 Aug 20	Ship	Drogheda	Beundige		Cardiff		Coal				J. T. Bourne		
1862 Aug 23	Str	Gladiator	Hord	467	Liverpool		General						

Date Of Arrival	Class	Name	Master	Tonnage	Where From	Where For	Cargo Inboard	Bales	Cargo Outboard	Bales	Agent	Date Of Departure	Remarks
1862 Aug 27	Brig	M. A. Horton	Wilks		Sidney	Halifax	Coal		Ballast		J. A. Atwood	Sep 13	
1862 Aug 27	Str	H. Pinckney	Halpin		London		General				J. T. Bourne		
1862 Sep 3	Str	Minho	Parke		Charleston	St. Johns NB	Cotton	500	General		J. T. Bourne	Sep 26	
1862 Sep 3	Barque	Almoner	Lampha		Cardiff	Turks Island	Coal		Ballast		J. T. Bourne	Sep 18	
1862 Sep 5	Str	Merrimac	Rowe		London		General				J. T. Bourne		
1862 Sep 15	Str	Ouachita	Gilpin		England	Madeira	General		Inward		J. T. Fisher	Sep 30	
1862 Sep 20	Barque	Monequash	Griffith		Nassau		Coal				J. T. Bourne		
1862 Sep 20	Str	Gladiator	Hord	467	Nassau	Liverpool	Cotton		Inward		J. T. Bourne	Sep 30	
1862 Oct 11	Ship	Harisburg	Wiswell		Cardiff		Coal				J. T. Bourne		
1862 Oct 17	Ship	Ella	Carter		Liverpool		Coal						
1862 Oct 17	Str	Herald	Coxetter		Nassau	St. Johns NB	Cotton	340	General		J. T. Bourne	Oct 25	
1862 Dec 31	Schr	Golden Line			Halifax		Powder, Caps				J. T. Bourne		Wrecked off the Islands
1862 Dec 31	Str	Princess Royal			Halifax	Nassau	General				J. T. Bourne		

Date of Arrival	Class	Name	Master	Tonnage	Where From	Where For	Cargo Inboard	Bales	Cargo Outboard	Bales	Agent	Date of Departure	Remarks
1863 Jan 20	Str	Miriam			London	Nassau	General		Inward		J. T. Bourne		
1863 Jan 20	Str	Cornubia	Burroughs				General	300			J. T. Bourne		
1863 Jan 20	Str	H. Pinckney		571	London		Cotton	304			J. T. Bourne		
1863 Jan 20	Str	Cornubia	Burroughs	588	Wilmington	Nassau			Inward		J. T. Bourne		
1863 Jan 20	Schr	Alma	Hicks		Beaufort, NC				Liquor, etc.		J. T. Bourne	Mar 6	
1863 Mar 20	Brig	Dashing Wave			London		General						
1863 Mar 22	Str	Cornubia		588	Wilmington		Cotton	314					
1863 Mar 22	Schr	St. George	Fennel		Baltimore							Apr 10	
1863 Mar 24	Str	Genl. Beauregard	Coxetter		Charleston	Nassau	Cotton	1026				Apr 7	
1863 Apr 10	Schr	Alma			From sea	Beaufort			Liquor, etc.			May 12	
1863 Apr 16	Str	R. E. Lee	Wilkinson		Wilmington		Cotton	520				Apr 24	
1863 Apr 16	Str	Merrimac	Porter			Nassau						Apr 24	
1863 Apr 16	Str	Laura Anne			Liverpool		Cotton			331		Apr 17	

Date Of Arrival	Class	Name	Master	Tonnage	Where From	Where For	Cargo Inboard	Bales	Cargo Outboard	Bales	Agent	Date Of Departure	Remarks
1863 Apr 22	Str	Cornubia	Burroughs	588	Wilmington		Cotton	371				May 8	
1862 May 6	Str	Eugenie	Halpin	239	London	Nassau						May 18	
1863 May 15	Brig	Vivid			Sunderland		Coal					Jun 5	
1863 May 22	Str	R. E. Lee	Wilkinson		Wilmington		Cotton		Cotton	251		Jun 5	
1863 May 22	Str	Miriam	Pitman		Nassau		Cotton		Inward			May 24	
1863 May 23	Str	Raccoon	Harris		Hamburgh	Nassau	Ballast		Ballast			May 23	
1863 May 29	Str	Eugenie	Halpin		Wilmington		Cotton					Jun 11	
1863 May 29	Str	Cornubia	Burroughs		Wilmington		Cotton					Jun 5	
1863 Jun 1	Brig	Chebucto?	Brown		Cardiff		Coal						
1863 Jun 11	Str	Emma	Leslie		Wilmington		Cotton	895				Jul 7	
1863 Jun 11	Str	Venus	Goldsmidt		London		General		Inward			Jun 13	
1863 Jun 15	Str	Lord Clyde	Willie		Cardiff		General		General			Jun 20	
1863 Jun 22	Str	Lady Davis	Gayle		Wilmington	Nassau	Cotton	17	General			Jul 9	Cornubia

Date Of Arrival	Class	Name	Master	Tonnage	Where From	Where For	Cargo Inboard	Bales	Cargo Outboard	Bales	Agent	Date Of Departure	Remarks
1863 Jun 22	Str	H. Pinckney	Johns		Liverpool	Halifax	General		Cotton	440		Jun 30	
1863 Jun 24	Str	Eugenie		239	Wilmington	Nassau	Cotton	318				Jul 11	
1863 Jun 7	Str	Ella			Halifax	Nassau	Ballast					Nov 2	
1863 Jul 11	Str	R. E. Lee	Wilkinson		Wilmington		Cotton	583				Nov 22	
1863 Jul 13	Str	Hansa	Randle		London		General					Nov 21	
1863 Jul 13	Brig	Resolution	Taylor			London			Cotton	583		Nov 9	
1863 Jul 16	Str	Florida	Maffitt		From sea	Cruise	Silver bars					Jul 22	C. S. Privateer
1863 Jul 18	Str	Venus	Goldsmidt		Wilmington	Nassau	Cotton	780	General			Aug 12	
1863 Jul 20	Str	Spaulding			St. John's, N.B.		General		Inward			Jul 22	
1863 Jul 20	Brig	Eagle			Liverpool				Cotton	367		Jul 17	
1863 Jul 21	Str	Gladiator	Hora		Wilmington		Cotton	1130				Aug 1	
1863 Jul 22	Str	H. Pinckney	Johns		Halifax		General		Cotton	950		Aug 29	
1863 Jul 22	Str	Despatch	Johnson		Liverpool	Nassau	General					Jul 25	

Date Of Arrival	Class	Name	Master	Tonnage	Where From	Where For	Cargo Inboard	Bales	Cargo Outboard	Bales	Agent	Date Of Departure	Remarks
1863 Jul 25	Str	Miriam	Holmes		London	London	General		Cotton	936		Aug 22	
1863 Jul 27	Str	Lady Davis			Wilmington	Nassau	Cotton	236				Aug 14	Cornubia
1863 Jul 27	Str	Advance	Willie		Wilmington	Nassau	Cotton	500				Aug 15	Lord Clyde
1863 Jul 27	Str	Banshee			Wilmington	Nassau	Cotton	446	General			Aug 15	
1863 Jul 27	Str	Eugenie		264					General			Aug 8	
1863 Jul 30	Str	Mail	Gilpin	99	Nassau		Ballast		Ballast			Jul 31	
1863 Jul 30	Brig	Lizzie Bernard	Bernard	380	New York	New York	Provisions		General			Aug 14	
1863 Jul 30	Schr	Kent	Perry	81	New York	Nassau	General						
1863 Jul 31	Brig	Levant	Evans	198	St. John's, N.B.	Liverpool	General		Ballast				
1863 Jul 31	Str	Gibraltar	Reed	387	Liverpool	Nassau	Inward					Aug 12	
1863 Aug 3	Str	Juno	Taylor	155	Bristol	Nassau	Inward					Sep 10	
1863 Aug 4	Str	Fanny & Jenny	Blakely	509	Halifax	Nassau	General					Aug 26	
1863 Aug 5	Str	Don Pinchon		244	London		General						

Date Of Arrival	Class	Name	Master	Tonnage	Where From	Where For	Cargo Inboard	Bales	Cargo Outboard	Bales	Agent	Date Of Departure	Remarks
1863 Aug 6	Str	Florida		1451	Nassau		Coal		Cotton	2600		Sep 19	
1863 Aug 11	Barque	E. Jenkins	Conway	666	Cardiff		Coal						
1863 Aug 10	Str	Phantom	Porter	266	Wilmington		Cotton						
1863 Aug 13	Schr	Dundee	Lomar	125	Nassau		Coal						
1863 Aug 13	Brig	Kenstral	Qurk	212									
1863 Aug 14	Brig	Eliza	Simpson	195									
1863 Aug 14	Brig	Eliza Wilson	Scott	270	Nassau	Liverpool	Coal		Cotton	589		Sep 25	
1863 Aug 14	Str	Elizabeth	Luckwood	676	Wilmington		Cotton	701					
1863 Aug 18	Str	Ella and Annie	Bonnear	766	Wilmington	Kingston, Ja.	Cotton	1049				Sep 9	
1863 Aug 18	Schr	Harriet	Pitchard	46	Nassau		Wines						
1863 Aug 18	Str	Flora	James	359	London		General						
1863 Aug 18	Brig	James				London			Cotton	400			
1863 Aug 19	Brig	Isabell	Howell		Nassau		Coal						

Date Of Arrival	Class	Name	Master	Tonnage	Where From	Where For	Cargo Inboard	Bales	Cargo Outboard	Bales	Agent	Date Of Departure	Remarks
1863 Aug 19	Str	Bondigo	Webber	178	Liverpool	Nassau	General					Sep 2	
1863 Aug 19	Str	R. E. Lee	Wilkinson	360	Wilmington	Nassau	Cotton	607					
1863 Aug 22	Brig	Minstrell	Tardy	182	Cardiff	Nassau	General						
1863 Aug 22	Str	Boston	Hilton	224	Halifax	Nassau						Jun 29, 1864	
1863 Aug 24	Ship	Ernestine	Benson	410	Cardiff		Coal						
1863 Aug 24	Barque	Westfield	Crispin	301	Nassau		General						
1863 Aug 26	Str	Eugenie	Fry	239	Wilmington	Nassau	Cotton	401				Sep 4	
1863 Aug 26	Schr	Harkaway	Frith	59	Nassau		General						
1863 Aug 26	Ship	St. Paul	Durant	299	Nassau	New York	General		Ballast			Aug 28	
1863 Aug 27	Schr	Resolution	Sutherland	56	Nassau		General						
1863 Aug 27	Schr	Jessie Banfield	Mitchell	122	Cardiff		Coal		Cotton	420			
1863 Aug 29	Brig	Millicent	Gilden	219	Cardiff	Liverpool	General		Cotton	420			
1863 Sep 1	Barque	Oden	Greenough	440	Cardiff	Nassau	Coal		Ballast			Oct 23	

Date Of Arrival	Class	Name	Master	Tonnage	Where From	Where For	Cargo Inbound	Bales	Cargo Outboard	Bales	Agent	Date Of Departure	Remarks
1863 Sep 2	Schr	Julia	Stream	79	Nassau	Nassau	General		Ballast			Sep 14	
1863 Sep 5	Ship	Nebucer	Fishwick	285	London							Oct 23	
1863 Sep 7	Str	Hansa	Randall	257	Wilmington	Nassau	Cotton	493				Sep 14	
1863 Sep 8	Str	Venus	Murry	365	Wilmington	Nassau	Cotton	410				Sep 16	
1863 Sep 8	Brig	Ann Catherine	Lloyd	210	Cardiff	New York	Coal		Ballast			Nov 9	
1863 Sep 8	Str	Cornubia	Gayle	585	Wilmington	Nassau	Cotton	384	General			Sep 18	
1863 Sep 11	Ship	Corona	Bailey	250	Cardiff								
1863 Sep 15	Str	Phantom	Porter	266	Wilmington	Nassau	General					Sep 19	
1863 Sep 15	Str	Ella and Annie	Bonnear	766	From sea	Nassau						Oct 23	Disabled and returned
1863 Sep 15	Brig	Melina	Stabb	150	Nassau							Oct 1	
1863 Sep 16	Str	Flora	James	359	Wilmington	Nassau		537	General			Oct 3	
1863 Sep 19	Schr	H. Gardner	Name?		Cardiff		Coal						
1863 Sep 19	Barque	Pedanticus	Buckholder		Swansea	St. Thomas	Coal		Ballast			Nov 21	

Date Of Arrival	Class	Name	Master	Tonnage	Where From	Where For	Cargo Inboard	Bales	Cargo Outboard	Bales	Agent	Date Of Departure	Remarks
1863 Sep 21	Barque	Neried	Jolly		Liverpool		Coal and general						
1863 Sep 21	Brig	J. Howell			Nassau	Liverpool			Cotton	309		Nov 18	
1863 Sep 27	Str	St. Thomas	Peters		Liverpool	Liverpool	General		Cotton	247		Oct 19	
1863 Sep 27	Brig	Lewellen	Gibson	262	Cardiff	Liverpool	Coal		Cotton	434	J. T. Bourne	Nov 18	
1863 Sep 27	Brig	Nero	Hamlyn	199	Cardiff	St. Mary's	Coal		Ballast		J. T. Bourne	Oct 8	
1863 Sep 27	Ship	Lemuella	James		London	Demerara	General		Ballast		J. T. Bourne	Oct 31	
1863 Sep 27	Str	A. D. Vance	Cresbow	902	Wilmington	Nassau	Cotton	530				Oct 6	
1863 Sep 27	Brig	Eliza Nelson	Scott	270		Liverpool	Cotton	509				Oct 20	
1863 Sep 28	Str	Dee	Holmes	215	London	Nassau	General		General			Oct 3	
1863 Sep 28	Barque	Nutfield	Crispin	301	London	Liverpool	General		Cotton	627		Nov 1	
1863 Oct 6	Barque	Morning Star	Key	480	Cardiff		Coal				W. P. Campbell		
1863 Oct 8	Schr	Zygia	Simpkins	137	Liverpool	St. John's, N.B.	General		Ballast		W. P. Campbell	Oct 16	
1863 Oct 12	Str	Alice	Egan	803	Wilmington	Nassau	Cotton	782	General			Oct 16	

Date of Arrival	Class	Name	Master	Tonnage	Where From	Where For	Cargo Inboard	Bales	Cargo Outboard	Bales	Agent	Date of Departure	Remarks
1863 Oct 12	Brig	Rover's Bride	James	111	London	Liverpool	General		Cotton	380		Nov 12	
1863 Oct 13	Brig	Glendower	Walsham	317	London	Liverpool	General		Cotton	625		Jan 8	
1863 Oct 15	Str	Cornubia	Gayle	585	Wilmington	Nassau	Cotton	854	General			Jan 4	
1863 Oct 15	Str	Flora	Gillham	359	Wilmington	Nassau	Cotton	540	General			Jan 2	
1863 Oct 20	Brig	A. V. Goodhue	Bissir	151	New York	New York	General		Ballast			Jan 6	
1863 Oct 20	Str	Dee	Buss	215	Wilmington		Cotton	316			J. T. Bourne		
1863 Oct 24	Schr	J. Smith	Gorley	157	London	London	General		Cotton	316	J. T. Bourne	Jan 24	
1863 Oct 24	Schr	Zampher	Wakeman	154	London	Liverpool	General					Jan 24	
1863 Oct 26	Brig	James Menchis	Mitchell	209	Cardiff	New York	Coal		Ballast		J. T. Bourne	Jan 18	
1863 Oct 26	Str	R. E. Lee	Knox	360	Halifax	Nassau	General		General		J. T. Bourne	Jan 4	
1863 Oct 26	Barque	Panama	Dondall	312	Newport		Coal				J. T. Bourne		
1863 Oct 27	Str	A. D. Vance	Gosher	902	Wilmington	Liverpool	Cotton	540	Cotton	526	J. T. Bourne		
1863 Oct 27	Ship	Neubla	Leggett		Cardiff		Coal						

Date Of Arrival	Class	Name	Master	Tonnage	Where From	Where For	Cargo Inboard	Bales	Cargo Outboard	Bales	Agent	Date Of Departure	Remarks
1863 Oct 27	Ship	Aline	Legarde	801	Cardiff		Coal						
1863 Oct 28	Barque	Lady Bute	Brown	348	Swansea		Coal						
1863 Oct 28	Ship	Hilga	Russell		Liverpool		Coal						
1863 Oct 29	Brig	Mary Garland	James	227	Cardiff		Coal				J. T. Bourne		
1863 Nov 2	Str	Heroine	Page	108	Glasgow		Ballast		360 cases merchandixe			Dec 12	
1863 Nov 2	Barque	Glacier	Fisher	480	Halifax		Coal						
1863 Nov 2	Schr	Eaton	Locket	122	Cardiff		Coal				W. P. Campbell		
1863 Nov 2	Schr	Eitae	Lacht	122	London		Saltpeter				W. P. Campbell		
1863 Nov 2	Barque	Ceres	Parson	217	Cardiff	Demerara	Coal		Ballast			Dec 15	
1863 Nov 5	Str	Powerful		119	Quebec	Havana	General		Inward			Oct 6 [sic]	
1863 Nov 9	Str	Ceres	Horsey	217	London	Nassau	General		Inward & 50 boxes [illegible]			Dec 3	
1863 Nov 9	Barque	Jane Gordie	Hunter	246	Swansea		Coal						

Date Of Arrival	Class	Name	Master	Tonnage	Where From	Where For	Cargo Inboard	Bales	Cargo Outboard	Bales	Agent	Date Of Departure	Remarks
1863 Nov 9	Str	City of Petersburgh	Fuller	426	Greenock	Nassau	General		Inward			Nov 14	
1863 Nov 16	Schr	Mary Banfield	Thomas	123	Liverpool	Western Island	Salt		Ballast		W. P. Campbell	Dec 9	
1863 Nov 16	Str	Gibraltar	Reed	387	Wilmington	Liverpool	Cotton	330	Cotton	330	J. T. Bourne	Nov 21	
1863 Nov 16	Schr	H. Gordon	Nance			Liverpool	Cotton	284			J. T. Bourne		
1863 Nov 16	Schr	Alert	Newman		Nassau		Tobacco				J. T. Bourne		
1863 Nov 18	Barque	Prowess	Brown		Cardiff		Coal				J. T. Bourne		
1863 Nov 18	Str	Flora	Horner		Wilmington	Nassau	Cotton	654	800 Casks Mdse		J. T. Bourne	Dec 4	
1863 Nov 19	Str	Coquette	Cosbett	390	Liverpool	Nassau	Str Machinery		Inward		J. T. Bourne	Dec 12	
1863 Nov 19	Barque	Jane Dowell	Page	410	Cardiff	Nassau	Coal		Cotton	338	J. T. Bourne	Jan 23	
1863 Nov 20	Brig	Ella Sophia	Bandell	202	Cardiff		Coal						
1863 Nov 20	Schr	Honesta	Drury	135	Liverpool	Nassau	General		Ballast		Johnson & Crofts	Jan 22	
1863 Nov 22	Ship	Ariosta	Patten	837	Cardiff	Nassau	Coal		Inward		J. T. Bourne	Nov 23	
1863 Nov 23	Brig	Talod	Strand	240	Cardiff		Coal				T. J. Hurst		

Date of Arrival	Class	Name	Master	Tonnage	Where From	Where For	Cargo Inboard	Bales	Cargo Outboard	Bales	Agent	Date of Departure	Remarks
1863 Nov 28	Brig	Daisy	Pyerson	337	Cardiff		Coal				J. T. Bourne		
1863 Nov 30	Str	Denbigh	McNevin	162	Waterford Island	Nassau	Ballast		31 Casks Mdse		J. T. Bourne	Dec 5	
1863 Nov 30	Brig	Frank	Jones	131	Halifax		General				J. T. Bourne		
1863 Nov 30	Ship	Enterprise	Scott	291	Liverpool		Coal				J. T. Bourne		
1863 Nov 30	Schr	G. O. Bigelow	Sabeston				Coal		Salt		J. T. Bourne	Nov 25	
1863 Dec 10	Str	Ranger	Holmes		Plymouth		Ballast				J. T. Bourne		
1863 Dec 10	Schr	The Dare	Skinner		Liverpool	Nassau	280 Pkgs Mdse				J. T. Bourne	Jan 2	
1863 Dec 20	Str	Flora	Horner		Wilmington	Halifax	Cotton	600	Ballast		J. T. Bourne	Jan 9	Went down at sea
1863 Dec 24	Str	Will O' Wisp	Capper		Glasgow	Halifax	Ballast		General		J. T. Bourne	Jan 1	
1863 Dec 28	Barque	Cambia	Morris		Liverpool		Coal				J. T. Bourne		
1863 Dec 28	Str	Vesta	Eustace		Falmouth		102 cases mdse		128 cases mdse		J. T. Bourne	Jan 2	
1863 Dec 28	Ship	Ann Adale	Norton		Cardiff		Coal				J. T. Bourne		
1863 Dec 28	Schr	Legate			Turks Island		Salt				J. T. Bourne		

Date Of Arrival	Class	Name	Master	Tonnage	Where From	Where For	Cargo Inboard	Bales	Cargo Outboard	Bales	Agent	Date Of Departure	Remarks
1863 Dec 28	Schr	Purse	Hester		Wilmington		Turpentine						Struck on reefs and sunk
1864 Jan 1	Str	Nola	Pitman		Greenock		General				J. T. Gilbert		
1864 Jan 1	Brig	Nina	Squires	205	Liverpool	Nassau	General				J. T. Bourne	Jan 14	
1864 Jan 4	Schr	Union	Corwin	74	St. Thomas		General				Johnson & Crofts		
1864 Jan 7	Brig	Lissie Bliss	Pearson	369	Cardiff		Coal						
1864 Jan 9	Str	A. D. Vance	Crossan	902	Nassau		20 Casks Mdse						
1864 Jan 11	Str	Dee	Bier	215	Wilmington	Nassau	Cotton	465	General			Jan 30	
1864 Jan 11	Barque	Agrippina	McQueen	275	London		General				J. T. Bourne		
1864 Jan 12	Str	City of Petersburgh	Fuller	426	Wilmington	St. John's, N.B.	Cotton	798	General		R. S. Musson & Co.	Jan 15	
1864 Jan 13	Str	Nutfield	Hawks	402	London	Nassau	Ballast		General		W. P. Campbell	Jan 30	
1864 Jan 14	Str	Don	Roberts	235	Wilmington	Nassau	Cotton	561	General			Jan 29	
1864 Jan 18	Str	Index	Jarvis	363	Falmouth				848 Pkg Mdse		W. P. Campbell	Mar 29	

Date Of Arrival	Class	Name	Master	Tonnage	Where From	Where For	Cargo Inboard	Bales	Cargo Outboard	Bales	Agent	Date Of Departure	Remarks
1864 Jan 19	Str	Emily	Halpin	253	Cardiff	Nassau			1426 Pkg Mdse		J. T. Bourne	Feb 3	
1864 Jan 22	Ship	Ella	Leggett	889	Liverpool	Liverpool	Coal & General		Cotton	1521	J. T. Bourne	May 18	
1864 Jan 22	Brig	Hans Gude	Due	260	France		450 Tons Salt		Cotton	524	W. P. Campbell	Mar 5	
1864 Jan 25	Str	Minnie	Gilpin	253	Cardiff	Nassau			869 Pkg Mdse		J. T. Bourne	Mar 26	
1864 Jan 27	Barque	Indefatigable	Ramstadt	584	Cardiff	Nassau	Coal	829			W. P. Campbell		
1864 Jan 27	Str	Eugenie	Porter	239	Nassau	Liverpool	Ballast				J. T. Bourne	Apr 8	
1864 Jan 27	Str	Caladonia	Dutton	115	Glasgow	Nassau			149 Pkg Mdse		F. W. G. Hurst	Feb 6	
1864 Jan 30	Barque	Costennico	Moulin	229	London	Kingston, Ja.	General				J. T. Bourne	Mar 1	
1864 Feb 9	Str	Will O' Wisp	Capper	117	Halifax	Nassau			278 Pkg Mdse		F. W. G. Hurst	Mar 13	
1864 Feb 10	Str	A. D. Vance	Guthrie	902	Wilmington	Nassau	Cotton	570	592 Pkg Mdse		F. W. G. Hurst	Mar 13	
1864 Feb 12	Str	H. Pinckney	Johns	571	Plymouth		443 Pkg Mdse				J. T. Bourne	May 17	
1864 Feb 12	Str	City of Petersburgh	Fuller	502	Wilmington	St. John's, N.B.			General			May 29	
1864 Feb 12	Str	Hansa	Atkinson	257	Wilmington	Nassau			General			May 26	

Date Of Arrival	Class	Name	Master	Tonnage	Where From	Where For	Cargo Inbound	Bales	Cargo Outboard	Bales	Agent	Date Of Departure	Remarks
1864 Feb 12	Str	Coquette	Carter	390	Wilmington	Nassau	Cotton	850				May 3	
1864 Feb 12	Str	Thistle	Hora	305	Liverpool	Nassau			General			May 29	
1864 Feb 14	Brig	Donor	Fayer	211	Liverpool		350 Tons Coal				J. T. Bourne		
1864 Mar 1	Str	Florie	Eger[?]	215	England	Halifax					C. L. Hobson	Mar 11	
1864 Mar 3	Brig	Carl Emile	Peterson	165	Liverpool	New York	General		Salt & Tea		J. W. Musson	Apr 9	
1864 Mar 3	Barque	Enterprise	Phillips	427	Newport		627 Tons Coal				J. T. Bourne		
1864 Mar 5	Ship	Storm King	McDougall	1147	Cardiff		Coal & General						In port
1864 Mar 5	Str	Caledonia	Dutton	115	Wilmington	Nassau	Cotton	308	115 Pkg Mdse		F. W. G. Hurst	May 25	
1864 Mar 11	Str	North Heath	Burroughs	345	Cardiff		Ballast		933 Pkg Mdse		J. T. Bourne	Mar 29	Returned to port leaky
1864 Mar 15	Str	Greyhound	Berwick	290	Liverpool		887 Pkg Mdse		968 Pkg Mdse			Mar 29	
1864 Mar 15	Str	City of Petersburgh	Fuller	426	Wilmington		Cotton	165			R. S. Musson		
1864 Mar 16	Barque	Harvest	McDougall	367	Cardiff		454 Tons Coal				C. L. Holson		
1864 Mar 17	Str	Index	Henry	363	Wilmington		Cotton	811			W. P. Campbell		

Date of Arrival	Class	Name	Master	Tonnage	Where From	Where For	Cargo Inboard	Bales	Cargo Outboard	Bales	Agent	Date of Departure	Remarks
1864 Mar 19	Str	A. D. Vance	Willie	902	Nassau		Ballast				F. W. G. Hurst		
1864 Mar 21	Brig	Mathilde	Peiper	105	Liverpool	Halifax	General				Johnson & Crofts	Apr 8	
1864 Mar 22	Schr	J. Davis	Gordie	23	Wilmington		Cotton & Pitch				J. T. Bourne		In Port
1864 Mar 22	Schr	Legate	Masters	47	Demerara		Rum, etc.				J. T. Bourne		
1864 Apr 4	Ship	William Graham	Bain	653	Cardiff		Coal & General				J. T. Bourne	May 23	
1864 Apr 5	Str	Edith	Gregory	237	Falmouth	Marimacki [?]	General		General		Hall & Craig	May 9	
1864 Apr 6	Brig	Queen of Britain	Harry [?]	144	Liverpool		General		Ballast		J. T. Bourne	May 25	
1864 Apr 7	Str	Helen	Leslie	342	London	Nassau	General		886 Pkg Mdse		J. T. Bourne	May 26	
1864 Apr 9	Str	Hansa	Atkinson	257	Nassau	Falmouth	Ballast					May 10	
1864 Apr 12	Str	Pevensey	Hawks	455	London	Nassau	450 Pkg Mdse		1178 Pkg Mdse		W. P. Campbell	May 6	
1864 Apr 15	Brig	Banneys	Ashfold	139	Liverpool		General				R. S. Musson		In Port
1864 Apr 15	Str	Minnie	Gilpin	253	Wilmington		Cotton	732	784 Pkg Mdse		J. Thorrold	May 26	
1864 Apr 16	Schr	Bonnie Bell	Bont	131	Liverpool				Ballast		J. W. Musson	May 23	

Date Of Arrival	Class	Name	Master	Tonnage	Where From	Where For	Cargo Inboard	Bales	Cargo Outboard	Bales	Agent	Date Of Departure	Remarks
1864 Apr 18	Str	Constance	Stewart	161	Greenock	Halifax	Ballast		Ballast			May 28	
1864 Apr 19	Barque	Tweed	McDougall	34	Cardiff	New York	583 Tons Coal				W. P. Campbell		
1864 Apr 19	Str	Atalanta	Pittman	253	London						C. L. Hobson	Jun 28	
1865 Apr 19	Barque	Bessie Young	Holmes	348	Cardiff	Nassau	400 Tons Coal		258 Pkg Mdse		J. Thorrold		
1864 Apr 22	Barque	Belladona	Leblanc	277	Cardiff	Liverpool	494 Tons Coal				W. P. Campbell	Jun 13	
1864 Apr 23	Barque	Lilian	Mahon	439	Liverpool	New Brunswick	716 Tons Coal				W. P. Campbell	May 18	
1864 Apr 23	Barque	Mary	Lewis	367	Cardiff		503 Tons Coal				J. Thorrold		
1864 Apr 27	Brig	Village Girl	Douglas	216	Cardiff	Liverpool	334 Tons Coal		Cotton	425	J. Thorrold	May 26	
1864 Apr 27	Brig	Princess Royal	Jones	170	Liverpool	Liverpool	General		Cotton	316	J. T. Bourne	Jun 11	
1864 Apr 29	Barque	Plaides	Knowlton	330	Cardiff		500 Tons Coal				W. P. Campbell		In Port
1864 Apr 30	Barque	Nutfield	Crispin	301	Cardiff		424 Tons Coal				W. P. Campbell		
1864 May 2	Str	Index	Marshall	363	Wilmington	Nassau	Cotton	770	713 Pkg Mdse			May 7	
1864 May 3	Brig	Congress	Smith	412			583 Tons Coal						In Port

Date Of Arrival	Class	Name	Master	Tonnage	Where From	Where For	Cargo Inboard	Bales	Cargo Outboard	Bales	Agent	Date Of Departure	Remarks
1864 May 5	Barque	Lady of the Lake	Barnes	492			619 Tons Coal				J. T. Bourne		
1864 May 6	Str	Georgianna McCaw	Corbett	373	Liverpool	Nassau	General		Inward		J. T. Bourne	May 11	
1864 May 7	Brig	Martha	Sawyer	200	Cardiff		316 Tons Coal				W. P. Campbell		In Port
1864 May 7	Barque	Echo	Crowing	888	Cardiff	Nassau	509 Tons Coal		Inward		J. T. Bourne	May 7	
1864 May 7	Barque	Rubemon	Studeman	386	Cardiff		610 Tons Coal				J. T. Bourne		
1864 May 7	Barque	Pallas	Eggert	259	Cardiff		443 Tons Coal				J. T. Bourne		
1864 May 7	Str	Mathilde	Peiper	105	Halifax	Halifax	General		Ballast		Johnson & Crofts	May 13	
1864 May 9	Str	Lynx	Reid	232	Liverpool	Nassau	Ballast		Ballast		F. B. Stacy	May 23	
1864 May 10	Str	City of Petersburgh	Fuller	425	Halifax	St. John's	Ballast				R. S. Musson	May 11	
1864 May 11	Str	Thistle	Hora	305	Wilmington	Nassau	Cotton	927	612 Pkg Mdse		F. B. Stacy	May 31	
1864 May 12	Str	Atalanta	Horner	253	Wilmington	Nassau	Cotton	665	General		C. L. Hobson	May 23	
1864 May 12	Str	Fox	Raisbeck	230	Liverpool	Nassau	Ballast				F. B. Stacy	Jun 28	
1864 May 13	Str	Rouen	Place	165	England	Nassau	Ballast				W. P. Campbell	May 15	

Date Of Arrival	Class	Name	Master	Tonnage	Where From	Where For	Cargo Inbound	Bales	Cargo Outboard	Bales	Agent	Date Of Departure	Remarks
1864 May 16	Str	Helen	Leslie	342	Wilmington	Nassau	Cotton	965	465 Pkg Mdse		J. Thorrold	May 28	
1864 May 16	Str	Mary Celestia	Usina	207	Liverpool	Nassau			General			May 23	
1864 May 21	Str	Lilian	Gilmore	246	Glasgow	Nassau	806 Pkg Mdse				C. L. Hobson	Jun 1	
1864 May 21	Brig	Sovereign	Walsh	167	Swansea		270 Tons Coal				Johnson & Crofts		In Port
1864 May 23	Barque	Harkaway	Cundy	685	Liverpool		General				Hall & Craig		In Port
1864 May 28	Str	Florie	McDougall	215	Halifax	Nassau			948 Pkg Mdse		C. L. Hobson	Jun 1	
1864 May 28	Barque	Vingoff	Holsen	319	Cardiff		450 Tons Coal				W. P. Campbell		In Port
1864 May 30	Str	Pevensey	Burroughs	455	Wilmington		Cotton	1003			W. P. Campbell		
1864 May 30	Schr	Maria Victoria	Caron	89	Montreal						Johnson & Crofts		In Port
1864 Jun 4	Str	Lynx	Reid	233	Wilmington	Nassau	Cotton	621	952 Pkg Mdse		F. B. Stacy	Jun 8	
		North Heath	Burroughs		From sea in distress	Nassau	Ballast					Jun 3	
1864 Jun 7	Str	Index	Marshall		Wilmington	London	Cotton	803			W. P. Campbell	Jun 20	
1864 Jun 8	Str	Atalanta	Horner		Wilmington	Nassau	Cotton	536				Jun 20	

Date Of Arrival	Class	Name	Master	Tonnage	Where From	Where For	Cargo Inboard	Bales	Cargo Outboard	Bales	Agent	Date Of Departure	Remarks
1864 Jun 9	Str	Mary Celestia	Usina		Wilmington	Nassau	Cotton	594				Jun 20	
1864 Jun 9	Str	Little Hettie	Collier	246	Glasgow						Hall & Craig		In Port
1864 Jun 11	Str	Virgin	Halplin	291	Cardiff	Nassau						Jun 14	
1864 Jun 11	Str	City of Petersburgh	Fuller	426	Wilmington	Nassau	Cotton	810	General			Jun 25	
1864 Jun 13	Str	Fanny	Dunning	803	Nassau	Greenock					W. P. Campbell	Jun 15	
1864 Jun 16	Str	Old Dominion	Page	518	Bristol	Nassau	General		Inward			Jun 25	
1864 Jun 17	Schr	Choice Fruit	Cowell	119			Coal				J. T. Bourne		In Port
1864 Jun 17	Str	Lynx	Reid	232	From sea in distress							Jun 20	
1864 Jun 20	Str	Edith	Murray	237	Nassau	Nassau	241 Pkg Mdse		Inward		Hall & Craig	Jun 23	
1864 Jun 21	Brig	Helen	Lovet	252	Nassau		403 Tons Coal				Hall & Craig		In Port
1864 Jun 23	Brig	Ann & Mary	Jones	145	Liverpool		General				R. S. Musson		In Port
1864 Jun 27	Str	North Heath	Burroughs	345	Wilmington		Cotton	759			J. Thorrold		In Port
1864 Jun 27	Str	Lilian	Martin	246	Wilmington		Cotton	709			J. H. Phinizy		In Port

Date Of Arrival	Class	Name	Master	Tonnage	Where From	Where For	Cargo Inboard	Bales	Cargo Outboard	Bales	Agent	Date Of Departure	Remarks
1864 Jun 28	Barque	Aid	Greenough	191	Cardiff		400 Tons Coal				C. L. Hobson		In Port
1864 Jun 28	Str	Florie	DeHorsey	215	Wilmington		Cotton	476			J. H. Phinizy		In Port
1864 Jun 28	Brig	Clara	Stubenvach	282	Cardiff		436 Tons Coal						In Port
1864 Jun 29	Brig	Ada	Scott	210	Liverpool		304 Tons Coal						In Port
1864 Jun 30	Str	Hawk	Cobby	630	London		General						In Port

Notes

1. "The most self-effacing of men"

1. Nahum Mitchell, *History of the Early Settlement of Bridgewater in Plymouth County, Massachusetts: Including an Extensive Family Register* (Boston: Kidder and Wright, 1840; repr., Bowie, Md.: Heritage Books, 1983), 98.

2. *Vital Records of Bridgewater, Massachusetts, to the Year 1850* (Boston: New England Historical and Genealogical Society, 1916), vol. 1, Births, 30.

3. Secretary of the Commonwealth, *Massachusetts Soldiers and Sailors in the Revolutionary War: A Compilation from the Archives Prepared and Published by the Secretary of the Commonwealth* (Boston: Wright and Potter Printing, 1896), 1:188.

4. Franklin County, Massachusetts, was created in 1811. It was originally part of Hampshire County, Massachusetts.

5. *Heath, Massachusetts, Town Clerk, Births, Deaths, Marriages and Intentions, 1735–1900* (Salt Lake City: filmed by the Genealogical Society of Utah, 1972; Family History Library Film No. 0768340), 143 [hereafter cited as Heath Town Clerk].

6. Howard Chandler Robbins, ed., *1785–1935, Sesquicentennial Anniversary of the Town of Heath, Massachusetts, August 25–29, 1935* (Greenfield, Mass.: Heath Historical Society, printed by E. A. Hall & Co., ca. 1935), 74–75. The Allen family was enumerated in Charlemont in 1790. Silas Allen household, United States, Department of Commerce and Labor, Bureau of the Census, *Heads of Families at the First Census of the United States Taken in the Year 1790: Massachusetts,* Heath Town, Massachusetts (Washington, D.C.: GPO, 1908).

7. Heath Town Clerk, 143.

8. Edward Calver, *Heath, Massachusetts: A History and Guidebook,* 2d ed. (Heath, Mass.: Heath Historical Society, 1995), 114.

9. Ibid., 114.

10. *Vital Records of Heath, Massachusetts to the Year 1850* (Boston: New England Historical and Genealogical Society, 1915), Deaths, 115.

11. *Vital Records, Heath,* Births, 11.

12. Calver, 71.

13. James Allen household, United States, Department of Commerce and Labor, Bureau of the Census, *1820 U.S. Federal Census,* Heath, Franklin County, Massachusetts.

14. *Vital Records, Heath,* Marriages, 79.

15. Daniel Wait Howe, *Howe Genealogies: John Howe of Sudbury and Marlborough, Massachusetts* (Boston: New England Historical and Genealogical Society, 1929), 212.

16. July 28, 1822, is the generally accepted date of Charles Maxwell Allen's birth. No record of his birth or baptism has been found. Although the year of Allen's birth is indicated on his tombstone as 1821, this is likely an error because family genealogical records are in agreement that Allen was born in 1822.

17. Calver, 74.

18. Winhall was and still is part of the larger town of Bondville. There are deeds documenting that James Allen was buying and selling land in Winhall as early as 1823. *Land Records, Microfilm of Original Records in the Town Hall, Winhall, Vermont, Vols. 1–3, 1796–1843* (Salt Lake City: Filmed by the Genealogical Society of Utah, Family History Library Film No. 29203).

19. Allen Collection, Vermont Historical Society, Barre, Vt. [hereafter Allen Collection, Vt.]. Sarah Howe Allen is buried in Winhall Cemetery.

20. Zadock Thompson, *Gazetteer of the State of Vermont* (Montpelier, Vt.: n.p., 1824), 196–197.

21. Stereoscopic view in the possession of Alice Ross de Kok. Mrs. de Kok is a descendant of James and Polly Vaile Allen.

22. Allen Collection, Vt. William Dennis Allen, Jonathan Vaile Allen, and Mary Ogilvia Allen were teachers.

23. The business was phased out when the poisonous sulfur tips were declared illegal in the late 1800s. *Orono, Maine: A Bicentennial View* (publisher and date of publication unknown, copy obtained from the Orono Historical Society), 27. *A Collection of "Old Orono Oddments" by Dr. A Douglas Glanville as published in the Old Town-Orono Times, compiled and presented by the Orono Historical Society* (Milford, Maine Print Show, n.d.), 35. The building that housed the match factory still stands.

24. Reverend Ezekiel Emerson, a Free Will Baptist, was one of the earliest settlers at Georgetown, Maine.

25. Allen Collection, Vt. William Dennis Allen died November 28, 1849, at Bidwell's Bar, California.

26. Charles Maxwell Allen household, United States, Department of Commerce and Labor, Bureau of the Census, *1850 U.S. Federal Census,* Amity, Allegany County, New York.

27. David Maldwyn Ellis, "The Yankee Invasion of New York, 1783–1850," *New York History* 32, no. 1 (1951): 3-17.

28. F. W. Beers, *History of Allegany County, N.Y. with illustrations, description of scenery, private residences, public buildings, fine blocks, and important manufactories, from original sketches by artists of the highest ability; and portraits of old pioneers and prominent residents* (New York: F. W. Beers and Company, 1879), 177.

29. In 1853, Amity and Miltonville were incorporated and named Phillipsville, but the name was later changed to Belmont.

30. Amity Sesquicentennial, Inc., *Sesquicentennial: A Collected History of a Town and Its People. Town of Amity, 1830–1980* (Belmont, N.Y.: Amity Press, 1980), 87; map of Belmont, N.Y., reproduced from *Atlas of Allegany County, NY,* compiled and published by D. G. Beers and Company, New York, 1869, 23.

31. The Fugitive Slave Act of 1850 mandated the return of runaway slaves.

32. Arch Merrill, *The Underground (Freedom's Road) and Other Upstate Tales* (Rochester, N.Y.: American Book-Stratford Press, 1963), 117–18.

33. Persons assisting runaway slaves were subject to fines and imprisonment by the terms of the Fugitive Slave Act of 1850.

34. Beers, 82.

35. Several years later, a fire destroyed the office of the *Genesee Valley Free Press.* No copy of the newspaper that contained the call has been located.

36. The New York meeting of October 17, 1854, had been preceded by similar meetings earlier that year in Ripon, Wisconsin, and Jackson, Michigan.

37. Beers, 84.

38. Evergreen Cemetery, Milo, Maine, monumental inscription: [Richards] Mary A., daughter, d. Nov. 12, 1857, 25 years.

39. Charles Maxwell Allen household, United States, Department of Commerce and Labor, Bureau of the Census, *1860 U.S. Federal Census,* Amity, Allegany County, New York.

40. Artemus C. Ward was the pen name of Charles Farrar Browne (1834–67). "Meet Brother Gregory." www.brooklyn.cuny.edu/bc/ahp/mbg/mbg2/Cameron.html/ (accessed Oct.12,2007).

41. Charles Stuart Kennedy, *The American Consul: A History of the United States Consular Service, 1776–1914* (New York: Greenwood Press, 1990), 71–72.

42. William H. Seward (1801–72), leader of the Republican Party in New York State, was appointed secretary of state by Abraham Lincoln and served until 1869.

43. For a detailed study of Lincoln's use of patronage, see Harry J. Carman and Reinhard H. Luthin, *Lincoln and the Patronage* (New York: Columbia Univ. Press, 1943). The subject is also covered in three journal articles by Neill F. Sanders, "Unfit for Consul? The English Consulates and Lincoln's Patronage Policy," *Lincoln Herald* 82, no. 3 (1980): 464-74; "'When a House is on Fire': The English Consulates and Lincoln's Patronage Policy," *Lincoln Herald* 83, no. 1 (1981): 579-91; "Even the Less

Important Consular Posts: The English Consulates and Lincoln's Patronage Policy," *Lincoln Herald* 85, no. 2 (1983) 61-79.

44. *Thirty-seventh Congress, First Session, H.R. 74,* July 23, 1861.

45. Edward Trowbridge, who had been nominated for the consular post at Bermuda, declined that position in favor of the post at Barbados on June 19, 1861. *United States Lists of Consular Officers, 1789–1939,* National Archives RG 59, Microfilm Reel M587, Roll 3, hereafter referred to as Lists of Consular Officers.

46. Ibid.

47. Ibid.

48. *Senate Executive Journal,* Monday, Dec. 23, 1861. On this date, more than four months after Allen's nomination, the Senate voted that the nominations of all consuls be referred to the Committee on Commerce, a routine practice given the commercial nature of the consuls' role.

49. *Senate Executive Journal,* Monday, Apr. 14, 1862.

50. *The United States consular system, a manual for consuls, and also for merchants, shipowners and masters in their consular transactions, comprising the instructions in regard to consular emoluments, duties, privileges and liabilities* (Washington, D.C.: Taylor and Maury, 1856).

51. Kennedy, 22.

52. *Bermuda Royal Gazette,* Nov. 12, 1861.

53. Many of the dispatches written by Charles Maxwell Allen were published in the *Official Records of the Union and Confederate Navies in the War of the Rebellion,* 30 vols. (Washington, D.C.: GPO, 1894–1922) [hereafter cited as *ORN*]. Portions of Allen's dispatches were also published in various editions of *Foreign Relations of the United States* and *North Atlantic Blockading Squadron Bulletins.*

54. National Archives, Washington. RG 84, *Consular Despatches for Bermuda,* Microfilm Reels T262, 5–9.

2. "Such a God-forsaken place"

1. Frederick W. Seward (1830–1915), the son of William H. Seward, served as his father's assistant secretary of state during the Civil War. For an account of his service in the Department of State, see Frederick W. Seward, *Reminiscences of a Wartime Statesman and Diplomat, 1830–1915* (New York: G. P. Putnam's Sons, 1916).

2. *Thirty-fourth Congress,* 1st sess., chap. 127, 1856. A bond was required to ensure "the true and faithful accounting for, paying over, and delivering up all fees, moneys, goods, effects, books, records, papers, and other property."

3. *Courthouse Records,* Belmont, New York: "Indenture dated October 3, 1861 from Charles M. Allen and his wife, Susan E. Allen to Silas Richardson of the town, county and state aforesaid, for the sum of $500 for a parcel of land in the Village of Belmont and in that portion of said village known as Milton Ville [illegible] that contains lot or parcel of land known as lots number fifty one (51) and fifty two (52) in the Village of Miltonville, Allegany County, State of New York, according to map and survey."

4. The transcript prepared by Allen's daughter, Edith Wistowe Allen, is a more complete transcript than that of Allen's granddaughter-in-law, Patricia Allen Chaplin. There are a small number of instances where details included in the Chaplin transcript were omitted in the Allen transcript. The personal letters included in this book are primarily from the transcript of Edith Wistowe Allen. The Patricia Allen Chaplin transcript is used only when text appears there that does not appear in the Edith Wistowe Allen transcript. Both transcripts are preserved in the Bermuda Archives.

5. Patricia Allen Chaplin, "Allen Letters to His Wife," Allen Collection, Bermuda Archives. This transcript was presented at Bermuda's Somers' Day celebration in 1959.

6. Frederick B. Wells of New Hampshire served three terms as U.S. consul at Bermuda. He was appointed by each of the three Democratic presidents who preceded Lincoln. Wells served from 1846–50, 1854–56, and 1859 until Allen's appointment. *Lists of Consular Officers.*

7. *Market Square from Ordnance Island,* St. George's, ca. 1864 by Lt. H. S. Clive, Bermuda National Trust Collection, Bermuda Archives.

8. Allen's request was approved by the Department of State, and Darrell continued to serve as consular agent at Hamilton. Darrell served from December 10, 1859, until May 1872, when the U.S. Consulate moved to Hamilton, making a consular agent there no longer necessary. *Lists of Consular Officers.*

9. Henry Wheaton, an American jurist and diplomat (1785–1848), published *A Digest of the Law of Maritime Captures and Prizes* in 1815, which was possibly the digest to which Wells referred.

10. As one of his first military acts as president, Lincoln proclaimed a blockade on April 19, 1861, of the Southern ports in the states of South Carolina, Georgia, Florida, Alabama, Mississippi, Louisiana, and Texas. On April 27, 1861, the blockade was extended to include North Carolina and Virginia.

11. For an account of Lincoln's role in foreign affairs, see Dean B. Mahin, *One War at a Time: The International Dimensions of the American Civil War* (Washington, D.C.: Brassey's, 2000).

12. Edith Wistowe Allen, "Contributions from Miss Edith Allen to the Somers' Day 'At Home' on July 28th, 1930," transcript, Allen Collection, Bermuda Archives.

13. Chaplin.

3. "They are a big lot of scamps"

1. Most of the enclosures submitted with Allen's quarterly reports are not included in the microfilm copies of Allen's diplomatic dispatches, having been disseminated to various government departments. There are a small number of enclosures that were microfilmed, but these have not been included in this work.

2. Passengers and crews of ships arriving at Bermuda who had been exposed to smallpox were routinely quarantined to control the spread of this then untreatable disease.

3. Consular regulations at this time prohibited U.S. consuls from corresponding "in regard to the public affairs of any foreign government with any private person, newspaper, or other periodical." Allen did not violate this regulation because he was correcting misconceptions reported in the *Bermuda Royal Gazette* and not commenting on any Bermudian government affairs. See Statutes at Large, 34th Congress, 1st Session, 52–65, August 18, 1856, chap. 127, "*An Act to Regulate the Diplomatic and Consular Systems of the United States.*"

4. Sir Alexander Milne, Bart. G. C. B., Vice Admiral, 1860–64, North America and West Indies Station, British Royal Navy. For an account of the British Royal Navy in Bermuda, see Ian Stranack, *The Andrew and the Onions: The Story of the British Royal Navy in Bermuda 1795–1975* (Bermuda: Island Press, ca. 1975). Also see Regis A. Courtemanche, *No Need of Glory: The British Navy in American Waters, 1860–1864* (Annapolis, Md.: United States Naval Institute, 1977).

5. In fact, the U.S. consul at Nassau, Samuel G. Whiting, suffered a similar indignity. See James Sprunt, *Derelicts: An Account of Ships Lost at Sea in General Commercial Traffic and a Brief History of Blockade Runners Stranded along the North Carolina Coast, 1861–1865* (Baltimore: Lord Baltimore Press, 1920), 216–17.

6. Edith Wistowe Allen.

7. The lengthy correspondence that this incident generated was reproduced in the *Bermuda Royal Gazette,* Sept. 30, 1862.

8. An exhibit of the works of Edward James was held in Hamilton, Bermuda, in 2001: "*Man of Mystery: The Artwork of Edward James, 1861–1877,*" Bermuda National Gallery. Many of James's watercolors are located in the Bermuda Archives.

9. Admiral Milne's residence was at the dockyard on Ireland Island, a distance of about twenty miles from St. George's at the west end of Bermuda.

10. Edith Wistowe Allen.

11. Sir Harry St. George Ord was governor of Bermuda from March 1861 through June 1864.

12. The *Bermuda Royal Gazette,* Feb. 25, 1862, reported, "The *Nashville* obtained a supply of coal from the Ship *Mohawk,* lying in St. George's harbour, and proceeded to sea yesterday."

13. This refers to Brig. Gen. Ambrose E. Burnside's (1824–81) combined land and naval campaign that resulted in the capture of Roanoke, North Carolina, on February 7–8, 1862. On March 14, 1862, the city of New Bern, North Carolina, was also captured by U.S. forces. New Bern, up to this time, had been a principal port for the blockade-runners.

14. Chaplin.

15. The Burnside expedition.

16. The *Bermuda Royal Gazette,* Jan. 13, 1863, in their review of the year 1862, reported on this incident: "A most deplorable affair at Hamilton opened the month of March. An adventurer of the name of Kendrick who had speculated in a sort of questionable hotel contrived to get himself involved in a disreputable uproar with some

liberty men from the fleet, fired into the mob, killed one man outright and wounded another severely. For this, he subsequently stood his trial, was convicted and sentenced to death, but the sentence was subsequently commuted to 14 years imprisonment."

17. Edith Wistowe Allen.

18. Frank E. Vandiver, *Confederate Blockade Running through Bermuda, 1861–1865: Letters and Cargo Manifests* (Austin: Univ. of Texas Press, 1947), 94.

19. In a later dispatch, Allen explains that he had misidentified the *Sedgewick*. The vessel's correct name was *Southwick*.

20. A supercargo was an individual appointed by the shipowners or the owner of the cargo whose duty it was to manage the commercial concerns of the voyage.

21. James A. Atwood, mayor of St. George's from 1861 to 1862. Bermuda National Trust, *Bermuda's Architectural Heritage: St. George's* (Bermuda: Bermuda National Trust, 1998), 178 [hereafter cited as BNT St. George's].

22. Vandiver, 12–14. For further information on Bourne's efforts to remove Captain Tate, see Vandiver, 14–21.

23. Vandiver, xl.

24. There is some discrepancy regarding the date of this letter. Edith Wistowe Allen's transcript dates this letter April 5, 1862. Patricia Allen Chaplin's transcript dates the letter April 24, which seems to be the correct date, as Allen mentions an article in the *Herald* dated April 14. Also, his comment that the "South has whipped the Northern army" most likely refers to the Battle of Shiloh, which took place April 6–7, 1862.

25. At this time, Joseph H. Rainey, a freed slave from South Carolina who was conscripted at the beginning of the war to work for the Confederates, fled to Bermuda with his wife. Rainey lived very near the U.S. consulate at St. George's and remained in Bermuda through the war years, supporting himself as a barber. Because of the physical proximity of Rainey's living quarters to the consulate, it is interesting to speculate that these are the people to whom Allen referred. After the war, Rainey and his wife returned to South Carolina, and Rainey became the first African American to be elected to the U.S. House of Representatives. For an account of Rainey's life in Bermuda and in the United States, see Cyril Outerbridge Packwood, *Detour— Bermuda, Destination—U. S. House of Representatives: The Life of Joseph Rainey* (Bermuda: Baxter's Ltd., 1977).

26. It is unclear where Allen's sleeping quarters were located at this time.

27. Allen often mentioned the severe storms and gales that hit Bermuda as well as the storm-wrecked vessels that arrived in St. George's. More than three thousand miles from England and more than five hundred miles from the United States, Bermuda was a welcome refuge for storm-tossed vessels in the western Atlantic.

28. Edith Wistowe Allen.

29. Sarah Agnes Wallace and Frances Elma Gillespie, eds., *The Journal of Benjamin Moran, 1857–1865* (Chicago: Univ. of Chicago Press, 1948–49), 2:1082.

30. Capt. W. C. Poe had been appointed by the shipowners to take over the captaincy of the *Wheatland* from Captain Peacock, a Confederate sympathizer. Mr. A. V.

Fraser was the representative from the New York Board of Underwriters overseeing the safe return of the vessel to the owners.

31. A colorful portrait of Coxetter is given in Robert Carse, *Blockade: The Civil War at Sea* (New York: Rinehart & Company, 1958), 50–51.

32. The *Jeff Davis* was formerly the slave ship *Echo,* captured by Lieut. John Newland Maffitt, United States Navy, in 1858 and sold to a South Carolinian. See Naval History Division, Navy Department, *Civil War Naval Chronology 1861–1865* (Washington, D.C.: GPO, 1971), VI-256 [hereafter cited as *Chronology*].

33. Wilmington, North Carolina, and Charleston, South Carolina, were the two primary Confederate ports of the blockade-runners in 1862.

34. James A. Ker Wilson, of the firm Cunard, Wilson & Co., Liverpool, who worked with John Tory Bourne. Vandiver, 21.

35. Because of the unusual circumstances of the capture of the *Bermuda* the case eventually reached the U.S. Supreme Court. It was captured on the open ocean in transit between two neutral ports, and evidence was found onboard of her intention to run the blockade. For details of the case, see www.justia.us/us/70/514/case.html.

36. An interesting account of the capture of this vessel appeared in the June 17, 1862, issue of the *Bermuda Royal Gazette.* It was written by the chief officer, screw steamer *Bermuda,* dated Philadelphia, May 14, 1862.

37. Chaplin.

38. Zachariah C. Pearson, owner of the London firm Z. C. Pearson & Co., was once the mayor of Hull in northern England. He became involved in blockade-running with John Tory Bourne. Ian Crook, "British Blockade-Running Ship '*Modern Greece,*'" originally published as "The Lasting Legacy of the Blockade Runner '*Modern Greece,*'" in *Crossfire, the Journal of The American Civil War Round Table* (UK).

39. At this time these three ports were under U.S. occupation.

40. Possibly Jacob M. Thompson (1810–85), a Confederate secret agent. Jefferson Davis appointed Thompson chief of the Confederate mission to Canada. See James D. Horan, *Confederate Agent: A Discovery in History* (New York: Crown, 1954), 80–81.

41. Allen's suspicions were confirmed when the *Lodona* was captured attempting to run the blockade at Hell's Gate, Georgia, on August 4, 1862.

42. Charles Fletcher Allen, "Blockade Runners," *Pittsburgh Dispatch,* a series of articles published in 1887.

43. It is not known if the president himself expressed his thanks to Allen for his efforts. No letter from Lincoln to Allen appears in the *Collected Works of Abraham Lincoln.*

44. Allen was misinformed on this point, because Semmes was not in Bermuda at this time. Capt. Raphael Semmes (1809–77) commanded the CSS *Sumter* and later the notorious Confederate commerce raider, the CSS *Alabama.* Semmes captured or destroyed sixty-nine vessels between 1862 and 1864, in addition to the eighteen vessels he had captured while commanding the CSS *Sumter* in 1861. The CSS *Alabama* was sunk June 19, 1864, off Cherbourg, France. See Adm. Raphael Semmes, *Memoirs of Service Afloat during the War between the States* (Baltimore: Kelly, Piet & Co., 1869).

45. Edith Wistowe Allen.

46. This refers to Consul Allen's actions in the *Wheatland* affair.

47. Alex V. Fraser of the New York Board of Underwriters became a good friend of Allen's after the *Wheatland* affair.

48. Gen. George B. McClellan (1826–85). Commander of the Army of the Potomac who was defeated in his attempt to capture Richmond in the Peninsular campaign of March–July 1862.

49. This may have been Richard Minor Higgs of St. George's. BNT St. George's, 111.

50. Edith Wistowe Allen.

51. This is the first instance in which Allen mentions the use of camouflage colors by the blockade-runners. The blockade-runners were often painted grey to make them less visible to United States Navy vessels.

52. BNT St. George's, 9.

53. Edith Wistowe Allen.

54. Chaplin.

55. The *Merrimac* in this instance is a British ship, not to be confused with the CSS *Virginia,* formerly the USS *Merrimack.*

56. Mortimer M. Jackson of Wisconsin, U.S. consul at Halifax from 1861 to 1882, with whom Allen corresponded on several occasions with regard to blockade-runners headed for Nova Scotia.

57. Matthew Fontaine Maury (1806–73), renowned hydrographer and Confederate navy commander. For an interesting view of Maury on a Bermuda-bound blockade-runner, see James Morris Morgan, *Recollections of a Rebel Reefer* (Boston: Houghton Mifflin, 1917), chap. 11, pp. 98–105.

58. *ORN*, ser. 1, vol. 1, The Operation of the Cruisers (Jan. 19, 1861–Jan. 4, 1863), 515. This letter is not included in the microfilm of Allen's diplomatic dispatches.

59. The *Urana* was a U.S. coal brig.

60. Earl Van Dorn (1820–63), Confederate army general, and Sterling Price (1809–67), Confederate army general, were defeated at the Battle of Corinth, October 3–4, 1862, in northeastern Mississippi by William S. Rosecrans (1819–98), Union general.

61. At this time, Edward James was employed by the Bermudian government as surveyor-general of the colony.

62. *Bermuda Royal Gazette,* Oct. 21, 1862.

63. John Russell, 1st Earl Russell, KG, GCMG, PC (1792–1878). Served twice as prime minister of the United Kingdom and was foreign secretary during the American Civil War.

64. Appointed U.S. consul at Vienna on December 23, 1861. *Senate Executive Journal,* Monday, Dec. 23, 1861.

4. "A GREAT MANY BLOCKADE RUNNERS IN THE HARBOR NOW"

1. Written across the top of this dispatch were the words "All portraits acceptable."

2. The CSS *Alabama* was known as the "*290.*" It was the 290th vessel launched from Laird's shipyard in Liverpool, England.

3. After service in the Peninsular campaign with the Army of Northern Virginia, Maj. Norman S. Walker of Virginia was appointed Confederate states agent in Bermuda on November 13, 1862. Duke Nordlinger Stern, "The First Lady of Confederate Bermuda," *Bermuda Journal of Archaeology and Maritime History* 7 (1995): 109–20.

4. See the journal of Georgina F. Ghoulson Walker, *Private Journal, 1862–1865, with Selections from the Post-War 1866–1876* (Tuscaloosa, Ala.: Confederate Publishing, 1963).

5. Fraser & Co. was a respected Charleston-based importing and exporting company.

6. Sprunt, 230–31.

7. "Contraband" was a slang term referring to slaves and free men of color.

8. Allen began to renumber his reports as requested by the Department of State.

9. For a study of this little-known aspect of blockade-running, see Ludwell H. Johnson, "Commerce between Northeastern Ports and the Confederacy, 1861–1865," *Journal of American History* 54, no. 1 (1967): 30–42. Also see Charles Peery, "Clandestine Commerce: Yankee Blockade Running," *Journal of Confederate History* IV, Special Commemorative Naval Issue, 111–68.

10. William C. J. Hyland had served as U.S. acting consul in charge in the absence of the consul, Frederick B. Wells, in 1848 and again in 1850. *Lists of Consular Officers.*

11. For a life of Vallandigham, see Frank L. Klement, *The Limits of Dissent: Clement L. Vallandigham and the Civil War* (Lexington: Univ. Press of Kentucky, 1970).

12. Yellow fever was a constant fear. "The prosperity which stemmed from the British military presence [in Bermuda] came at a price. Naval vessels and mail steamers returning from the West Indies brought the dreaded yellow fever which swept through the town on no fewer than eight occasions between 1796 and 1864, with fatal consequences for townspeople and garrison troops alike." BNT St. George's, 8.

13. The commercial firm of Higgs & Hyland, owned by Benjamin Higgs and William C. J. Hyland, merchants in St. George's during the Civil War.

14. Gen. John C. Pemberton (1814–81) was in command of Confederate forces at Vicksburg, Mississippi. Joseph E. Johnston (1807–91) commanded a Confederate force in the field that opposed Grant's advance on Vicksburg.

15. Capt. John Newland Maffitt (1819–86), Confederate navy, commander of the CSS *Florida,* which captured or destroyed thirty-seven vessels before it was captured in Brazil in 1864. See Emma Martin Maffitt, *The Life and Services John Newland Maffitt* (New York: Neale, 1906).

16. Michael Jarvis, "The Long, Hot Summer of 1863," *RG Magazine,* Heritage month, vol. 4, no. 5 (1996): 26-28

17. *Bermuda Royal Gazette,* Jan. 13, 1863.

18. Frank Lawrence Owsley Jr., *The CSS* Florida: *Her Building and Operations* (Philadelphia: Univ. of Pennsylvania Press, 1964), 74–75.

19. Chester G. Hearn, *Gray Raiders of the Sea* (Baton Rouge: Louisiana State Univ. Press, 1992), 96.

20. Jim McNeil, *Masters of the Shoals: Tales of the Cape Fear Pilots Who Ran the Union Blockade* (Cambridge: Da Capo Press, 2003), 46.

21. Rear Adm. Samuel P. Lee (1812–97) was commander of the North Atlantic Blockading Squadron.

22. Capt. Samuel Barron, Confederate navy, was ordered to England "by the first suitable conveyance from Wilmington or Charleston." Confederate navy secretary Mallory hoped to have Barron command one of the ships being constructed there under the direction of Commander Bulloch. *Chronology*, 135. Professor Benslow's identity has not been established.

23. Edith Wistowe Allen.

24. It is not known for certain what Allen's illness was. Since he suffered from chronic asthma, this most likely was at least a contributing factor in his lengthy illness.

25. Chaplin.

26. Allen's report was submitted July 13, 1864.

27. John H. Morgan, Confederate general and cavalry raider (1825–64). Captured in July 1863, he was sent to the Ohio State Penitentiary and escaped from there on November 26 of that year. It is unlikely that Morgan was on this ship inasmuch as he fled Ohio overland to the Confederate states.

28. Gideon Welles, *Diary of Gideon Welles, Secretary of the Navy under Lincoln and Johnson* (Boston: Houghton Mifflin, 1911), 1:499–500.

5. "I HAVE USED MY UTMOST ENDEAVORS"

1. Captain Roberts's true identity was Augustus Charles Hobart-Hampden, the son of the second Duke of Buckingham. A very successful blockade-runner, he left an interesting account of his adventures. See Capt. Roberts, "Never Caught: Personal Adventures Connected with Twelve Successful Trips in Blockade Running during the American Civil War, 1863–64," *William Abbatt, Magazine of History*, extra number, no. 3 (1908): 143-205. Hobart-Hampden had an exciting career before and after the Civil War. He fought in the Crimean War and later served as an admiral in the Turkish service as Hobart Pasha.

2. "*Agrippina* coaled and rearmed the *Alabama* at uninhabited Blanquilla Island in the Caribbean, at Praya again in mid-January 1864, and elsewhere, while Federal cruisers searched in her wake all over the Caribbean and South Atlantic." *Chronology*, VI-190.

3. This refers to the seizure of the U.S. vessel *Chesapeake*, captained by John C. Braine.

4. *Lodge registers*, Masonic Lodge St. George's No. 200, Bermuda.

5. Master Mason certificate, Allen Collection, Bermuda Archives.

6. This most likely refers to Capt. Richard Squire, who served as an undercover agent for the U.S. government. See *Dictionary of American Naval Fighting Ships Online: Confederate States Navy, "C" Ships*, www.hazegray.org/danfs/csn/ (accessed Oct. 24, 2007).

7. This traffic was a persistent problem, Allen having first reported it as early as May 1863. See Allen's dispatches of May 19, 1863, and June 17, 1863.

8. George Proctor Kane (1817–78), marshal of Baltimore, Maryland, was arrested in 1861 as a traitor and was imprisoned in Fort McHenry. *Harper's Weekly,* July 13, 1861. Kane was released after fourteen months and went to the South.

9. It is known that Confederate blockade-runners sometimes patronized photography studios in Bermuda.

10. This was the USS *Shenandoah* rather than the Confederate commerce raider of the same name, which did not go to sea until October 1864.

11. William Henry Chase Whiting (1824–65). Confederate general who served at Fort Fisher, which guarded the port of Wilmington, North Carolina.

12. This most likely refers to Fort Lafayette in New York harbor, where Confederate prisoners of war were incarcerated.

13. Perhaps a Freudian slip on Allen's part. The vessel's name was correctly *Little Hattie.* "Hettie" was the nickname of Allen's twelve-year-old daughter, Henrietta.

14. For details of the capture and destruction of the U.S. steamer *Roanoke,* see Allen's dispatch of October 17, 1864.

15. William G. Hamley was acting governor of Bermuda during this period.

16. The *Atalanta* was sold to the Confederate government in July 1864 and commissioned as the CSS *Tallahassee.* In an Atlantic voyage from Wilmington to Halifax the ship burned fifteen Northern merchant ships and scuttled ten others. An interesting account of this can be found in McNeil, 65.

17. This letter is located in the papers of William H. Seward, University of Rochester. For details of this incident, see Welles, vol. 2, pp. 125–27.

18. Joseph Emerson Brown (1821–95), Confederate governor of Georgia.

19. The *Hawk* was purchased from Scotland by the Virginia volunteer navy for use as a privateer. The company ran out of funds, and the vessel never operated as a privateer or as a blockade-runner. Stephen R. Wise, *Lifeline of the Confederacy: Blockade Running during the Civil War* (Columbia: Univ. of South Carolina Press, 1988), 321–22.

20. British authorities released Braine and his party after Braine produced a Confederate navy commission. In the opinion of the authorities, this "commission and instructions relieved them from personal responsibility to neutral nations." The correspondence regarding the *Roanoke* affair is to be found in papers relating to foreign affairs, accompanying the annual message of the president to the first session of the thirty-ninth congress (Washington, D.C.: GPO, 1865), pt. 1, p. 60, http://digital.library.wisc.edu/1711.dl/FRUS.FRUS1865p1, and pt. 2, pp. 361–67, http://digital.library.wisc.edu/1711.dl/FRUS.FRUS1864p2.

21. For an account of his service, see John Wilkinson, *The Narrative of a Blockade Runner* (New York: Sheldon, 1877).

22. William Monroe, lieutenant governor, Bermuda, June–July 1864.

6. "There could hardly have been greater consternation"

1. Originally published in the *Bermuda Advocate,* Oct. 12, 1864, the same notice was republished in the *Bermuda Royal Gazette,* Jan. 31, 1865.

2. CSS *Shenandoah*, commanded by Lt. James I. Waddell. The *Shenandoah* destroyed Northern whaling ships in the Pacific long after the end of the war. Upon learning of the war's end, Waddell sailed the ship to Liverpool, England, where it was surrendered on November 6, 1865. It was the last Confederate surrender of the Civil War.

3. The *Stonewall* was a Confederate ironclad ram built in France and purchased by Confederate agents in Denmark. Commanded by Thomas Jefferson Page, Confederate navy, the ship sailed from Denmark in January 1865 but did not see active service before the end of the war.

7. "In the place where the tree falleth"

1. Luke Prior Blackburn (1816–87), governor of Kentucky (1879–83).

2. Not until many years later was yellow fever known to be transmitted by a species of mosquito.

3. *Bermuda Royal Gazette,* May 2, 1865.

4. Allen dispatch dated June 5, 1865, enclosing condolence letters.

5. The Apr. 28, 1865, condolence letter from the colored people of Bermuda included the signature of Joseph H. Rainey.

6. Allen's dispatches dated July 10, 1865, and Aug. 18, 1865.

7. John Tavenier Bartram (1811–89), Bermuda naturalist.

8. Allen dispatch dated Jan. 22, 1870.

9. *Bermuda Pocket Almanack* 1877. The photograph of the family appears in an exceedingly rare book, *Bermuda Through the Camera of James B. Heyl: 1868–1987,* compiled by Edith Stowe Godfrey Heyl. Regretfully, it has not been possible to reproduce the photograph in this book.

10. Allen dispatch dated Oct. 20, 1881.

11. Olof O. Nylander, "The Lymnaeidae of Northern Maine and Adjacent Canadian Provinces and Notes on Anson Allen and His Collection," *Maine Bulletin* 46, no. 2 (1943): 31-37.

12. William Dennis, Sarah Elizabeth, James, and the youngest, who died at birth, had preceded Anson in death. Charles Maxwell had also lost his younger brother, Jonathan Vaile, who had died in the battle of Cedar Creek in 1864.

13. Mary Genevieve, Charles Fletcher, and Henrietta Eliza.

14. Publication date and place unknown, clipping in the Bermuda Archives.

15. Date of publication unknown, clipping in the Bermuda Archives.

16. Photograph may have been taken by Allen's brother, Henry Seldon Allen in 1874. Engraved portrait after the photograph, Allen Collection, Bermuda Archives.

17. *Bermuda Royal Gazette,* January 1, 1889.

18. St. Mark's Churchyard, Smith's Parish, Bermuda.

19. Charles Fletcher Allen, *David Crockett: Scout, Small Boy, Pilgrim, Mountaineer, Soldier, Bear-Hunter, and Congressman, Defender of the Alamo* (Philadelphia: J. B. Lippincott, 1911).

Bibliography

MANUSCRIPT SOURCES

Allen Collection, Bermuda Archives, Hamilton, Bermuda.

Allen Collection, Vermont Historical Society, Barre, Vt.

Courthouse Records, Belmont, N.Y.

Heath, Massachusetts, Town Clerk, Births, Deaths, Marriages and Intentions, 1735–1900. Salt Lake City. Filmed by the Genealogical Society of Utah, 1972. Family History Library Film No. 0768340.

Land Records, Microfilm of Original Records in the Town Hall, Winhall, Vermont, Vols. 1–3, 1796–1843. Salt Lake City. Filmed by the Genealogical Society of Utah; Family History Library Film No. 29203.

Lodge Registers, Masonic Lodge St. George's No. 200, Bermuda.

National Archives, Washington. RG 84. *Consular Despatches for Bermuda,* Microfilm Reels T262, 5–9.

United States Lists of Consular Officers, 1789–1939. National Archives RG 59, Microfilm Reel M587, Roll 3.

United States. *Department of Commerce and Labor, Bureau of the Census, Heads of Families at the First Census of the United States Taken in the Year 1790: Massachusetts.* Heath Town, Massachusetts. Washington, D.C.: GPO, 1908.

United States. *Department of Commerce and Labor, Bureau of the Census, 1820 U.S. Federal Census,* Heath, Franklin County, Massachusetts.

United States. *Department of Commerce and Labor, Bureau of the Census, 1850 U.S. Federal Census,* Amity, Allegany County, New York.

United States. *Department of Commerce and Labor, Bureau of the Census, 1860 U.S. Federal Census,* Amity, Allegany County, New York.

Allen, Charles Fletcher. "Blockade Runners." *Pittsburgh Dispatch,* 1887.

Allen, Edith Wistowe. "Contributions from Miss Edith Allen to the Somers' Day 'At Home' on July 28th, 1930." *Allen Collection,* Bermuda Archives.

Capt. Roberts. "Never Caught: Personal Adventures Connected with Twelve Successful Trips in Blockade Running during the American Civil War, 1863–64." *William Abbatt, Magazine of History,* extra number, no. 3 (1908): 143–205.

Chaplin, Patricia Allen. "Allen Letters to His Wife," *Allen Collection,* Bermuda Archives.

Harper's Weekly, July 13, 1861.

Howe, Daniel Wait. *Howe Genealogies: John Howe of Sudbury and Marlborough, Massachusetts.* Boston: New England Historical and Genealogical Society, 1929.

Maffitt, Emma Martin. *The Life and Services of John Newland Maffitt.* New York: Neale, 1906.

Morgan, James Morris. *Recollections of a Rebel Reefer.* Boston: Houghton Mifflin, 1917.

Official Records of the Union and Confederate Navies in the War of the Rebellion. 30 vols. Washington, D.C.: GPO, 1894–1922.

Secretary of the Commonwealth. *Massachusetts Soldiers and Sailors in the Revolutionary War: A Compilation from the Archives Prepared and Published by the Secretary of the Commonwealth.* Vol. 1. Boston: Wright and Potter Printing, 1896.

Semmes, Raphael. *Memoirs of Service Afloat during the War between the States.* Baltimore: Kelly, Piet & Co., 1869.

Seward, Frederick W. *Reminiscences of a Wartime Statesman and Diplomat, 1830–1915.* New York: G. P. Putnam's Sons, 1916.

The United States consular system: a manual for consuls, and also for merchants, shipowners and masters in their consular transactions, comprising the instructions in regard to consular emoluments, duties, privileges and liabilities. Washington, D.C.: Taylor and Maury, 1856.

United States. *Senate Executive Journal,* Dec. 23, 1861, and Apr. 14, 1862.

United States. Thirty-fourth Congress, 1st sess., chap. 127 (1856).

United States. *Thirty-seventh Congress, First Session, H.R. 74* (July 23, 1861).

U.S. Department of State. *Papers Relating to Foreign Affairs, accompanying the annual message of the president to the first session of the thirty-ninth congress.* Part I. Washington, D.C.: GPO, 1864. http://digital.library.wisc. edu/1711.dl/FRUS. FRUS1864p2.

U.S. Department of State. *Papers Relating to Foreign Affairs, accompanying the annual message of the president to the first session of the thirty-ninth congress.* Part II. Washington, D.C.: GPO, 1865. Available from the University of Wisconsin Digital Collections. http://digital.library.wisc. edu/1711.dl/FRUS.FRUS1865p1.

Vandiver, Frank E., ed. *Confederate Blockade Running through Bermuda, 1861–1865: Letters and Cargo Manifests.* Austin: Univ. of Texas Press, 1947.

Vital Records of Bridgewater, Massachusetts, to the Year 1850. Vol. 1. Boston: New England Historical and Genealogical Society, 1916.

Vital Records of Heath, Massachusetts, to the Year 1850. Boston: New England Historical and Genealogical Society, 1915.

Walker, Georgina F. Ghoulson. *Private Journal, 1862–1865, with Selections from the Post-War 1866–1876.* Tuscaloosa, Ala.: Confederate Publishing, 1963.

Wallace, Sarah Agnes, and Frances Elma Gillespie, eds. *The Journal of Benjamin Moran, 1857–1865.* Vol. II. Chicago: Univ. of Chicago Press, 1948–49.

Welles, Gideon. *Diary of Gideon Welles, Secretary of the Navy under Lincoln and Johnson.* Vols. 1–2. Boston: Houghton Mifflin, 1911.

SECONDARY PRINTED SOURCES

Allen, Charles Fletcher. *David Crockett: Scout, Small Boy, Pilgrim, Mountaineer, Soldier, Bear-Hunter, and Congressman, Defender of the Alamo.* Philadelphia: J. B. Lippincott, 1911.

Amity Sesquicentennial, Inc. *Sesquicentennial: A Collected History of a Town and Its People. Town of Amity, 1830–1980.* Belmont, N.Y.: Amity Press, 1980.

Beers, F. W. *History of Allegany County, N.Y. with illustrations description of scenery, private residences, public buildings, fine blocks, and important manufactories, from original sketches by artists of the highest ability; and portraits of old pioneers and prominent residents.* New York: F. W. Beers and Company, 1879.

Bermuda National Trust. *Bermuda Architectural Heritage: St. George's.* Bermuda: Bermuda National Trust, 1998.

Calver, Edward. *Heath, Massachusetts: A History and Guidebook.* 2d ed. Heath, Mass.: Heath Historical Society, 1995.

Carman, Harry J., and Reinhard H. Luthin. *Lincoln and the Patronage.* New York: Columbia Univ. Press, 1943.

Carse, Robert. *Blockade: The Civil War at Sea.* New York: Rinehart & Company, 1958.

A Collection of "Old Orono Oddments" by Dr. A. Douglas Glanville as published in the Old Town-Orono Times, compiled and presented by the Orono Historical Society. Milford, Maine: Print Show, n.d.

Crook, Ian. "British Blockade-Running Ship 'Modern Greece.'" Originally published as "The Lasting Legacy of the Blockade Runner 'Modern Greece'" in *Crossfire: The Journal of the American Civil War Round Table* (UK).

Courtemanche, Regis A. *No Need of Glory: The British Navy in American Waters, 1860–1864.* Annapolis, Md.: United States Naval Institute, 1977.

Dictionary of American Naval Fighting Ships Online: Confederate States Navy. www.hazegray.org/danfs/csn.

Ellis, David Maldwyn. "The Yankee Invasion of New York, 1783–1850." *New York History* 32, no. 1 (1951): 3–17.

Hearn, Chester G. *Gray Raiders of the Sea.* Baton Rouge: Louisiana State Univ. Press, 1992.

Horan, James D. *Confederate Agent: A Discovery in History.* New York: Crown, 1954.

Jarvis, Michael. "The Long, Hot Summer of 1863." *RG Magazine,* Heritage month, vol. 4, no. 5 (1996): 26–28.

Johnson, Ludwell H., "Commerce between Northeastern Ports and the Confederacy, 1861–1965." *Journal of American History* 54, no. 1 (1967): 30–42.

Kennedy, Charles Stuart. *The American Consul: A History of the United States Consular Service, 1776–1914.* New York: Greenwood Press, 1990.

Klement, Frank L. *The Limits of Dissent: Clement L. Vallandigham and the Civil War.* Lexington: Univ. Press of Kentucky, 1970.

Mahin, Dean B. *One War at a Time: The International Dimensions of the American Civil War.* Washington, D.C.: Brassey's, 2000.

McNeil, Jim. *Masters of the Shoals: Tales of the Cape Fear Pilots Who Ran the Union Blockade.* Cambridge: Da Capo Press, 2003.

Merrill, Arch. *The Underground (Freedom's Road) and Other Upstate Tales.* Rochester, N.Y.: American Book-Stratford Press, 1963.

Mitchell, Nahum. *History of the Early Settlement of Bridgewater, in Plymouth County, Massachusetts: Including an Extensive Family Register.* Boston: Kidder and Wright, 1840; repr., Bowie, Md.: Heritage Books, 1983.

Naval History Division, Navy Department. *Civil War Naval Chronology, 1861–1865.* Washington, D.C.: GPO, 1971.

Nylander, Olof O. "The Lymnaeidae of Northern Maine and Adjacent Canadian Provinces and Notes on Anson Allen and His Collection," *Maine Bulletin* 46, no. 2 (1943): 31–37.

Orono, Maine: A Bicentennial View. Publisher and date of publication unknown, copy obtained from the Orono Historical Society.

Owsley, Frank Lawrence, Jr. *The CSS* Florida: *Her Building and Operations.* Philadelphia: Univ. of Pennsylvania Press, 1964.

Packwood, Cyril Outerbridge. *Detour—Bermuda, Destination—U.S. House of Representatives: The Life of Joseph Rainey.* Bermuda: Baxter's Ltd., 1977.

Peery, Charles. "Clandestine Commerce: Yankee Blockade Running." *Journal of Confederate History IV* Special Commemorative Naval Issue.

Robbins, Howard Chandler, ed. *1785–1935, Sesquicentennial Anniversary of the Town of Heath, Massachusetts, August 25–29, 1935.* Greenfield, Mass.: Heath Historical Society, printed by E. A. Hall & Co., 1935.

Sanders, Neill F. "Even the Less Important Consular Posts: The English Consulates and Lincoln's Patronage Policy." *Lincoln Herald* 85, no. 2 (1983): 61–79.

———."Unfit for Consul? The English Consulates and Lincoln's Patronage Policy." *Lincoln Herald* 82, no. 3 (1980): 464–74

———. "'When a House Is on Fire': The English Consulates and Lincoln's Patronage Policy," *Lincoln Herald* 83, no. 1 (1981): 579–91.

Sprunt, James. *Derelicts: An Account of Ships Lost at Sea in General Commercial Traffic and a Brief History of Blockade Runners Stranded Along the North Carolina Coast, 1861–1865.* Baltimore: Lord Baltimore Press, 1920.

Stern, Duke Nordlinger. "The First Lady of Confederate Bermuda." *Bermuda Journal of Archaeology and Maritime History* 7 (1995): 109–20.

Stranack, Ian. *The Andrew and the Onions, The Story of the British Royal Navy in Bermuda, 1795–1975.* Bermuda: Island Press, ca. 1975.

Thompson, Zadock. *Gazetteer of the State of Vermont.* Montpelier, Vt.: n.p., 1824.

Wilkinson, John. *The Narrative of a Blockade Runner.* New York: Sheldon, 1877.

Wise, Stephen R. *Lifeline of the Confederacy: Blockade Running during the Civil War.* Columbia: Univ. of South Carolina Press, 1991.

Index